Florian Znaniecki

ON HUMANISTIC SOCIOLOGY

THE HERITAGE OF SOCIOLOGY

A Series Edited by Morris Janowitz

Florian Znaniecki

ON

HUMANISTIC SOCIOLOGY

Selected Papers

Edited and with an Introduction by
ROBERT BIERSTEDT

THE UNIVERSITY OF CHICAGO PRESS

CHICAGO AND LONDON

Standard Book Number: 226-98842-2 (clothbound)
226-98843-0 (paperbound)

Library of Congress Catalog Card Number: 73-83534

THE UNIVERSITY OF CHICAGO PRESS, CHICAGO 60637
The University of Chicago Press, Ltd., London

Printed in the United States of America

Acknowledgments

FOR HELPFUL SUGGESTIONS the Editor expresses his grateful appreciation to Eileen Markley Znaniecki, to Helena Znaniecki Lopata, and to Tamara Obrebska.

Contents

Introduction

FLORIAN WITOLD ZNANIECKI was born on January 15, 1882, in Swiatniki, Poland. As one of three children of an estate manager, he received his earliest instruction at the hands of tutors, a private curriculum that included Greek, Latin, French, German, and Russian. At the gymnasium, or secondary school, he studied literature and wrote poetry. In 1903 at the age of twenty-one, he published a volume of verse entitled *Cheops: A Poem of Fantasy,* his first words to appear in print. At the University of Warsaw, where he undertook his undergraduate studies, he belonged to an underground group that was in rebellion against the Russian authorities; the students lectured to one another on forbidden subjects—namely, books that had been written by Polish authors. When the students staged a protest against the administration, Znaniecki, chosen by his comrades to represent them, politely sent his card to the rector to announce his presence and was promptly expelled from the university. He thus never received a baccalaureate degree.

Znaniecki thereupon began a period of romantic travel and study in Switerland, France, and Italy. He attended the universities of Geneva, Zurich, and Paris, from the first of which he received an M.A. degree. Then he returned to Poland, where he received the Ph.D. degree from the University of Cracow in 1909. His *Wanderjahren* included a brief period in the French Foreign Legion—although a man less militarily inclined than Znaniecki can hardly be imagined—from which he was discharged with a shoulder wound, and also a period during which he served as editor of a French literary magazine. During these years his interests turned from poetry to philosophy; it was the latter field in which he took his doctorate, and in which he won an early distinc-

1

tion both for his articles and for his Polish translation of Bergson's *L'Évolution Créatrice*.

For political reasons Znaniecki was ineligible for appointment to an academic post in his native country, then as now under the hegemony of Russia, and he accordingly accepted a position as director of an Emigrants' Protective Association. It was here that W. I. Thomas met him, in 1913, on one of his frequent trips to Europe. Thomas had begun to study the problems of immigrants to the United States, and particularly the Polish immigrants who were settling in large numbers in Chicago and Detroit. When Thomas learned that Znaniecki had no opportunity to pursue an academic career in Poland, he suggested that the young scholar go to the United States, which he did in 1914. Thomas later arranged for him an appointment at the University of Chicago.[1] Together they worked on their monumental *The Polish Peasant in Europe and America*, published in five volumes during the years 1918–1920 and in a new two-volume edition in 1927. In 1919 Znaniecki also published his own first book in the English language, *Cultural Reality*, intended as the first part of a general introduction to the philosophy of culture.

In 1920 Znaniecki returned to Poland, where he became professor of sociology (first professor of philosophy but changed at his request) at the University of Poznan, and where he founded the Polish Sociological Institute and the *Polish Sociological Review*. At Poznan he trained many students whose own works were later to add luster to the history of Polish sociology, and there

---

[1]   There is some discrepancy in the record here. Morris Janowitz, in his introduction to *W. I. Thomas: On Social Organization and Social Personality*, (Chicago: University of Chicago Press, 1966), says that Thomas "neither invited him nor encouraged him to come" and "was completely unaware of his journey from Poland until he actually arrived penniless at Thomas' home." Znaniecki, on the other hand, says that Thomas suggested that he go to Chicago and help him with his work, a suggestion mentioned both in his paper, "William I. Thomas as a Collaborator," *Sociology and Social Research* 32 (1948): 765, and in a letter Znaniecki addressed to Kimball Young, in response to direct questions from Champaign, Illinois, under date of August 31, 1951. The discrepancy is not great. The suggestion is one that a traveler would normally make under the circumstances.

he wrote his *Introduction to Sociology* (1922) and his massive *Sociology of Education* (1928–1930). His book, *The Laws of Social Psychology*, was published in English in 1925.

In 1932–1934 Znaniecki was back in the United States; he served as visiting professor at Columbia University, where he supervised a number of dissertations in the Columbia Department of Sociology, then headed by Robert M. MacIver. In 1934 he published in English *The Method of Sociology*, and in 1936, back again in Poznan, he produced his large volume, *Social Actions*, also in English. In the summer of 1939 he was once more in the United States, where he had been invited to deliver a series of lectures, again at Columbia University. These lectures were published in 1940 under the title *The Social Role of the Man of Knowledge*. At the end of summer, 1939, European clouds were heavy with the threat of war. MacIver tried to persuade Znaniecki to remain in this country, but Znaniecki insisted on returning. His ship, however, was intercepted by the Royal Navy and taken to a British port. On the day of its scheduled arrival in Gdynia the Nazi armies crossed the border of Poland to begin World War II. Znaniecki's name was on the list of Polish patriots and professors scheduled for execution.

Znaniecki then had no alternative but to return to the United States. He was offered an appointment as professor of sociology at the University of Illinois, and there he spent the last period of his active career with the exception of one post-retirement year as visiting professor at Wayne State University. His wife and daughter, interned briefly in a concentration camp in Poland, managed to escape the country and join him in Urbana. A son by an earlier marriage, Juliusz Znaniecki, a poet and novelist, participated in the Warsaw uprising and was incarcerated at Dachau, from which he was released by Allied forces at the end of the war.

Znaniecki was married twice, the first time in 1906 to Emilia Szwejkowska, who died in 1915. In 1916 he married Eileen Markley, and this proved to be a most remarkable and successful marriage. The young Miss Markley, a graduate of Smith College, had taken her M.A. in history at Columbia University under James

Harvey Robinson. She then experienced frustration in her efforts to matriculate at the Columbia Law School, because its doors at that time were closed to women. She accordingly went to the University of Chicago Law School, where she graduated with a distinguished record. It was in Chicago that she met the young Polish scholar, and after marriage she submerged her own career entirely in his. Except for several articles and chapters which she wrote on Polish sociology, she devoted all of her efforts to Florian's writing, beginning with *The Polish Peasant*. It is difficult to estimate the extent of her contribution to his career but it was very large indeed, and there should be nothing but the most profound recognition of her work as brilliant assistant to her more famous husband. Only those who were close to both of them could understand and appreciate the significance of the role she played in his career. A daughter of this marriage, Helena Znaniecki Lopata, also became a sociologist.

The years at Illinois were pleasant ones for Znaniecki. He occupied a large and comfortable house on a tree-shaded street in Champaign, a typical Midwestern street, and enjoyed the most congenial relationships with his colleagues in the department, which at that time included J. William Albig, Donald R. Taft, and E. T. Hiller. His daily regimen was seldom varied. From Catholic and aristocratic lineage, he was wholly unhampered by the Puritan ethic and accordingly spent his mornings in bed. By the time he rose at noon, however, he had added a number of pages to the corpus of his work. His afternoons were devoted to lectures, when classes were in session, his evenings to quiet reading or, as often as he could manage it, to bridge, a game in which he took great delight. The end of a semester was always a time of agony for him. Not overly impressed by the grading system in the American university, he could not endure giving any of his students a lower grade than B, a system of evaluation that distressed the registrar and attracted hordes of students to his classes. He was a kind and gentle man, dangerous only on the streets of the city in which he drove his car, an activity for which he had no talent.

Znaniecki was a pure academician, one who was at home only

in the realm of ideas. His colleagues at one time elected him rector of the University of Poznan, but administration was a duty he viewed with distaste and he escaped the responsibility as soon as he decently could. He served as president of the American Sociological Society in 1954 and gave his presidential address on "Basic Problems of Contemporary Sociology." In 1952 he published his last major work, *Cultural Sciences*, succeeded in the same year by a smaller work, *Modern Nationalities*. The first of these was dedicated "to the University of Illinois, in gratitude for ten free, happy, and productive years as a member of its faculty," and the second to his students. His final years were devoted to writing a work he never finished, on systematic sociology, fragments of which were edited by his daughter and published posthumously in 1965 under the title *Social Relations and Social Roles*. He died at Urbana, Illinois, on March 23, 1958, at the age of seventy-six.

During the last years before his death Znaniecki spoke frequently of his desire to return to Poland. His friends dissuaded him from doing so, however, on the ground that a visit to that country might imply approval of the regime. He was always, of course, opposed to any restrictions on the freedom of inquiry, restrictions he had experienced in his student days, and he was particularly appalled by the fate of sociology in Poland after World War II. He was a scholar through and through, dedicated to the university, at home in its ambience, zealous in its purpose, and happy in its service. He lived with grace and distinction "the social role of the man of knowledge."

Early Philosophical Writings

Znaniecki's reputation suffered from the fact that almost half of his books were written in Polish, a language inaccessible to most of his American and English readers. Like his countryman Joseph Conrad before him, however, he developed an enviable style in English. His little book, *The Social Role of the Man of Knowledge*, is a masterpiece of the literary art, a book that can be read today not only for its sociological sophistication but also for the aesthetic pleasure to be derived from its English prose. All of his English sentences, in all of his English books, are free of the jargon that sometimes disfigures sociological writing. All of them shine with lucidity and this, in an adopted tongue, is a high order of achievement. On his first voyage to the United States, in 1914, he practiced the new and unfamiliar language by writing an article, "The Principle of Relativity and Philosophical Absolutism." Accepted by *The Philosophical Review*, it was his first publication in English.

Znaniecki's first article published in Polish, in 1909, was a methodological critique of Lévy-Bruhl's *La Morale et la science des mœurs*. The philosophical challenge to which he responded in his youth was an effort to develop a systematic theory of culture. In 1910 he published his first book, *The Problem of Values in Philosophy*, in which he formulated the hypothesis that all theories of culture require at their base a concept of values, which are the common data of human experience and which are not reducible to any combination either of natural objects or of subjective processes. They are unique and belong to a realm of their own, no part of the physical world and yet objectively accessible to inquiry. His second book, *Humanism and Knowledge*, published in 1912, belongs properly to the sociology of knowledge, although Znaniecki did not call it that. In it he developed the view that all knowledge, including scientific knowledge, is a product of the socio-cultural or historico-cultural situation in which it arises. It is in these terms that he aspired to trace the evolution of civilization.

The problem of values was of prime concern to Znaniecki in these early philosophical writings. He wanted very much to build a bridge, undergirded with strong epistemological and ontological support, between this realm and the empirical world of the natural sciences in which values would ultimately be validated. He was interested similarly in the problem of creativity, a phenomenon that seemed to have no counterpart in the natural order of things. In *Cultural Reality*, his first book in English (1919), he addressed himself to these problems. He was concerned about the separation, and growing tension, between idealism and realism in philosophy, by the fact that philosophy itself had surrendered some of its historical issues, and by the failure, in his opinion, of both Bergsonian intuitionism and Deweyan pragmatism to offer satisfactory answers and constructive principles with which the problems of creativity and culture could be solved.

As indicated in the excerpt from *Cultural Reality*, printed here, Znaniecki was puzzled by the fact that idealism, incomparably stronger from any fundamental logical point of view, had consistently given ground to realism, which proved itself able to solve a number of concrete problems. Idealism had thus become incapable of criticizing the internal organization and conclusions of the "realistic sciences," and had to derive only some small comfort by questioning their epistemological and metaphysical foundations. This abdication, however, does not serve the best interests of human culture, or of human knowledge; it violates indeed the highest standards of intellectual, moral, and aesthetic inquiry and reduces them to a mere by-product of a natural evolution. This is the framework in which Znaniecki pursued his thesis, often technical and often complicated, that culture constitutes a reality of its own and is no mere epiphenomenon of a natural universe. It is a reality that neither an unsuccessful idealism nor an illogical naturalism can explain. Among the many statements that express this view the following may be regarded as representative: "If therefore modern thought intends to avoid the emptiness of idealism and the self-contradictions of naturalism, it must accept the culturalistic thesis. It must maintain against idealism the universal historical relativity of all forms of reason and standards of valuation as being within, not above, the evolving empirical world. It must maintain against naturalism that man is not a product of the evolution of nature, but that, on the contrary, nature, in a large measure at least, is the product of human culture, and if there is anything in nature which preceded man the way to find it leads through historical and social science, not through biology, geology, astronomy, or physics."[2]

Although little of *Cultural Reality* is directly relevant to soci-

---

[2]   *Cultural Reality* (Chicago: University of Chicago Press, 1919), pp. 21–22.

ology for the reason that its aims and purposes are primarily to guarantee an ontological status to the realm of culture, Znaniecki nevertheless touches upon sociology in his discussion of the kinds or "orders" of reality. These are four in number: the physical, the psychological, the sociological, and the ideal. With respect to the psychological order, Znaniecki approved of behaviorism insofar as it studied the natural processes of organisms in environment, but he pointed out that in doing so it became a part of biology and thus left the study of conscious data to other schools.[3] The basic problems of psychology are problems of situations and not of objects. It is the situation that gives us a ground for the explanation of personal experiences: "A reality is supposed to assume similar aspects in similar situations; and if it has a certain aspect for the given individual at the given moment, it is because it is determined for his actual experience by some actual situation of which it is a part. Therefore whenever similar situations are found, we expect similar experiences of given reality, and, on the contrary, in different situations we expect different aspects of this reality to appear."[4] Furthermore, what we might be tempted to view as an objective, natural reality—whether thing, property, relation, or process—does not in its own identity afford the conditions of being experienced always and everywhere in the same way. Only when experienced in similar situations can such realities be compared. It is the situation that thus assumes significance. As a matter of fact, objects can have meanings only when we include the social dimension, and a dynamic psychology must therefore be a social psychology. Objects have meanings only when they are seen as elements of situations. In his discussion of the psychological order of reality, Znaniecki discourses at length on attitudes and values and refers to the methodological conception of social psychology and sociology "which Professor Thomas and I have developed together" in the Methodological Note to *The Polish Peasant*.[5]

3   *Ibid.*, p. 274.
4   *Ibid.*, p. 276.
5   *Ibid.*, p. 281, note.

In his treatment of the sociological order of reality, Znaniecki endeavors to show that it is independent both of physical and of psychological reality. For him the social and the psychological are two separate "schemes." It is a self-contradiction to reduce the social to the psychological as it is indeed to reduce the psychological to the social. "By conceiving society as a synthesis of psychological individuals we preclude the possibility of a rational solution of all particular problems which can be solved only with the help of common social schemes acting in and through individuals and yet existing independently of each of them. By conceiving the individual as synthesis of social schemes, we preclude the possibility of the solution of all those problems in which the continuity of personal life or the uniformity of experiences in all conscious individuals independent of the social groups to which they belong are the necessary presuppositions."[6] It is not possible to divide the empirical word into two ontologically separate categories, the psychological and the social; they are rather two different ways of treating the same phenomenon.

When Znaniecki turns his attention to the conditions that are logically indispensable for the construction of an autonomous social science he states his fundamental proposition that social reality is formally constituted of schemes or rules, whether or not consciously formulated, "giving uniform and permanent definitions of personal situations."[7] If schemes or rules are the form, the matter is constituted of social values, which are products of the social order and which stand in an intermediate position between concrete historical reality on the one hand and the objects of natural reality on the other. These must necessarily be communicated, of course, and since there are limits to communication the schemes themselves are limited to particular social groups.

Although we find in *Cultural Reality* echoes of things already written and anticipations of things to come, the book is basically an essay in ontology and methodology—the latter of course in the sense of the logic of inquiry—and, as mentioned above, it would

6   *Ibid.*, pp. 285–286.
7   *Ibid.*, p. 290.

satisfy only a minimum criterion of relevance to sociology. When Znaniecki went to Chicago he had already won a mention of himself and his work in Windelband's monumental *Geschichte der Philosophie*. But he had had no instruction in sociology and for him the discipline was a "new experience." He had hoped to begin an academic career in America in philosophy, and it is testimony to the influence that Thomas benevolently exerted upon him during his period as research assistant that he rejected the old mistress and happily embraced the new. It was a decision he never regretted. But *Cultural Reality* belongs almost entirely to his philosophical phase. Only many years later, in *Cultural Sciences*, did he return again to the issues that had attracted his restless and roving mind in his youth.

The Polish Peasant in Europe and America

So much has been said and written about *The Polish Peasant*, in articles about both Thomas and Znaniecki, that it hardly seems necessary to expatiate upon it again. There is no doubt that it is a classic work in the history of American sociology. Even today, long after the Polish peasants who were the subjects of the book have been assimilated, it maintains its fascination and its significance for the insights it contains about the human person, his attitudes and values, his disorganization and reorganization, as he moves from one culture to another.

For a number of years prior to the meeting of Thomas and Znaniecki in Poland in 1913, Thomas had interested himself in the backgrounds, problems, and adjustments of immigrants then coming to the United States, especially those from central and eastern Europe—Poles, Russians, Rumanians, Czechs, Hungarians, and Jews. He had begun to collect materials about them, and especially about those in the peasant classes, for these made up the large majority of those who chose to emigrate. At some time or other Thomas decided that the exigencies of research would force him to limit his study to one of these groups; and it was the Poles that he selected, primarily because the Polish community in Chicago was a large one and one that seemed to exhibit special kinds of personal and social disorganization. In accordance with this design he visited Poland, talked with everyone he could find who knew anything about the emigrants—professors, newspaper editors, heads of agricultural bureaus, economists—and it was in pursuit of this trail that he was led to Znaniecki. By this time he had already collected a large amount of material, to which Znaniecki, as director of the Emigrants' Protective Association, was able to add a great deal more. It was the beginning of a long and unusually harmonious relationship, both intellectually and personally, with Znaniecki serving Thomas as research assistant, editing and translating Polish documents, helping to formulate the ideas that Thomas and he discussed in their conversations, and preparing drafts of various portions of the manuscript. The work was Thomas's in inception and plan, but it was Znaniecki who persuaded him to include an introductory note that would deal with the methodology of the enterprise. Thomas himself was not attracted to methodological or other philosophical issues, whereas these were the problems that lay at the center of Znaniecki's concerns. It was after Znaniecki wrote the Methodological Note, in at least three drafts, that Thomas decided to add his name to the title page of the book.

Although the careers of the two authors diverged considerably after 1920 and although they were fairly far apart not only in intellectual emphasis but also in temperament, it may be said that their collaboration, precisely because of these differences, was an unusually successful one. It is doubtful indeed if either one of them alone could have brought *The Polish Peasant* to fruition in anything like the form in which we know it or made it the sociological classic it is generally conceded to be. Thomas's contribution was a psychological penetration, a comprehensive curiosity, and a rare wisdom; Znaniecki's a philosophical sophistication, an historical erudition, and a talent for systematization. Unfortunately, friends of each were sometimes tempted in later years to emphasize the contributions of one of them at the expense of the other. It was a game in which neither of the authors indulged. As one who knew both Thomas and Znaniecki well, the former at Harvard and the latter at Illinois, I never heard either of them say anything that would in any degree denigrate the contribution of the other to their joint enterprise. Indeed, Znaniecki, in an article entitled "William I. Thomas as a Collaborator," wrote, "Never have I known, heard, or read about anybody with such a wide, sympathetic interest in the vast diversity of sociocultural patterns and such a genius for understanding the uniqueness of every human personality. The famous statement of Terence: 'I am a man and nothing human seems alien to me,' expresses an ideal which few men have ever realized as fully as Thomas."[8]

Whatever Znaniecki's final view of the Note, and *The Polish Peasant* in general, it is necessary to say that the book nevertheless made major contributions to the developing science of sociology. The first of these was the extensive use of personal documents as an instrument of research. Indeed, even before Thomas turned to this particular subject he had encouraged his students at Chicago to submit to him their autobiographies, including their sexual histories, all of which he regarded as important data for sociological purposes. The autobiography of a young Polish immigrant, Wladek, published originally as Volume 3 and then at the end of Volume 2 in the two-volume edition, is still perhaps the finest example of the use of an autobiographical resource. The credit for this, however, probably belongs to Wladek himself as much as it does to Thomas and Znaniecki. It is an unusual document. Znaniecki continued to use personal documents in his research, and at one time collected biographical material from his students at the University of Illinois, but the ensuing work, entitled "The Social Role of the University Student," was never published.

Of the theoretical contributions of *The Polish Peasant* it is necessary to say only that they were joint products, one the emphasis upon the famous four wishes, and two the emphasis upon attitudes, which provided a stimulus to attitude research in the history of American social psychology. Finally, there is, in the later volumes, the treatment of human personalities and their participation in social life, a participation that often issues, as in the case of the Polish peasant, in disorganization at first and then in reorganization.

In the Methodological Note itself a number of positions are advanced which represent the sociological thought of Thomas and Znaniecki at the time of writing it. First of all, science is regarded as a conscious and rational technique for controlling the physical world, and it is no less important that rational techniques be similarly applied to social reality. The rapid pace of social evolution requires it. For this purpose "common sense" does not suffice. In the first place, we do not "know" social reality simply because we have a certain "empirical acquaintance" with it; the acquaintance that each one of us has is always limited and cannot supply the required generalizations. In the second place, sociology, like the physical sciences, has to win a certain independence from practice. The reformer and the idealist have their roles to play, and important roles they are, but indignation and idealism have no place in sociological inquiry. Unfortunately, what is important in practice may not be important in theory. In the third place, sociology ought not to use current norms as a basis for inquiry because it is precisely in times of rapid social evolution and crisis that the norms themselves are changing. Nor is it desirable or even possible to separate any special set of social facts from the total context of a given society—except, of course, for purely analytical purposes. In the fourth place, theoretical work must not be bent to the service of immediate solutions to practical problems. Science must sooner or later pay its debt to society in the practical application of its results, but if utility is the ultimate criterion it must never be the immediate one.

The following section of the Note is addressed to the task of constructing some kind of synthesis in which both attitudes and values will assume their appropriate places and perform their necessary roles. This was clearly an effort—which Znaniecki later came to regard as an unsuccessful one—to bring Thomas's emphasis upon attitudes into some kind of a viable theoretical relationship with his own concept of values. In the course of the discussion sociology, unlike social psychology with which it has a close affinity, is viewed as a special and not a general science of culture. The authors arrive at a basic methodological principle, in language that is wholly Durkheimian but not altogether Durkheimian in substance, when they say in italics: "The cause of a value or of an attitude is never an attitude or a value alone, but always a combination of an attitude and a value."[9]

The authors reject the view that the sheer complexity of the social world precludes the search for laws or generalizations. The physical world is equally complex. Whether, in spite of the illustrations supplied, the method of *The Polish Peasant* has produced such social laws is a question that animated the critique of Herbert Blumer, a critique with which the authors largely agreed.[10] One of Blumer's observations was that the relationship between the method employed and the quality of the book may not be as close as was then commonly supposed. The distinction of *The Polish Peasant* may be attributable not to the method but rather to the talents of the authors—insight, imagination, intimate knowledge of their subject, and a superior sophistication.

Toward the end of the Note we have a discussion of the "four wishes" which, to Thomas's subsequent surprise, occupied so large a place in the histories of sociology. Here the wish for mastery is listed although it was later to be replaced, by Thomas, by the wish for response, largely in order to include the sexual factor whose importance Thomas had come increasingly to recognize. The Note concludes with the modest affirmation that the book is devoted primarily to a study of the attitudes and values that obtain in a specific social group, namely, the migrating Polish peasants, with the intent to show that both of these attributes are important factors in any effort to understand and define the situation.

Excerpts from the Methodological Note, surely the longest "note" in the history of the literature, appear in a number of places. The Note is so important, however, that we reprint it here in

9   William I. Thomas and Florian Znaniecki, *The Polish Peasant in Europe and America* (New York: Alfred A. Knopf, 1927), 1:44.

10   *Critiques of Research in the Social Sciences.* vol. 1 (New York: Social Science Research Council, 1939).

its entirety. It is an eloquent and enduring contribution to the science of sociology.

The Method of Sociology

A claim can be made for the proposition that of all of Znaniecki's books in English, *The Method of Sociology* offers the most complete and satisfactory system, even though it is dedicated largely to issues of method rather than to issues of substance. It is concerned, that is, with the selection and determination of scientific data in general, with the principles of selection of cultural data, with the data of sociology, with a criticism of certain methodological tendencies of which Znaniecki disapproved, and finally wth his own recommended method, the method of analytic induction. The book also offers us almost all of the specific notions that informed Znaniecki's approach. When he wrote it he was conscious of the fact that sociology was passing through a critical period, that what had once been a synthetic science interested in "society" or "civilization"—a special kind of philosophy of history—was in process of becoming an analytic science directed to the investigation of detailed, particular, and specific kinds of empirical data. It was becoming not only distrustful of the sweeping generalization but in fact indifferent to it. This shift in the focus of the science seemed to Znaniecki to require a more thoroughgoing methodological sophistication than had previously been exhibited, and this was a prime factor in his decision to write this particular book. The time had come for sociology to indulge in "fundamental discussion concerning the general possibilities and conditions of its future development."[11]

Znaniecki gives in his preface a clear indication of three of the views that informed his methodological theory. The first of these is that sociology is a special and not a general social science; that it has its own special subject-matter, its own "specific category of data" shared by no other science; and that, without being

[11]   *The Method of Sociology*, (New York: Farrar and Rinehart, 1934), p. vii.

as formalistic as Simmel, for example, would have liked, it is nevertheless, and of methodological necessity, limited to the treatment of a restricted but important range of facts. The second is that, in opposition to positivistic approaches to the study of society, Znaniecki decided to emphasize what he called "the primary and essential meaningfulness of social reality, to accept human values and activities as facts, just as human agents themselves accept them, but to study them objectively and with the application of the same formal principles as the physicist and the biologist apply to material nature." And finally, the third is that over-zealous efforts to quantify social data often "sacrifice the substance of valuable knowledge and true discovery for the shadow of mathematical formulae devoid of significant content." At the same time, with respect to the last, Znaniecki recognized the importance of maintaining in his qualitative studies "the highest standard of logical exactness compatible with the nature of social data."[12]

The three principles attracted a number of polemical dissents from those who maintained, on the contrary (like Sorokin for example), that sociology is a general and not a special social science; from those (like Lundberg for example) who denied that there is any "social reality" that is ontologically distinguishable from "physical reality," whatever these two expressions may mean; and from those (like perhaps a majority of American sociologists) who insisted that only through the use of quantitative methods could sociology achieve its proper stature as a science. These controversies were rife in American sociology during the four decades of Znaniecki's productive life, and it is only to be expected that, as a prolific writer in the field, he was drawn into them. It was for the same reason that he became one of the principal targets of the opposing schools. It is amusing to recall in this connection that Lundberg, no mean polemicist, once scored a debating point against him. Znaniecki had been incautious enough to observe that "wherever the statistical method definitely gains the ascendency, the number of students of a high intellectual level who are attracted to sociology tends to fall off considerably."[13] To this

12   *Ibid.*
13   *Ibid.*, p. 234, note.

Lundberg had the apparently devastating answer that Znaniecki had had recourse to a statistical argument to prove the inferiority of statistics.[14]

In any event, a number of salient points attract our attention in this book. Znaniecki argues, for example, that although practical experience has already taught us a great deal about social life, and indeed these teachings have both empirical importance and pragmatic relevance, they do not nevertheless suffice as groundwork for scientific knowledge in sociology. Observations like these, based upon individual experience, cannot themselves do more than serve as building blocks in the construction of a systematic science. The same observations can be made about centuries of ethical and political reflection. All of it is suggestive, much of it is useful, and some of it may even be "true." But again, it has no relevance to a systematic sociological theory until it is organized into propositions that lead to generalizations about social actions and social relations. Furthermore, as asserted also in *Cultural Reality*, a theoretic science cannot be built upon practical considerations. Even though some theoretical knowledge should prove to be completely useless, as is almost certainly the case, a science can grow only as it conforms to the theoretic criteria involved in the acquisition and advancement of knowledge. As Znaniecki says, "No theoretic science can, therefore, afford to have the selection of its object-matter prescribed to it by any practical considerations."[15] A theoretic science like sociology can grow and prosper only when it uses theoretic criteria and theoretic standards in the selection of its problems, and in the determination of its data.

Znaniecki was enamoured of closed systems in sociological thought. Such systems involve a degree of abstraction—perhaps a considerable degree—from the volume of concrete experiences in the empirical realm of social life. Abstraction, however, is necessary for two reasons. First of all, it is entirely useless to require the sociologist to attend to every event in which every human individual is involved. It would be similarly useless to require the

14   George A. Lundberg, *Foundations of Sociology* (New York: Macmillan Company, 1939), p. 53.
15   *Method of Sociology*, p. 7.

botanist to describe every leaf on every tree. Only God can watch the sparrow fall. Secondly, in the explanation of social change, the only way of avoiding the insoluble problem of infinite antecedents is by constructing systems in which every possible kind of change will find its appropriate place. In Znaniecki's own words, "Only when we are able to connect a process with some closed system and interpret it as a change of this system do we gain a standard of the relative importance of its antecedents as factors in its occurrence."[16]

On the relationship between facts and theories—a lacuna particularly noticeable in sociology—Znaniecki is especially incisive. He writes, "There is only one course open for sociology, if it wishes definitely to avoid both the Charybdis of theorizing with no firmer ground than the hypotheses of the other sciences accepted as dogmas, and the Scylla of an irrational mass of motley information, however interesting in itself. This course is *to determine exactly the general type of those closed systems which it is the special right and duty of the sociologist to study,* and to concentrate primarily on these."[17] It is clear from these remarks that neither an undisciplined rationalism nor a planless empiricism will satisfy Znaniecki's criteria for the determination of the problems and data of sociology and that, although both rationalism and empiricism are susceptible to the excesses of enthusiasm, both must be used as instruments for the discovery and ordering of sociological knowledge. Discovering and ordering, investigating and systematizing—these are the activities that jointly build a science.

Znaniecki insists, in the neo-Kantian manner, upon a fundamental distinction between two different kinds of systems—natural systems on the one hand and cultural systems on the other—which exhibit differences not only in composition and structure but also in the character of the elements that account for their coherence. He summarizes the differences with the assertion that natural systems are objectively given and exist in independence of the experience and activity of men. Cultural systems, on the other

16   *Ibid.*, p. 19.
17   *Ibid.*, pp. 28–29; italics in original.

hand, depend not only for their meaning but also for their very existence upon the participation of conscious and active human agents and upon their relations with one another. Znaniecki has his own label for this difference. It is the humanistic coefficient that distinguishes cultural from natural systems. The data of the former always belong to somebody, exist in the experience of conscious agents, and are objects of theoretic reflection. It is the humanistic coefficient which characterizes Znaniecki's sociology and which separates it rather sharply from the behavioristic theories of many of his contemporaries on the American scene, although it bears a resemblance, of course, to the category of meaning in Sorokin's "logico-meaningful method," to the "dynamic assessment" in Mac-Iver, and to the choice factor in Parson's voluntaristic theory of action.[18]

As a footnote to this point—namely, the distinction between natural and cultural systems—it may be observed that the elements of the former Znaniecki calls "things," and the elements of the latter, "values." A value has both a content and a meaning, whereas a thing has only a content. Thus, he still clings tenaciously to one of his favorite philosophical concepts, and one he tried to bring into some kind of a synthesis with Thomas's concept of attitude in *The Polish Peasant.* Znaniecki has a great many things to say about values, and strives in fact to remove them from the sphere of volitions, but other sociologists—probably because of the long and complicated history of the concept of value in ethical theory—have preferred to avoid the word altogether.

On another issue, however, the issue of *Wertfreiheit,* Znaniecki firmly associates himself with those who contend that sociology is a categorical and not a normative discipline, that it deals with what is and not with what ought to be. He is far from denying, of course, the importance and indeed the necessity of such normative disciplines as social and political philosophy, but he wants to emphasize that such pursuits have nothing to do with the positive

18   Znaniecki had already formulated his concept of the humanistic coefficient in his *Introduction to Sociology.* See *Wstęp do socjologji* (Poznań: Poznańskie Tow, 1922), p. 452.

science of sociology. For, as he says, "when theoretic investigation of activities is combined with their normative standardization, there is always the danger that the former will be subordinated to the latter with results detrimental to scientific validity."[19]

As suggested above, sociology was a very special kind of discipline for Znaniecki. It was not a natural science; it was not social or political philosophy, or indeed any kind of normative discipline; it was not psychology or social psychology; it was not the purely formal discipline that Simmel might have liked, at least in part of its endeavors; it was not a general theory of cultural data as Durkheim thought (parts of *The Division of Labor* excepted) ; and above all it was not the synthetic science that Barth envisaged in his *Philosophie der Geschichte als Soziologie.* Perhaps the outstanding significance of *The Method of Sociology* is that in this book in its entirety Znaniecki gives his readers the sense of sociology as a distinctive discipline, a discipline with its own method and subject matter, and a discipline, needless to say, for which he had the highest aspirations.

If sociology is none of the things just mentioned, it is important to say positively and precisely what it is in Znaniecki's conception. The answer is readily forthcoming. Sociology is a science of social systems and these systems in turn fall into four main subdivisions which are, respectively, the theory of social actions, the theory of social relations, the theory of social persons, and the theory of social groups. The data of these subdivisions reveal as clearly as anything can that sociology is a special science and has its own special field of investigation; that social systems as such differ from other cultural systems like, for example, technical, economic, religious, and linguistic systems; and that it is time for sociologists to abandon the superannuated claims of creating a "synthetic" or "fundamental" science of society or of culture. Sociology is a special and not a general social science, and on this point Znaniecki was adamant.

Nothing has been said so far about the role of conscious agents, or active subjects as Znaniecki sometimes called them, in his sys-

[19]   *Method of Sociology*, pp. 47–48.

tem of sociology. It may suffice to say that everywhere in his work he emphasized the subjective point of view, the importance of seeing social action from the actor's side and not only from the observer's. In this respect, of course, although from a different tradition, he anticipated Parsons and Parsons might have found in him a mentor superior to any of the three—Durkheim, Pareto, Weber—whose theories allegedly converged into a voluntaristic theory of action. Certainly no one in the history of the discipline concentrated so steadfastly upon action as a basic category of sociological inquiry, and no one before or since analyzed actions in such comprehensive detail. Indeed, his next book was entitled *Social Actions* (1936). And no one could have written with more insistence than Znaniecki that sociology has nothing to do with human beings as organisms or as "natural entities" in any psychological or biological sense. It is social persons both as conscious agents and as objects of the actions of others that qualify as sociological data. Every man is an aspect of himself as he appears to someone else—and here the influence of Cooley is also manifest—and to himself as well. This is a crucial point in Znaniecki's theory. For here we find the locus of the primary data of sociology. These aspects of selves and others are "realities." They are *there*, so to speak, in the universe of values, and they are the building blocks—not to say the very foundation—of a science of sociology.

Sociology therefore draws its data from several sources: (1) the personal experience of the sociologist, both original and vicarious; (2) observation by the sociologist, both direct and indirect; (3) the personal experience of other people; and (4) observation by other people. To these four he added a fifth, subsidiary, source; namely, generalizations made by other people with or without scientific purposes in mind. The emphasis upon personal experience, however, is clear, whether that of the sociologist or that of the subject he is studying. It is this emphasis which served as the methodological foundation for the ultilization of personal documents in *The Polish Peasant* and elsewhere. Znaniecki never hesitated in his attacks upon the limitations of statistical methods and never ceased his insistence that only by the use of personal and even intimate sources, such as diaries, letters, and autobiographies, could the sociologist make full utilization of the humanistic co-efficient which above all distinguished the social from the physical sciences. Surely the autobiography of Wladek in *The Polish Peasant* contributed to this goal, in spite of, or indeed because of, the fact that it was so frank in every sphere of life, including the sexual. But that autobiography, explicit as it was, was nowhere near as outspoken with respect to sexual experience as another one that Znaniecki later published in Polish, under the auspices of the Polish Sociological Institute, which first aroused a storm of protest in Poland and then came to be regarded in that country—so rapidly do the mores change—as one of Znaniecki's important contributions.

In one respect, however, Znaniecki, doubtless in a moment of carelessness, went too far. Although the term "participant-obser-vation" had not yet been invented, he nevertheless insisted that just as we cannot experience a sentence without speaking it, a game of golf without playing it, and a geometrical theorem without proving it, so also we could not know what friendship was without being a friend, what a marital relationship was without being married, and so on. He concludes therefore that "The only way actually to experience a social system at first-hand is to be active in its construction, for only thus are we directly aware of the tendencies involved in its structure and the actual significance of the values included in its composition."[20] With these assertions, however, Znaniecki gave hostages to those who would deride the use of subjective data in sociology. It would follow that one could not understand such phenomena as the commission of a crime, the conducting of an orchestra, and the government of a monarchy without oneself being a criminal, a conductor, or a king. Fortunately, as Znaniecki concedes in a subsequent paragraph, the range of anyone's own experience is fairly narrow and to have to remain within its boundaries would result in a limited discipline. He is still concerned to claim, however, that the personal experiences of sociologists have the same objective validity as the

[20]   *Ibid.*, p. 157.

"methodical observations" made by students of the physical universe, even though the risks of error are greater.

In the last sections of his book Znaniecki criticizes certain methodological tendencies that are apparent in sociology. Among these are simple enumerative induction (Spencer, Sumner and Keller) and the effort to increase the precision of such induction by statistical techniques. Formal precision has nothing to do with material significance. Indeed, statistical methods are not only useless but are actually harmful in that they substitute mechanical tabulation for creative thought. There are, of course, certain legitimate uses of the statistical method, but on the whole it can contribute little to scientific progress. He prefers instead a method he calls analytic induction, a method whose introduction into sociological research he attributes almost entirely to W. I. Thomas. The point is that in the use of statistical method each case is treated exactly like every other case, whereas in analytic induction the differences between cases receive methodological recognition. Whether the method of analytic induction is simply another name for orthodox casual analysis by way of case study, or whether it is something much more sophisticated, is an issue that cannot occupy additional space here. Although the controversy it aroused has since subsided,[21] and although analytic induction is not a label in current use, the subject retains sufficient interest to warrant reprinting a brief discussion of it in this book.

Znaniecki supplies no general summary to *The Method of Sociology*. One can nevertheless be found in the preface, where he says that the book "embodies the result of long and strenuous efforts to harmonize ideals with reality, to reconcile the standards of highest scientific perfection, derived partly from philosophy, partly from the methodologies of physical and biological sciences, with the need for preserving intact those characteristics which concrete social facts possess in our experience. It has been worked

---

[21]   See W. S. Robinson, "The Logical Structure of Analytic Induction," *American Sociological Review* 16 (1951): 812–818; also comments by Alfred R. Lindesmith, *Ibid.*, 17 (1952): 492–493; S. Kirson Weinberg, *Ibid.*, 17 (1952): 494; and Robert C. Angell, *Ibid.*, 19 (1954): 476–477.

out in a continual conflict between the interests of exact analysis and strictly rational systematization on the one hand, and the interests of unprejudiced observation and empirical research with their inexhaustible variety of materials, on the other."[22] Znaniecki's success in satisfying these two contrary criteria is evident in everything he wrote, and especially in *The Method of Sociology*.

Social Actions

Social Actions (1936), although it is a book of over seven hundred pages, requires less attention than its size and its chronological position in Znaniecki's career would seem to warrant. He tells us in his preface that he worked on the book for fifteen years, rewriting parts of it no fewer than six times; indeed, internal evidence also suggests that much of it was written prior to *The Method of Sociology*, whose publication date is two years earlier. In any event, it is less well organized than the earlier book, less incisive in its view of sociology, and it offers to the reader less sense of system. Its importance lies in its insights into the internal meaning of various types of actions and the manner in which investigation and analysis of such meanings can contribute to sociological theory.

The pivotal concept, of course, is actions. Znaniecki insisted that a systematic treatment of various types of social actions—indeed as many types as possible—was a necessary prerequisite for all sociological studies: "Without knowing what the various ways are in which men tend to deal actively with other men and how those ways have evolved, we cannot understand their efforts to regulate normatively their mutual activities by customs, mores, and laws, or the social positions which they individually occupy and the functions they perform in their communities, or the organized groups which they create, maintain, and destroy."[23] Znaniecki's primary task, therefore, as he conceived it, was the de-

[22]   *Method of Sociology*, pp. vii–viii.
[23]   *Social Actions* (New York: Farrar & Rinehart, 1936), p. ix.

scription, analysis, and classification of social actions. The major portion of the book, therefore, is devoted to analyses of various kinds of actions including among others, invitation, suggestion, incitement, persuasion, cooperative guidance, educational guidance, participative submission, purposive submission, imitation, primary opposition (*i.e.*, self-defense), coercion, repression (especially of criminal behavior), revolt, inter-collective opposition, aggression, altruism, hostility, and compromise.

The emphasis here continues to rest upon *social* actions. There is in addition a very large category of non-social actions—for example, technical actions, linguistic actions, religious actions, economic actions, and so on—which, though often intimately related to social actions, nevertheless lie outside the purview of the sociologist. One might be tempted to say that all actions indulged in by human beings are social because, except for those rare cases that are quite anomic, they all conform to norms of one kind or another, and that writing a book, painting a picture, or changing a tire are therefore social actions. One could say indeed that everything we do or even refrain from doing—above the level of sheer reflexive behavior—is social action. For Znaniecki, however, this view is unacceptable if sociology wants to carve out a domain of its own and thus take its place among the other sciences, each of which can justify on ontological grounds a separate and necessary field of inquiry. In his view social actions are those actions that deal with human beings, with human beings, furthermore, who are themselves experienced as conscious objects by the authors of the actions. The object of a social action is another individual (or a collectivity) who has a capacity to be influenced by the action. Otherwise the action, even though surrounded and constrained by norms, is not a social action. Social actions are thus actions directed solely to persons (or collectivities) and would seem, therefore, to be always interactions, although Znaniecki does not use this word until *Cultural Sciences*, a book which appeared some sixteen years later, and there is no mention of it in the index of *Social Actions*.

The autonomy of sociology in relation to psychology was a

point of considerable importance to Znaniecki and he always resisted, once with unaccustomed vehemence,[24] any suggestion that his treatment of actions was in fact social psychology rather than sociology. His view of the matter is well expressed in the first chapter of *Social Actions*, reprinted in this book, which indicates clearly that he opposed any effort to deduce propositions about actions from psychology, whether the psychology was of the Freudian, behavioristic, or any other variety, and insisted that social actions had to be investigated and studied independently, as independent empirical data, without any relationship to psychological theory. One finds here, as in other places in Znaniecki's work, agreement with and no doubt also the influence of Durkheim. He would have rejected out of hand the reductionist tendency that has recently reappeared in American sociology.

In the years 1928 and 1930 Znaniecki published in Polish the first and second volumes respectively of a book on the sociology of education. Much of it is summarized, although only very briefly, in the chapter in *Social Actions* entitled "Educational Guidance," and in the essay that accompanies the references to this chapter. Sociology and education, though combined in the sociology of education, are in fact two different disciplines which should not be confused. Educators as such write on the history of education, on the learning process, on the school system, on the ends of education, and so on. None of this is sociology. The sociology of education has a different task to perform and that is to make an objective, theoretical study of the social facts involved in the educational process, the social action that goes on between the educator and what Znaniecki called the "educand," the teacher on the one hand and the learner on the other. A general sociology will of course concern itself with more than actions—it includes also social relations, social persons, and social groups—and so also a

[24] On a train trip between Chicago and Champaign, Illinois, Theodore Abel and I went too far in teasing him about this, suggesting that he was a psychologist at heart and had no business attending a meeting of the American Sociological Association, from which we were returning. The old gentleman, as he then was, became quite angry with us and stoutly defended his position.

sociology of education will some day attend to all four categories of theory. For the present, however, it is sufficient to begin with the first of these, the social actions of educators.

Educational guidance, as opposed to cooperative guidance, is concerned with the actions of some persons in teaching other persons what the latter do not yet know or know how to perform. In the first instance the mother teaches the child the various things he needs to know, and of course this is a process that occurs in all societies. The young are also taught in a primary way to cooperate with those who teach them originally, their parents, and in a secondary way with other adults. As the demands of adult society increase in scope and difficulty, however, the parents are no longer able, especially since they have a life of their own, to give all of the guidance required, and consequently an increasing part of the responsibility is assigned to people known as teachers or educators. The prototype of the educator is the old man of the tribe, full of the lore and the mysteries and eager to pass them on to the young. Hunters, warriors, priests, physicians, and rhetoricians often performed this function too, but in modern societies the role of educator is differentiated and requires special training for those who wish to play it. The chapter continues with discussions of patterns of educational guidance, education as a process in which the educand's social personality is formed, the guidance of the educand's "reflected self" (Znaniecki acknowledges his indebtedness to Cooley here), the system of apprenticeship, the teaching of formal skills, the teaching of ideas, thinkers as educators, professional education, education as a means to a career, and the significance of authority and prestige in educational guidance.

Volume I of the larger work is concerned primarily with the social function of education and Volume II with the educational process as such. The latter begins, incidentally, with the humanistic coefficient, which played so prominent a part in everything that Znaniecki wrote. In both volumes he insisted that education is a social process, once again with emphasis upon the adjective. In a long passage Znaniecki also has occasion to discuss the sick role and, in conformity with contemporary medical so-

ciology, to regard the sick individual as one of the most significant of all personality types, and one that changes in different
societies and in different periods of history. He also included a
chapter on the sociology of sport, a subject which, despite its importance in every modern society, has received almost no scientific attention. In this book too, Znaniecki used the expression
"reference group" in almost the same sense in which Merton was
later to give it conceptual significance.

One final issue invites a modicum of attention before we leave
Social Actions, and that, once more, is Znaniecki's emphasis upon
the dynamic quality of social relations. Znaniecki always regarded
Comte's distinction between social statics and social dynamics as
pernicious and he expressed his opposition to it with an earnest
enthusiasm. The social world is a world becoming and not a world
in being, and for this reason studies of social structure as such
can only lead to distortion of social reality. Studies of this kind,
in fact, are erroneous in basic premise because there is no such
thing as a static action. Taking an ancient cue from Heraclitus,
Znaniecki insisted that all is action in society and that it is thus
inconsistent and unwarranted to inquire into a social structure.
One can no more talk about social structure than one can change
a tire while the automobile is in motion. The opposing view,
urged upon him without Eleatic malice by some of his associates,
that society nevertheless exhibits patterns, constants, and regularities, and that these too might be legitimate subjects for inquiry, left him wholly unimpressed. In this connection too it is
interesting to recognize that he seldom used such concepts as
"community" or "society," usually maintaining that he did not
know what they meant. As static concepts they violated his sense
of the flux and changefulness of the human scene. He was a follower of Bergson rather than of Descartes.

The Social Role of the Man of Knowledge

The Social Role of the Man of Knowledge, as mentioned
before, consists of a series of lectures that Znaniecki delivered at
Columbia University in the summer of 1939, before his last fate-

ful effort to return to Poland. It is, as I have also said, a book so beautifully written that students today can read it for pleasure as well as profit. In it Znaniecki insists again that sociology is a special social science and not a general cultural science, and that legitimate sociological interest in the "sociology of knowledge"— probably an unfortunate label, as Louis Wirth also was inclined to suspect—would properly focus not upon the relationships that may obtain between knowledge and the sociocultural conditions that give rise to it, not upon questions of validity in changing historical contexts, but rather upon the social relations that those who are engaged in the discovery of knowledge, its dissemination, and its use have to one other and to those who receive its benefits. If the sociology of knowledge meant, for example, a sociological theory of knowledge, then sociology would be in the curious— and untenable—position of articulating and determining its own character as sociology.

In this book also Znaniecki placed heavy reliance upon the two concepts of social person and social circle, both of which played a major role in his subsequent thinking. They appear, for example, in his description of a social role, as follows: "Every social role presupposes that between the individual performing the role, who may thus be called a 'social person,' and a smaller or larger set of people who participate in his performance and may be termed his 'social circle' there is a common bond constituted by a complex of values which all of them appreciate positively."[25] The circle gives to the person a social status, indeed a set of social roles, or "role-set" in more recent parlance, and he in turn performs a number of discernible functions for the circle. These Znaniecki regards as the essential components of social roles and it is in these terms that he discusses the social role of the man of knowledge.

In the course of this discussion Znaniecki has occasion to treat in turn the roles of technologists, priests, sages, scholars, and "explorers," the last being those who create new knowledge. He traces

[25]   *The Social Role of the Man of Knowledge* (New York: Columbia University Press, 1940), pp. 14–15.

the history of these roles and accents the manner in which they have changed from century to century in the West. He answers the question, far from rhetorical, why men of knowledge have been tolerated and even encouraged by those whose active pursuits, on the contrary, are politics or business or war, and why they have been granted the status they enjoy in most modern societies. It is again a changeful status, always in flux, but one that always possesses some measure of prestige. Once more we acclaim this book as a small masterpiece, one of the most illuminating essays in the literature of sociology, and one whose last chapter, "The Explorer as Creator of New Knowledge," we are glad to reprint in this book.[26]

Cultural Sciences: Their Origin and Development

In *Cultural Sciences* (1952), a large and learned book, Znaniecki traveled beyond the boundaries of sociology proper—boundaries that he himself had tried to chart—and wrote again, as in his first English book, as a philosopher of culture. He had intended, he tells us in the preface, to outline the historical evolution of sociology, but he could not isolate its threads from the history of philosophy and science and consequently had to attend to the origin and development of the cultural sciences in their entirety. Beginning with the problem of order, Znaniecki distinguishes between order as the intentional creation of conscious agents and order as a condition of successful activity, and then proceeds to a discussion of certain metaphysical postulates of universal order. He is next concerned with various theories of man which have emerged in Western thought and attends to three controversial issues in this realm of inquiry including (1) biological versus psychological determinants of culture, (2) individual entities versus collectivities, and the problems that have arisen concerning the ontological status of the group, and (3)

[26]   For a thoughtful and sympathetic review see Robert K. Merton, *American Sociological Review* (1941): 111–115.

determinism versuş creativity in the history of man and culture. After another look at order, this time the natural order among different kinds of data, Znaniecki arrives at one of his central concerns, namely human actions, which leads him further into a consideration of three of the basic concepts in his general approach to sociology. These are human actions themselves, active tendencies, and standards and norms. Attention to standards and norms in a separate treatment indicates that toward the end of his career Znaniecki came to stress increasingly that social actions belong to axio-normatively ordered systems and cannot be understood without axiological reference. Here again he returns, from the sociological direction so to speak, to his earlier interest in values. The book concludes with discussions of cultural patterns and systems of actions, the disorganization and reorganization of cultural systems, an important chapter on the function of sociology as a cultural science, part of which we reprint in this book, and finally a brief discourse on the practical applications of the cultural sciences.

The book is full of insights, and rich in erudition. In some respects, of course, Znaniecki reiterates or expands upon points of view treated in earlier works. Throughout, however, we find him insisting that sociology is a specialized discipline, not a general science of culture or of society, and that it deals specifically wth social actions, social relations, social groups, and social roles. But in this regard there is a new note, namely, that sociology, though specialized, is nevertheless the basic cultural science and performs the same function in this respect that physics does for the natural sciences. These two facets of sociology, in fact, are related to each other. As his own words make perfectly clear, "Sociologists are gradually becoming aware that the importance of sociology for other cultural sciences *increases* in the very measure in which it *limits its task* to a comparative study of those social systems upon which the existence of every realm of culture depends."[27] Sociology, in short, though specialized, is nevertheless

[27]   *Cultural Sciences* (Urbana, Ill.: University of Illinois Press, 1952), p. 396, note.

the basic social science and one which makes possible the existence and guarantees the viability of the others. It makes these others possible because they too involve human actions, which are social actions. This is the unique contribution that sociology can make, and in doing so it accepts a responsibility that no other social science shares, a responsibility that gives it its own place in the universe of ideas.

Znaniecki's observations on the practical applications of the cultural sciences, with which he concludes his book, are brief. His final paragraph, however, sheds some light not only upon the nature of his thought but also upon the character of the man himself:

As a sociologist and a philosophical optimist, I like to imagine that sooner or later the solution of all important human problems will be entrusted to cultural scientists, and that sociologists will assume the task of ascertaining how innovations of specialists in various realms of culture (including the realms of natural sciences and of techniques) can be cooperatively used by social groups of practical agents for the best advantage of humanity. This does not mean that the future of mankind would be planned and controlled by sociologists, as Comte imagined, or that the human world would become not only socially united, but culturally uniform. It means rather that sociologists would function as intellectual leaders in the ceaseless course of differentiation and integration of social roles and social groups throughout the world. By performing this function, they would indirectly contribute to the continuous creative growth of new varieties of cultural systems and the enrichment and diversification of individual lives.[28]

Znaniecki was an optimist to the end, believing firmly and even fiercely in the prospects, both theoretical and practical, of the discipline to which he devoted his life.

Conclusion

I have not sought in this introduction to provide a complete résumé of Znaniecki's writings. Some of these, like *The Laws of Social Psychology* (1925) are superseded by later works;

[28]   *Ibid.*, p. 419, *finis.*

others, like *Modern Nationalities* (1952), however suggestive, are addressed to special subjects;[29] and still another, *Social Relations and Social Roles* (1965), posthumously edited and published by his daughter, consists of a series of essays which, enlightening in themselves, were planned for inclusion in a larger and unfinished volume on systematic sociology. In a sense that is a compliment to the author, all of his work was unfinished. Every book, no matter how comprehensive or complete in itself, was conceived as part of a larger and more systematic work. Znaniecki always looked ahead to the contributions that he would make in the future.[30]

Nor can I say anything about the Polish works for the simple reason that I do not read the language. I have had to rest content, therefore, with the contributions Znaniecki made in English, contributions that suffice, and more, to establish and maintain his reputation. One would like nevertheless to be able to read what he had to say, in his poetry, about Cheops, builder of the great pyramid at Giza, to study carefully his *Introduction to Sociology* (1922),[31] to read his book on the city, published in 1931, and most especially to follow his thoughts in the 1935 book whose title is translated as *The People of Today and the Civilization of Tomorrow*, a book that enjoyed a rather considerable reception among the Polish intellectuals of its time.

Nor finally, have I tried to write a definitive treatise on Znaniecki's contributions to sociology. No such treatise can be contained in a few pages and here, in any event, Znaniecki's words can speak for themselves. His reputation, though secure, will fluctuate with the tides of time and ideas, and it is still too early for those Olympian judgments in which the historians of sociology will one day indulge. It will be enough perhaps if we conclude with summary

---

[29]   See also, for example, *The Sociology of the Struggle for Pomerania* (1934) ; also in French and Polish.

[30]   I have also omitted several papers of importance, including "Social Organization and Institutions" (1945), "Social Groups in the Modern World" (1954), and his Presidential Address to the American Sociological Association, "Basic Problems of Contemporary Sociology" (1954). See bibliography for details.

[31]   *Wstęp do socjologji.* Znaniecki supplied a brief summary of the book in English, pp. 451–467.

statements of Znaniecki's principal points of view, which are five in number: (1) that sociology is a social and not a natural science and that culture is a reality in its own ontological right; (2) that sociology is a special and not a general social science, concerned not with everything that happens in society but only with conscious agents as they interact with one another and thus fit into systems of social actions; (3) that these systems, in turn, are constitutive of sociological knowledge; (4) that, notwithstanding the differences between natural and social systems, investigation of the latter can be as objective, as precise, and as penetrating as investigation in the other sciences; and (5) that sociology, though properly limited in scope, is nevertheless the basic cultural science.

The stars, it is said, have no sentiments, the atoms no anxieties that have to be taken into account. But sentiments and anxieties are intimately involved in the actions of human beings, and these actions require therefore for their understanding some comprehension of the humanistic coefficient. It is the humanistic coefficient that distinguishes sociology as a cultural science from the sciences of nature and gives meaning and significance to sociological inquiry.

Robert Bierstedt

1. The Subject Matter of Sociology

CULTURAL REALITY

1919

THE PREDOMINANT feature of intellectual evolution during the last hundred and fifty years has been the growing separation and struggle between realism, representing the relatively new and common ground of all sciences of nature, and idealism, representing partly a survival, partly a development of the fundamental points of that view of the world which was achieved by the synthesis of mediaeval religious doctrines and ancient philosophy. And—a curious historical problem—the faction which, from the standpoint of logical consistency, was and is decidedly and irremediably in the wrong has been continually victorious in this struggle, has gradually wrestled away from its opponent its whole domain, appropriated all the vital intellectual issues, and left to the spoiled, though not subjugated, enemy nothing but the empty and practically useless consciousness of his eternal right.

It is not difficult to see how this process went along. The triumph of realism, in any sphere of investigation, has not consisted in a successful logical demonstration of the validity of its claims and methods, but simply in an actual growth of the number and importance of the concrete particular problems which it set and solved, without concerning itself much as to the philosophical justification of the standpoint assumed in these problems. The defeat of idealism, in any sphere of investigation, was not due to a logical inferiority of its general philosophical doctrine, but simply

Chapter 1, "Culturalism," from *Cultural Reality* (Chicago: University of Chicago Press, 1919), pp. 1–15.

to the fact that it failed to develop a large and continually growing body of positive empirical knowledge based on idealistic premises.

Thus realism grew stronger with every step and no efforts could prevent idealism from losing ground continually in the wide field of intellectual life covered by empirical science, and popular reflection. Every particular realistic science, in its beginnings usually despised by idealistic philosophy for its lack of logical perfection, became more and more self-consistent as it developed, and some of these sciences have reached a level where idealism itself is forced to treat them as models of systematic construction. And it can scarcely deny to them this tribute, because it has in its past days emphasized the importance and the rational perfection of those very *organa* which realistic sciences use in systematizing their investigations, i.e., the logic of things-substances and the mathematical theory of functions. Idealism has become thus unable to attack the internal organization of realistic sciences; it can criticize only their foundations, their explicit or implicit epistemological and metaphysical presuppositions. Of course, as long as a realistic science claims an absolute validity for its foundations, idealistic criticism has an easy task in showing the absurdity of such claims, in demonstrating, for example, that the assumption of an absolute objectivity of geometrical space is self-contradictory or that the reduction of all sensual qualities to movements of matter is not a substitution of reality for illusion but merely an expression of all kinds of sensual data in terms of one particular kind of sensual data, a combination of certain sensations of sight with certain sensations of touch and of the muscular sense. If, however, a realistic science begins to base its claims not on the abstract philosophical justification of its presuppositions, but on the practical applicability of its results; if it concedes that its assumptions cannot be demonstrated a priori but that they show themselves valid a posteriori by the growing control of reality which they permit, the attacks of idealism lose much of their force. For in this line also idealism itself has unconsciously strengthened in advance the position of realism by bringing forth, in order to defend traditional religion and morality against realistic theoretic analysis, the idea that practical claims can have an objective validity of their own, independent of theoretic criteria; it can therefore hardly reject now the test of practical applicability to which realistic science appeals.

This is not all. During the first three centuries of its development scientific realism was practically unable to reach any general view of the world. Not only did a large part of experience remain for a long time outside of realistic investigations, but the connection between such investigations as were pursued in various sciences of nature was not close enough to become the foundation of a consistent realistic conception of the entire empirical world. The rise of a realistic psychology and sociology on the one hand, the doctrine of natural evolution on the other, obviated these difficulties and led to modern naturalism—the most comprehensive and consistent realistic doctrine ever reached. The application of positive realistic methods to individual consciousness and to social institutions brought within the scope of naturalistic science a domain from which idealism drew most of its materials; at the same time the theory of evolution not only gave a general foundation on which all sciences of nature could hope to attain their metaphysical unity, but bridged over the chasm between man as thinking subject and his object, the inorganic and organic natural reality which he studies and controls. By putting concrete problems concerning the development of human consciousness out of the elementary needs of organic life and up to its highest rational manifestations, modern naturalism claims to have actually and definitively incorporated man into nature. Reason itself, as manifested in science, is then only a continuation of the natural evolution of the animal world, the latest stage of adaptation of living beings to their environment; and all the forms of thinking on which idealism constructs its systems are products of the natural reality and, as instruments of adaptation, dependent both on their natural object-matter and on the natural organization of the living beings who use them.

On the other hand, indeed, idealism preserves some of the old arguments which enable it to prove that the naturalistic conception of the world as a whole moves in a vicious circle. It is clear that natural evolutionism presupposes for its own validity the ideal validity of those same principles of thought and standards of practical valuation which it tries to deduce genetically from natural reality. Ideas may be, indeed, instruments of real adaptation of the living being to its environment, but only if used not as realities but as ideas referring to reality and logically valid or invalid in this reference. The system of ideas constituting the evolutionistic theory itself certainly claims to be a valid *theory of reality* and not a mere *part of reality*. The entire content of evolutionism as a rational system is subjected to ideal criteria, to these very criteria which it wants to deprive of their ideality. In the measure in which it succeeds in reducing thought to biological functions it will make itself and this very reduction devoid of objective significance; that is, its claim of objective significance for its form proves it is false in its content.

An analogous reasoning can be used with regard to the practical test of natural science. If this test is to be objectively valid, it presupposes objective standards for appreciating practical activity as successful. But since the practical test is by hypothesis independent of theory, we cannot take as the standard of success the adaptation of the active being to its natural environment, for the conception of the active being as a living being, the conception of natural environment, and the whole conception of adaptation have been reached by a purely theoretic study subjected to criteria of theoretic validity. Therefore, the standards of practical success must be sought in the sphere of practical human values, and they can guarantee the objectivity of the practical test only if they are themselves objective as values, not merely as existential data; that is, if they are not merely reactions of living beings to their environment, as the biologist in his character of a theorist conceives them, but objective ideal values as the moralist, the artist, the religious man, etc., assumes them. The practical success of the applications of the natural sciences can be thus a proof of the objective bearing of these sciences as instruments of adaptation only if we accept, besides theoretic reason, some objective values, of the type of the moral values of Kantianism, which are not the products of biological evolution and by which the practical results of our activity can be measured. If there are no objective values independent of those produced during the biological evolu-

tion of the human race, the test of naturalism by its practical applicability has no objective significance.

But however binding the criticism which idealism opposes to
the theory of natural evolution, and we have here merely schematized the two central arguments among the many found in idealistic
literature, its weak point is that it has no positive doctrine to
oppose to it which can solve the problems put by the theory of
evolution. While naturalism has made an enormous progress and
undergone deep changes during the last fifty years, idealism has
remained on the same ground on which it stood in the beginning
of the past century; instead of nature as a dynamic and changing
process it is still facing nature as a changeless substance or a system
of substances, as it did when the timeless evolution of the Hegelian
Idea seemed the limit of dynamism. Is idealism merely unwilling
to enter into the heart of evolutionistic problems, or is it not rather
essentially incapable of doing it? The fact is that it has lost all
touch with modern science, that the present scientific issues are
unable to move it, and that Platonism, mediaeval realism, Kantianism, and Fichteanism still continue to be revived and accepted as if
nothing had happened since their first promulgation, as if our
intellectual life were the same as a hundred, a thousand, or even
two thousand years ago.

Yet it is clear that we cannot accept the naturalistic view of
the world without violating most of our highest standards of intellectual, moral, aesthetic, validity, standards which have been
reached after innumerable centuries of constructive and critical
activity, at the cost of incalculable efforts and sacrifices. We cannot voluntarily and consciously resign ourselves to a doctrine
which in the light of theoretic criticism proves irremediably self-
contradictory; we cannot voluntarily and consciously accept as
guide of our moral life a view which considers free creation a
psychological illusion and proclaims the impossibility of bringing
into the world anything that is not already virtually included in
it; we cannot admit an interpretation of our aesthetic life which
treats it as nothing but a play. Above all, we cannot consciously
agree to look at these our highest standards as mere by-products
of natural evolution, instruments of adaptation of one particular

species of living beings to their natural environment, having no other objective validity than the one derived from the success of this adaptation; we cannot resign ourselves, in spite of all realistic argumentation, to be nothing but insignificant and transient fragments of a whole which, while transcending us infinitely, remains almost unaffected by our existence, absolutely indifferent toward our claims, and absolutely inaccessible to our valuations. We might, indeed, train ourselves to become satisfied with naturalism by lowering our standards and limiting our aspirations, forgetting the general problems of life and knowledge for the sake of the many and various particular problems which confront us at every step of our personal and social activity. Such a course would be identical to that which Pascal prescribed against religious doubts by advising the doubter to follow in detail the ceremonies and prayers of the church instead of raising any fundamental problems of dogma and morality. Or we might, like James, accept as a matter of personal belief any doctrine we need to supplement, for our individual use, the deficiencies of naturalism, an attitude which has a curious analogy with the attitude of the workman who, dissatisfied with his everyday job, instead of trying to learn a wider and more interesting speciality, supplemented the monotony of his work by the excitement of day-dreams.

However insufficient and lacking in concreteness and vitality the idealistic philosophy may be, it certainly has the merit of being a permanent protest against these two extremes of powerless pessimism and of self-satisfied intellectual philistinism to which the naturalistic view of the world alternatively leads. Weak, inefficient, and unfruitful when brought into connection with concrete problems of actual life, idealism preserves nevertheless some vestige of its old importance in the abstract domain of the highest theoretic and practical standards, and this explains the attraction which it still has for all those who, while realizing the vitality of naturalism in particular fields and not wishing to intoxicate themselves with some rationally unjustifiable faith, still refuse to resign those aspirations of which Greek and mediaeval philosophy were the expressions, and cling desperately to what is left of the old values in modern philosophic abstraction.

This is, or rather was still a few years ago, the predominant situation of our intellectual life. The opposition of idealism and naturalism has completely absorbed the attention of scientists and philosophers. More than this: it has been carried over into practical fields and more or less consciously identified with the fight between social and religious conservatism and synthetic traditionalism on the one hand, and progressive radicalism and analytic rationalism on the other.

By one of the most curious failures of observation ever found in history, neither the theorists nor the men of practice involved in this great struggle have ever noticed how, alongside with the gradual development, unification, and systematization of naturalism, there had grown slowly, but ceaselessly, an independent domain of concrete theoretic and practical problems at least as wide as that covered by natural science and technique, but remaining completely outside of the entire opposition of idealism and realism and implying a view of the world entirely different from both. We mean, of course, the domain of investigations and practical problems concerning human culture in its historical past and its actual development—politics, economics, morality, art, language, literature, religion, knowledge. Certain schools of psychology and sociology have tried indeed to reduce cultural evolution to natural evolution; but, as a matter of fact, this reduction remains only a postulate and, as we shall see in detail later on, the essential and objectively significant side of cultural life remains forever inaccessible to naturalistic science. On the other hand, certain idealistic currents appealed to history for help in determining the content and the meaning of the absolute values which they exposed and defended; but they did not see that the historical and absolutistic standpoints are irreconcilable by their very logical essence and that to search in history for a justification of any absolute values is simply self-contradictory.

We can, however, hardly wonder that neither the realistic scientist nor the idealistic philosophers sees the full significance of the great problem of cultural evolution, since even those who are most immediately interested in this problem—the historians and the active and conscious builders of culture—scarcely begin to realize that their work has a much more general and fundamental intellectual meaning than a mere description of some past cultural happening or a mere modification of some present cultural situation. The reason is easy to understand. Whatever new and original contributions the cultural workers ever brought to our methods of studying and controlling the world were produced and offered in connection with particular problems put within the limits of special cultural sciences or special fields of cultural practice. Thus the wider meaning of each such contribution was seldom seen at once and the fundamental unity of standpoint underlying all cultural sciences and reflective cultural practice was very slow to develop, slower even than in natural sciences and technique, for as a matter of fact, there has always been a more far-going specialization in the sciences of culture than in the sciences of nature and the intellectual connection between special problems has been therefore more difficult to establish in this field. Moreover, the sciences of culture, for many reasons, have been so far unable to reach the same relative degree of methodical perfection as the sciences of nature, and this has prevented them from becoming as conscious of their own significance as the latter. Finally, as we shall have many opportunities to see, the entire logical and metaphysical foundation of both natural science and idealistic philosophy represents a more primary stage of intellectual activity than that required by cultural science, so that the statement of problems of knowledge in terms of natural realism or idealism seems so much simpler and easier in this relatively early period of theoretic evolution in which we live as to appear almost self-evident and to exclude any attempt to transgress its limitations.

But if all these reasons explain why the theoretic implications of cultural sciences have been scarcely noticed and intellectual interest has concentrated during the past century and a half on the various phases of the idealism-realism controversy, no reason can justify at present a continuation of this policy. Naturalism has reached the summit of its power with the theory of evolution and, while always still able to extend its presuppositions and methods to new data, it can no longer produce, at the present moment at least, any fundamentally new standpoints; it may still change in detail but not in its essential outlines as a general view of the world. It has become a complete system with definite foundations and a definite framework in a great measure filled out. There is, indeed, a very large place for new content, for new results of particular scientific investigations, but the framework cannot be modified any further without ruining the whole building. This may come some day, but certainly not now, when there is still so much to do before the building is completed. On the other hand we have seen traditional idealism unable not only to develop any fundamentally new standpoints, but even to extend its old doctrines to any new data. It is evident that the time has come to search for some new view of the world, more comprehensive, more productive, and more able to grow by creative additions.

By a view of the world we mean here not merely an abstract philosophical doctrine, but a complex of concrete intellectual functions manifested in numerous particular acts of investigation and reflection in various fields of theoretic and practical life and culminating in an intellectual ideal. As examples we can quote, besides modern naturalism, the Greek rationalism of the fourth century B.C., the later Stoicism and Epicureanism, neo-Platonism, mediaeval Aristotelism. It is evident that a view of the world in this sense cannot be created by a single thinker: it is the accumulated product of whole generations; it arises slowly, thanks to many efforts of synthesis, out of innumerable scattered activities, and, after being unified and formulated as an explicit ideal, goes on developing by many various and unexpected applications. It is clear therefore that no new view of the world can be substituted at the present moment in the place of naturalism, however unsatisfied we may be by the latter, unless such a view has already been gradually developing in concrete intellectual life and is sufficiently mature to find its explicit expression in an intellectual ideal. This makes it evident that a revolution of our intellectual life such as is demanded by the present situation cannot come from any other source than from the domain of cultural science and practice, because this is the only field outside of naturalism where a creative intellectual development has been going on in modern times. The only question is whether the synthetic activity in this domain has already reached the point where we can formulate the fundamental aims of cultural science and practice and attain thus an intellectual ideal sufficiently unified and sufficiently wide, not only to take the place of naturalism, but to include, besides the positive elements of naturalism itself, all those important principles of our intellectual life for which naturalism found no place.

Whether this is possible to fulfil only actual attempts can show. Certainly such attempts are now, if ever, indispensable. Not only is a new ideal needed to satisfy the demand for a harmonization and modification of our complex and scattered intellectual activities, but the time has come when, for all actual human purposes, the most intense reflection must be concentrated on the field of culture. It is more and more generally recognized, particularly since the outbreak of the present cultural crisis, that we have permitted ourselves to be blinded by the successes of natural science and material technique and have failed to bring a consistent, self-conscious, and critical intellectual attitude into the domain of cultural science and practice, so that the results attained in this domain, however important by themselves, are very insufficient if compared with the number of failures at the cost of which they have been reached and if measured by the scale of demands which can and should be put in the name of cultural progress. At present our attention is forcibly attracted to this domain, and it is clear that we shall have to face, for the next two or three generations at least, such problems of cultural construction as will require all our creative and critical powers. Needless to say that we are very inadequately prepared for this task, particularly in so far as theory is concerned, in spite of the enormous accumulation of materials during the past few centuries. This inadequacy manifests itself chiefly in two respects. First, we lack laws of cultural becoming which would give us means of controlling the cultural world as we control the natural world. Secondly, we lack objective and applicable standards of appreciation of cultural values which would permit us to organize the aims of our constructive activities so as to avoid wasting our energies in useless fights and destroying almost as much as we create.

Now, while laws are found only by empirical investigation of particular problems and aims are created only in particular actual pursuits, the history of cultural science and practice shows with a perfect evidence that the present unsatisfactory situation in both lines is directly due to the lack of a *general* understanding of culture, to the lack of a *view of the world* based on cultural experience. The theorist of culture associated scientific laws with naturalism, so that when he found that the laws of natural sciences did not apply to culture, his immediate reaction was to proclaim cultural becoming to be essentially inaccessible to any method which tries to determine laws of becoming. The builder of culture associated objective standards of appreciation and selection of aims with the idealistic search for absolute values, and when he saw that absolute valuation could not be applied to cultural experience he proclaimed concrete cultural life to be inaccessible to any standardization and hierarchization of values, to be a chaos of valuations whose only justification is their existence.

The fundamental and distinctive characters of cultural data which were discovered in the course of positive empirical investigations or found in concrete constructive activities were thus formulated negatively, in terms of opposition to naturalism or idealism, instead of being formulated positively in terms of their own. The scientist and the practical man were accustomed to see no other possible order of becoming than the order of nature, no other possible order of appreciation and aims than the idealistic order of absolute values, because their *world as a whole* was the world of material things and of individual or social conscious processes, subjected to laws of natural causality and, eventually, to principles of ideal finality. Cultural data had to comply with this double causal and final order as well as they could; they were not supposed to have any positive order of their own, because they did not constitute the world, because in reflecting about them, in philosophizing about them, the theorist or the builder of culture saw in them, not a unified and ordered totality of experience, but only a plurality of detached phenomena, each separately rooting in the consciousness of human beings and in their natural environment and each separately drawing whatever objective meaning it might possess from its reference to the "kingdom of ends," to the absolute order of superworldly values.[1]

If thus, on the one hand, the predominance of idealism and naturalism in modern thought has prevented the new view of the world implied by cultural knowledge and practice from developing more rapidly and manifesting itself explicitly in a conscious intellectual ideal, the lack of such an explicit formulation of this view has, on the other hand, contributed to keep cultural knowledge and practice under the domination of idealism and naturalism and prevented them from becoming more efficient and from developing consciously and methodically along their own independent lines. This shows with particular clearness the necessity of collaboration between philosophy and particular sciences, a collaboration which has become lately very imperfect. The rôle of philosophy in the past has been certainly incomparably more important than it is now. This importance was due to the fact that philosophy was a special discipline, with its own field of investigation, its own perfectly elaborated and efficient methods, and at the same time from its own standpoint was able to supervise the entire field of knowledge and practice and to outline general intellectual ideals which scientific and practical activities could follow with a profit to themselves. Now, the peculiar modern intellectual conditions sketched above had, among other consequences, the effect of almost entirely separating philosophy as a special discipline from philosophy as a synthetic, dynamic unity of other disciplines. As a particular branch of knowledge, with its own aims and standards, philosophy is idealistic and critical; it has preserved or

[1]   There were, as we know, attempts to conceive the totality of cultural phenomena as constituting a unified and ordered world, not *the world*, indeed, but *a world* at least distinct from the world of nature. But the Hegelian historical school to which these attempts were almost exclusively confined was completely dependent on idealism. By treating culture as gradual manifestation of absolute values, by exaggerating its unity, and by assuming an entirely arbitrary order of cultural becoming, it had discouraged subsequent efforts in this line even before realism extended the theory of natural evolution to this field and attracted general attention by this attempt to absorb definitively culture into nature.

even increased its methodical perfection, but, as we have seen, it has nothing new to say, no vital ideals to give to science and practice. As a dynamic unity of other disciplines, philosophy is realistic and constructive; it has, indeed, given new and vital ideals; without it natural science and social life would not be what they are; but these ideals, as we have seen, are narrow and uncritical and represent a striking lowering of philosophical standards as compared with the past.

If we claim therefore that it is time to substitute a new culturalistic philosophy for both idealism and naturalism, it is because we believe that a systematic and explicit philosophical study of culture will both regenerate philosophy, in the same way as in the sixteenth and seventeenth centuries contact with nature regenerated it when it was slowly dying between scholasticism and occultism, and give us the most powerful instrument possible for the progress of concrete cultural sciences and concrete cultural creation. Our scientific knowledge and reflective control of culture can reach a level superior or even equal to that of our knowledge and control of nature only with the help of an independent, systematic, and productive philosophy of culture.

2. Methodological Perspectives

METHODOLOGICAL NOTE

1919

ONE OF THE most significant features of social evolution is the growing importance which a conscious and rational technique tends to assume in social life. We are less and less ready to let any social processes go on without our active interference and we feel more and more dissatisfied with any active interference based upon a mere whim of an individual or a social body, or upon preconceived philosophical, religious, or moral generalizations.

The marvelous results attained by a rational technique in the sphere of material reality invite us to apply some analogous procedure to social reality. Our success in controlling nature gives us confidence that we shall eventually be able to control the social world in the same measure. Our actual inefficiency in this line is due, not to any fundamental limitation of our reason, but simply to the historical fact that the objective attitude toward social reality is a recent acquisition.

While our realization that nature can be controlled only by treating it as independent of any immediate act of our will or reason is four centuries old, our confidence in "legislation" and in "moral suasion" shows that this idea is not yet generally realized with regard to the social world. But the tendency to rational control is growing in this field also and constitutes at present an insistent demand on the social sciences.

From William I. Thomas and Florian Znaniecki, *The Polish Peasant in Europe and America* (New York: Alfred A. Knopf, 1927), 1:1–86.

This demand for a rational control results from the increasing rapidity of social evolution. The old forms of control were based upon the assumption of an essential stability of the whole social framework and were effective only in so far as this stability was real. In a stable social organization there is time enough to develop in a purely empirical way, through innumerable experiments and failures, approximately sufficient means of control with regard to the ordinary and frequent social phenomena, while the errors made in treating the uncommon and rare phenomena seldom affect social life in such a manner as to imperil the existence of the group; if they do, then the catastrophe is accepted as incomprehensible and inevitable. Thus—to take an example—the Polish peasant community has developed during many centuries complicated systems of beliefs and rules of behavior sufficient to control social life under ordinary circumstances, and the cohesion of the group and the persistence of its membership are strong enough to withstand passively the influence of eventual extraordinary occurrences, although there is no adequate method of meeting them. And if the crisis is too serious and the old unity or prosperity of the group breaks down, this is usually treated at first as a result of superior forces against which no fight is possible.

But when, owing to the breakdown of the isolation of the group and its contact with a more complex and fluid world, the social evolution becomes more rapid and the crises more frequent and varied, there is no time for the same gradual, empirical, unmethodical elaboration of approximately adequate means of control, and no crisis can be passively borne, but every one must be met in a more or less adequate way, for they are too various and frequent not to imperil social life unless controlled in time. The substitution of a conscious technique for a half-conscious routine has become, therefore, a social necessity, though it is evident that the development of this technique could be only gradual, and that even now we find in it many implicit or explicit ideas and methods corresponding to stages of human thought passed hundreds or even thousands of years ago.

The oldest but most persistent form of social technique is that of "ordering-and-forbidding"—that is, meeting a crisis by an arbitrary act of will decreeing the disappearance of the undesirable or the appearance of the desirable phenomena, and using arbitrary physical action to enforce the decree. This method corresponds exactly to the magical phase of natural technique. In both, the essential means of bringing a determined effect is more or less consciously thought to reside in the act of will itself by which the effect is decreed as desirable and of which the action is merely an indispensable vehicle or instrument; in both, the process by which the cause (act of will and physical action) is supposed to bring its effect to realization remains out of reach of investigation; in both, finally, if the result is not attained, some new act of will with new material accessories is introduced, instead of trying to find and remove the perturbing causes. A good instance of this in the social field is the typical legislative procedure of today.

It frequently happens both in magic and in the ordering-and-forbidding technique that the means by which the act of will is helped are really effective, and thus the result is attained, but, as the process of causation, being unknown, cannot be controlled, the success is always more or less accidental and dependent upon the stability of general conditions; when these are changed, the intended effect fails to appear, the subject is unable to account for the reasons of the failure and can only try by guesswork some other means. And even more frequent than this accidental success is the result that the action brings some effect, but not the desired one.

There is, indeed, one difference between the ordering-and-forbidding technique and magic. In social life an expressed act of will may be sometimes a real cause, when the person or body from which it emanates has a particular authority in the eyes of those to whom the order or prohibition applies. But this does not change the nature of the technique as such. The prestige of rulers, ecclesiastics, and legislators was a condition making an act of will an efficient cause under the old régimes, but it loses its value in the modern partly or completely republican organizations.

A more effective technique, based upon "common sense" and represented by "practical" sociology, has naturally originated in those lines of social action in which there was either no place for legislative measures or in which the *hoc volo, sic jubeo* proved too evidently inefficient—in business, in charity and philanthropy, in diplomacy, in personal association, etc. Here, indeed, the act of will having been recognized as inefficient in directing the causal process, real causes are sought for every phenomenon, and an endeavor is made to control the effects by acting upon the causes, and, though it is often partly successful, many fallacies are implicitly involved in this technique; it has still many characters of a planless empiricism, trying to get at the real cause by a rather haphazard selection of various possibilities, directed only by a rough and popular reflection, and its deficiencies have to be shown and removed if a new and more efficient method of action is to be introduced.

The first of these fallacies has often been exposed. It is the latent or manifest supposition that we know social reality because we live in it, and that we can assume things and relations as certain on the basis of our empirical acquaintance with them. The attitude is here about the same as in the ancient assumption that we know the physical world because we live and act in it, and that therefore we have the right of generalizing without a special and thorough investigation, on the mere basis of "common sense." The history of physical science gives us many good examples of the results to which common sense can lead, such as the geocentric system of astronomy and the mediaeval ideas about motion. And it is easy to show that not even the widest individual acquaintance with social reality, not even the most evident success of individual adaptation to this reality, can offer any serious guaranty of the validity of the common-sense generalizations.

Indeed, the individual's sphere of practical acquaintance with social reality, however vast it may be as compared with that of others, is always limited and constitutes only a small part of the whole complexity of social facts. It usually extends over only one society, often over only one class of this society; this we may call the exterior limitation. In addition there is an interior limitation, still more important, due to the fact that among all the experiences which the individual meets within the sphere of his social life a large, perhaps the larger, part is left unheeded, never becoming a

basis of common-sense generalizations. This selection of experiences is the result of individual temperament on the one hand and
of individual interest on the other. In any case, whether temper-
amental inclinations or practical considerations operate, the selection is subjective—that is, valid only for this particular individual in this particular social position—and thereby it is quite
different from, and incommensurable with, the selection which a
scientist would make in face of the same body of data from an
objective, impersonal viewpoint.

Nor is the practical success of the individual within his
sphere of activity a guaranty of his knowledge of the relations
between the social phenomena which he is able to control. Of
course there must be some objective validity in his schemes of social
facts—otherwise he could not live in society—but the truth of these
schemes is always only a rough approximation and is mixed with
an enormous amount of error. When we assume that a successful
adaptation of the individual to his environment is a proof that he
knows this environment thoroughly, we forget that there are degrees of success, that the standard of success is to a large extent
subjective, and that all the standards of success applied in human
society may be—and really are—very low, because they make
allowance for a very large number of partial failures, each of
which denotes one or many errors. Two elements are found in
varying proportions in every adaptation; one is the actual control
exercised over the environment; the other is the claims which this
control serves to satisfy. The adaptation may be perfect, either
because of particularly successful and wide control or because of
particularly limited claims. Whenever the control within the given
range of claims proves insufficient, the individual or the group
can either develop a better control or limit the claims. And, in fact,
in every activity the second method, of adaptation by failures, plays
a very important rôle. Thus the individual's knowledge of his environment can be considered as real only in the particular matters in which he does actually control it; his schemes can be true
only in so far as they are perfectly, absolutely successful. And if we
remember how much of practical success is due to mere chance
and luck, even this limited number of truths becomes doubtful.

Finally, the truths that stand the test of individual practice are always schemes of the concrete and singular, as are the situations in which the individual finds himself.

In this way the acquaintance with social data and the knowledge of social relations which we acquire in practice are always more or less subjective, limited both in number and in generality. Thence comes the well-known fact that the really valuable part of practical wisdom acquired by the individual during his life is incommunicable—cannot be stated in general terms; everyone must acquire it afresh by a kind of apprenticeship to life—that is, by learning to select experiences according to the demands of his own personality and to construct for his own use particular schemes of the concrete situations which he encounters. Thus, all the generalizations constituting the common-sense social theory and based on individual experience are both insignificant and subject to innumerable exceptions. A sociology that accepts them necessarily condemns itself to remain in the same methodological stage, and a practice based upon them must be as insecure and as full of failures as is the activity of every individual.

Whenever, now, this "practical" sociology makes an effort to get above the level of popular generalizations by the study of social reality instead of relying upon individual experience, it still preserves the same method as the individual in his personal reflection; investigation always goes on with an immediate reference to practical aims, and the standards of the desirable and undesirable are the ground upon which theoretic problems are approached. This is the second fallacy of the practical sociology, and the results of work from this standpoint are quite disproportionate to the enormous efforts that have recently been put forth in the collection and elaboration of materials preparatory to social reforms. The example of physical science and material technique should have shown long ago that only a scientific investigation, which is quite free from any dependence on practice, can become practically useful in its applications. Of course this does not mean that the scientist should not select for investigation problems whose solution has actual practical importance; the sociologist may study crime or war as the chemist studies dyestuffs. But from the method of the study itself all practical considerations must be excluded if we want the results to be valid. And this has not yet been realized by practical sociology.

The usual standpoint here is that of an explicit or implicit norm with which reality should comply. The norm may be intrinsic to the reality, as when it is presumed that the actually prevailing traditional or customary state of things is normal; or it may be extrinsic, as when moral, religious, or aesthetic standards are applied to social reality and the prevailing state of things is found in disaccord with the norm, and in so far abnormal. But this difference has no essential importance. In both cases the normal, agreeing with the norm, is supposed to be known either by practical acquaintance or by some particular kind of rational or irrational evidence; the problem is supposed to lie in the abnormal, the disharmony with the norm. In the first case the abnormal is the exceptional, in the second case it is the usual, while the normal constitutes an exception, but the general method of investigation remains the same.

There is no doubt that the application of norms to reality had a historical merit; investigation was provoked in this way and the "abnormal" became the first object of empirical studies. It is the morally indignant observer of vice and crime and the political idealist-reformer who start positive investigations. But as soon as the investigation is started both indignation and idealism should be put aside. For in treating a certain body of material as representing the normal, another body of material as standing for the abnormal, we introduce at once a division that is necessarily artificial; for if these terms have a meaning it can be determined only on the basis of investigation, and the criterion of normality must be such as to allow us to include in the normal, not only a certain determined stage of social life and a limited class of facts, but also the whole series of different stages through which social life passes, and the whole variety of social phenomena. The definition a priori of a group of facts that we are going to investigate as abnormal has two immediate consequences. First, our attention is turned to such facts as seem the most important practically, as being most conspicuously contrary to the norm and calling most insistently for reform. But the things that are practically important may be quite insignificant theoretically and, on the contrary, those which seem to have no importance from the practical point of view may be the source of important scientific discoveries. The scientific value of a fact depends on its connection with other facts, and in this connection the most commonplace facts are often precisely the most valuable ones, while a fact that strikes the imagination or stirs the moral feeling may be really either isolated or exceptional, or so simple as to involve hardly any problems. Again, by separating the abnormal from the normal we deprive ourselves of the opportunity of studying them in their connection with each other, while only in this connection can their study be fully fruitful. There is no break in continuity between the normal and the abnormal in concrete life that would permit any exact separation of the corresponding bodies of material, and the nature of the normal and the abnormal as determined by theoretic abstraction can be perfectly understood only with the help of comparison.

But there are other consequences of this fallacy. When the norm is not a result but a starting-point of the investigation, as it is in this case, every practical custom or habit, every moral, political, religious view, claims to be *the* norm and to treat as abnormal whatever does not agree with it. The result is harmful both in practice and in theory. In practice, as history shows and as we see at every moment, a social technique based upon pre-existing norms tends to suppress all the social energies which seem to act in a way contrary to the demands of the norm, and to ignore all the social energies not included in the sphere embraced by the norm. This limits still more the practical importance of the technique and often makes it simply harmful instead of useful. In theory, a sociology using norms as its basis deprives itself of the possibility of understanding and controlling any important facts of social evolution. Indeed, every social process of real importance always includes a change of the norms themselves, not alone of the activity embraced by the norms. Traditions and customs, morality and religion, undergo an evolution that is more and more rapid, and it is evident that a sociology proceeding on the assumption that a certain norm is valid and that whatever does not comply with it is abnormal finds itself absolutely helpless when it suddenly realizes that this norm has lost all social significance and that some other norm has appeared in its place. This helplessness is particularly striking in moments of great social crisis when the evolution of norms becomes exceptionally rapid. We notice it, for example, with particular vividness during the present war, when the whole individualistic system of norms elaborated during the last two centuries begins to retreat before a quite different system, which may be a state socialism or something quite new.

The third fallacy of the common-sense sociology is the implicit assumption that any group of social facts can be treated theoretically and practically in an arbitrary isolation from the rest of the life of the given society. This assumption is perhaps unconsciously drawn from the general form of social organization, in which the real isolation of certain groups of facts is a result of the demands of practical life. In any line of organized human activity only actions of a certain kind are used, and it is assumed that only such individuals will take part in this particular organization as are able and willing to perform these actions, and that they will not bring into this sphere of activity any tendencies that may destroy the organization. The factory and the army corps are typical examples of such organizations. The isolation of a group of facts from the rest of social life is here really and practically performed. But exactly in so far as such a system functions in a perfect manner there is no place at all for social science or social practice; the only thing required is a material division and organization of these isolated human actions. The task of social theory and social technique lies outside of these systems; it begins, for example, whenever external tendencies not harmonizing with the organized activities are introduced into the system, when the workmen in the factory start a strike or the soldiers of the army corps a mutiny. Then the isolation disappears; the system enters, through the individuals who are its members, into relation with the whole complexity of social life. And this lack of real isolation, which characterizes a system of organized activity only at moments of crisis, is a permanent feature of all the artificial, abstractly formed groups of facts such as "prostitution," "crime," "education," "war," etc.

Every single fact included under these generalizations is connected by innumerable ties with an indefinite number of other facts belonging to various groups, and these relations give to every fact a different character. If we start to study these facts as a whole, without heeding their connection with the rest of the social world, we must necessarily come to quite arbitrary generalizations. If we start to act upon these facts in a uniform way simply because their abstract essence seems to be the same, we must necessarily produce quite different results, varying with the relations of every particular case to the rest of the social world. This does not mean that it is not possible to isolate such groups of facts for theoretic investigation or practical activity, but simply that the isolation must come, not a priori, but a posteriori, in the same way as the distinction between the normal and the abnormal. The facts must first be taken in connection with the whole to which they belong, and the question of a later isolation is a methodological problem which we shall treat in a later part of this note.

There are two other fallacies involved to a certain extent in social practice, although practical sociology has already repudiated them. The reason for their persistence in practice is that, even if the erroneousness of the old assumptions has been recognized, no new working ideas have been put in their place. These assumptions are: (1) that men react in the same way to the same influences regardless of their individual or social past, and that therefore it is possible to provoke identical behavior in various individuals by identical means; (2) that men develop spontaneously, without external influence, tendencies which enable them to profit in a full and uniform way from given conditions, and that therefore it is sufficient to create favorable or remove unfavorable conditions in order to give birth to or suppress given tendencies.

The assumption of identical reactions to identical influences is found in the most various lines of traditional social activity; the examples of legal practice and of education are sufficient to illustrate it. In the former all the assumptions about the "motives" of the behavior of the parties, all the rules and forms of investigation and examination, all the decisions of the courts, are essentially based upon this principle. Considerations of the variety of traditions, habits, temperaments, etc., enter only incidentally and secondarily, and usually in doubtful cases, by the initiative of the lawyers; they are the result of common-sense psychological observations, but find little if any place in the objective system of laws and rules. And where, as in the American juvenile courts, an attempt is made to base legal practice upon these considerations, all legal apparatus is properly waived, and the whole procedure rests upon the personal qualifications of the judge. In education the same principle is exhibited in the identity of curricula, and is even carried so far as to require identical work from students in connection with the courses they follow, instead of leaving to everyone as much field as possible for personal initiative. Here again the fallaciousness of the principle is corrected only by the efforts of those individual teachers who try to adapt their methods to the personalities of the pupils, using practical tact and individual acquaintance. But as yet no objective principles have been generally substituted for the traditional uniformity.

The assumption of the spontaneous development of tendencies if the material conditions are given is found in the exaggerated importance ascribed by social reformers to changes of material environment and in the easy conclusions drawn from material conditions on the mentality and character of individuals and groups. For example, it is assumed that good housing conditions will create a good family life, that the abolition of saloons will stop drinking, that the organization of a well-endowed institution is all that is necessary to make the public realize its value in practice. To be sure, material conditions do help or hinder to a large extent the development of corresponding lines of behavior, but only if the tendency is already there, for the way in which they will be used depends on the people who use them. The normal way of social action would be to develop the tendency and to create the condition simultaneously, and, if this is impossible, attention should be paid rather to the development of tendencies than to the change of the conditions, because a strong social tendency will always find its expression by modifying the conditions, while the contrary is not true. For example, a perfect family life may exist in a Polish peasant community in conditions which would probably be considered in America as a necessary breeding-place of crime and pauperism, while uncommonly favorable external conditions in the Polish aristocratic class do not hinder a decay of family life. In Southern France and Northern Italy there is less drunkenness with the saloon than in the prohibition states of America. In Russian Poland, without a Polish university and with only a private philosophical association, more than twice as much original philosophical literature has been published recently as in Russia with her eleven endowed universities. And innumerable examples could be cited from all departments of social life. But it is easy to understand that in the absence of a science of behavior social reformers pay more attention to the material conditions of the people than to the psychology of the people who live in these conditions; for the conditions are concrete and tangible, and we know how to grasp them and to conceive and realize almost perfect plans of material improvements, while in the absence of a science the reformer has no objective principles on which he can rely, and unconsciously tends to ascribe a preponderating importance to the material side of social life.

And these fallacies of the common-sense sociology are not always due to a lack of theoretic ability or of a serious scientific attitude on the part of the men who do the work. They are the unavoidable consequence of the necessity of meeting actual situations at once. Social life goes on without interruption and has to be controlled at every moment. The business man or politician, the educator or charity-worker, finds himself continually confronted by new social problems which he must solve, however imperfect and provisional he knows his solutions to be, for the stream of evolution does not wait for him. He must have immediate results, and it is a merit on his part if he tries to reconcile the claims of actuality with those of scientific objectivity, as far as they can be reconciled, and endeavors to understand the social reality as well as he can before acting. Certainly social life is improved by even such a control as common-sense sociology is able to give; certainly no effort should be discouraged, for the ultimate balance proves usually favorable. But in social activity, even more than in material activity, the common-sense method is the most wasteful method, and to replace it gradually by a more efficient one will be a good investment.

While, then, there is no doubt that actual situations must be handled immediately, we see that they cannot be solved adequately as long as theoretical reflection has their immediate solution in view. But there is evidently one issue from this dilemma, and it is the same as in material technique and physical science. We must be able to foresee future situations and prepare for them, and we must have in stock a large body of secure and objective knowledge capable of being applied to any situation, whether foreseen or unexpected. This means that we must have an empirical and exact social science ready for eventual application. And such a science can be constituted only if we treat it as an end in itself, not as a means to something else, and if we give it time and opportunity to develop along all the lines of investigation possible, even if we do not see what may be the eventual applications of one or another of its results. The example of physical science and its applications show that the only practically economical way of creating an efficient technique is to create a science independent of any technical limitations and then to take every one of its results and try where and in what way they can be practically applied. The contrary attitude, the refusal to recognize any science that does not work to solve practical problems, in addition to leading to that inefficiency of both science and practice which we have analyzed above, shows a curious narrowness of mental horizon. We do not know what the future science will be before it is constituted and what may be the applications of its discoveries before they are applied; we do not know what will be the future of society and what social problems may arise demanding solution. The only practically justifiable attitude toward science is absolute liberty and disinterested help.

Of course this does not mean that the actual social technique should wait until the science is constituted; such as it is, it is incomparably better than none. But, just as in material technique, as soon as a scientific discovery is at hand an effort should be made to find for it a practical application, and if it can be applied in some particular field a new technique should take the place of the old in this field.

But if no practical aims should be introduced beforehand into scientific investigation, social practice has, nevertheless, the right to demand from social theory that at least some of its results shall be applicable at once, and that the number and importance of such results shall continually increase. As one of the pragmatists has expressed it, practical life can and must give credit to science, but sooner or later science must pay her debts, and the longer the delay the greater the interest required. This demand of ultimate practical applicability is as important for science itself as for practice; it is a test, not only of the practical, but of the theoretical, value of the science. A science whose results can be applied proves thereby that it is really based upon experience, that it is able to grasp a great variety of problems, that its method is really exact—that it is valid. The test of applicability is a salutary responsibility which science must assume in her own interest.

If we attempt now to determine what should be the object-matter and the method of a social theory that would be able to satisfy the demands of modern social practice, it is evident that its main object should be the actual civilized society in its full development and with all its complexity of situations, for it is the control of the actual civilized society that is sought in most endeavors of rational practice. But here, as in every other science, a determined body of material assumes its full significance only if we can use comparison freely, in order to distinguish the essential from the accidental, the simple from the complex, the primary from the derived. And fortunately social life gives us favorable conditions for comparative studies, particularly at the present stage of evolution, in the coexistence of a certain number of civilized societies sufficiently alike in their fundamental cultural problems to make comparison possible, and differing sufficiently in their traditions, customs, and general national spirit to make comparison fruitful. And from the list of these civilized societies we should by no means exclude those non-white societies, like the Chinese, whose organization and attitudes differ profoundly from our own, but which interest us both as social experiments and as situations with which we have to reconcile our own future.

In contrast with this study of the various present civilized societies, the lines along which most of the purely scientific sociological work has been done up to the present—that is, ethnography of primitive societies and social history—have a secondary, though by no means a negligible, importance. Their relation to social practice is only mediate; they can help the practitioner to solve actual cultural problems only to the degree that they help the scientist to understand actual cultural life; they are auxiliary, and their own scientific value will increase with the progress of the main sphere of studies. In all the endeavors to understand and interpret the past and the savage we must use, consciously or not, our knowledge of our civilized present life, which remains always a basis of comparison, whether the past and the primitive are conceived as analogous with, or as different from, the present and the civilized. The less objective and critical our knowledge of the present, the more subjective and unmethodical is our interpretation of the past and the primitive; unable to see the relative and limited character of the culture within which we live, we unconsciously bend every unfamiliar phenomenon to the limitations of our own social personality. A really objective understanding of history and ethnography can therefore be expected only as a result of a methodical knowledge of present cultural societies.

Another point to be emphasized with regard to the question of the object-matter of social theory is the necessity of taking into account the whole life of a given society instead of arbitrarily selecting and isolating beforehand certain particular groups of facts. We have seen already that the contrary procedure constitutes one of the fallacies of the common-sense sociology. It is also a fallacy usually committed by the observers of their own or of other societies—litterateurs, journalists, travelers, popular psychologists, etc. In describing a given society they pick out the most prominent situations, the most evident problems, thinking to characterize thereby the life of the given group. Still more harmful for the development of science is this fallacy when used in the comparative sociology which studies an institution, an idea, a myth, a legal

or moral norm, a form of art, etc., by simply comparing its content
in various societies without studying it in the whole meaning which
it has in a particular society and then comparing this with the
whole meaning which it has in the various societies. We are all
more or less guilty of this fault, but it pleases us to attribute it
mainly to Herbert Spencer.

In order to avoid arbitrary limitations and subjective interpretations there are only two possible courses open. We can study
monographically whole concrete societies with the total complexity
of problems and situations which constitute their cultural life; or
we can work on special social problems, following the problem
in a certain limited number of concrete social groups and studying
it in every group with regard to the particular form which it assumes under the influence of the conditions prevailing in this
society, taking into account the complex meaning which a concrete
cultural phenomenon has in a determined cultural environment. In
studying the society we go from the whole social context to the
problem, and in studying the problem we go from the problem
to the whole social context. And in both types of work the only
safe method is to start with the assumption that we know absolutely nothing about the group or the problem we are to investigate except such purely formal criteria as enable us to distinguish
materials belonging to our sphere of interest from those which do
not belong there. But this attitude of indiscriminate receptivity
toward any concrete data should mark only the first stage of investigation—that of limiting the field. As soon as we become acquainted with the materials we begin to select them with the
help of criteria which involve certain methodological generalizations and scientific hypotheses. This must be done, since the whole
empirical concreteness cannot be introduced into science, cannot
be described or explained. We have to limit ourselves to certain
theoretically important data, but we must know how to distinguish
the data which are important. And every further step of the investigation will bring with it new methodological problems—
analysis of the complete concrete data into elements, systematization of these elements, definition of social facts, establishing of social laws. All these stages of scientific procedure must be exactly

and carefully defined if social theory is to become a science conscious of its own methods and able to apply them with precision, as is the case with the more mature and advanced physical and biological sciences. And it is always the question of an ultimate practical applicability which, according to our previous discussion, will constitute the criterion—the only secure and intrinsic criterion —of a science.

Now there are two fundamental practical problems which have constituted the center of attention of reflective social practice in all times. These are (1) the problem of the dependence of the individual upon social organization and culture, and (2) the problem of the dependence of social organization and culture upon the individual. Practically, the first problem is expressed in the question, How shall we produce with the help of the existing social organization and culture the desirable mental and moral characteristics in the individuals constituting the social group? And the second problem means in practice, How shall we produce, with the help of the existing mental and moral characteristics of the individual members of the group, the desirable type of social organization and culture?[1]

If social theory is to become the basis of social technique and to solve these problems really, it is evident that it must include both kinds of data involved in them—namely, the objective cultural elements of social life and the subjective characteristics of the members of the social group—and that the two kinds of data must be taken as correlated. For these data we shall use now and in the future the terms "social values" (or simply "values") and "attitudes."

By a social value we understand any datum having an empirical content accessible to the members of some social group and a meaning with regard to which it is or may be an object of activity. Thus, a foodstuff, an instrument, a coin, a piece of poetry, a university, a myth, a scientific theory, are social values. Each of them

[1]   Of course a concrete practical task may include both problems, as when we attempt, by appealing to the existing attitudes, to establish educational institutions which will be so organized as to produce or generalize certain desirable attitudes.

has a content that is sensual in the case of the foodstuff, the instrument, the coin; partly sensual, partly imaginary in the piece of poetry, whose content is constituted, not only by the written or spoken words, but also by the images which they evoke, and in the case of the university, whose content is the whole complex of men, buildings, material accessories, and images representing its activity; or, finally, only imaginary in the case of a mythical personality or a scientific theory. The meaning of these values becomes explicit when we take them in connection with human actions. The meaning of the foodstuff is its reference to its eventual consumption; that of an instrument, its reference to the work for which it is designed; that of a coin, the possibilities of buying and selling or the pleasures of spending which it involves; that of the piece of poetry, the sentimental and intellectual reactions which it arouses; that of the university, the social activities which it performs; that of the mythical personality, the cult of which it is the object and the actions of which it is supposed to be the author; that of the scientific theory, the possibilities of control of experience by idea or action that it permits. The social value is thus opposed to the natural thing, which has a content but, as a part of nature, has no meaning for human activity, is treated as "valueless"; when the natural thing assumes a meaning, it becomes thereby a social value. And naturally a social value may have many meanings, for it may refer to many different kinds of activity.

By attitude we understand a process of individual consciousness which determines real or possible activity of the individual in the social world. Thus, hunger that compels the consumption of the foodstuff; the workman's decision to use the tool; the tendency of the spendthrift to spend the coin; the poet's feelings and ideas expressed in the poem and the reader's sympathy and admiration; the needs which the institution tries to satisfy and the response it provokes; the fear and devotion manifested in the cult of the divinity; the interest in creating, understanding, or applying a scientific theory and the ways of thinking implied in it—all these are attitudes. The attitude is thus the individual counterpart of the social value; activity, in whatever form, is the bond between them. By its reference to activity and thereby to individual consciousness the value is distinguished from the natural thing. By its reference to activity and thereby to the social world the attitude is distinguished from the psychical state. In the examples quoted above we were obliged to use with reference to ideas and volitions words that have become terms of individual psychology by being abstracted from the objective social reality to which they apply, but originally they were designed to express attitudes, not psychological processes. A psychological process is an attitude treated as an object in itself, isolated by a reflective act of attention, and taken first of all in connection with other states of the same individual. An attitude is a psychological process treated as primarily manifested in its reference to the social world and taken first of all in connection with some social value. Individual psychology may later re-establish the connection between the psychological process and the objective reality which has been severed by reflection; it may study psychological processes as conditioned by the facts going on in the objective world. In the same way social theory may later connect various attitudes of an individual and determine his social character. But it is the original (usually unconsciously occupied) standpoints which determine at once the subsequent methods of these two sciences. The psychological process remains always fundamentally a *state of somebody*; the attitude remains always fundamentally an attitude *toward something*.

Taking this fundamental distinction of standpoint into account, we may continue to use for different classes of attitudes the same terms which individual psychology has used for psychological processes, since these terms constitute the common property of all reflection about conscious life. The exact meaning of all these terms from the standpoint of social theory must be established during the process of investigation, so that every term shall be defined in view of its application and its methodological validity tested in actual use. It would be therefore impractical to attempt to establish in advance the whole terminology of attitudes.

But when we say that the data of social theory are attitudes and values, this is not yet sufficient determination of the object of this science, for the field thus defined would embrace the whole human culture and include the object-matter of philology and economics, theory of art, theory of science, etc. A more exact definition is therefore necessary in order to distinguish social theory from these sciences, established long ago and having their own methods and their own aims.

This limitation of the field of social theory arises quite naturally from the necessity of choosing between attitudes or values as fundamental data—that is, as data whose characters will serve as a basis for scientific generalization. There are numerous values corresponding to every attitude, and numerous attitudes corresponding to every value; if, therefore, we compare different actions with regard to the attitudes manifested in them and form, for example, the general concept of the attitude of solidarity, this means that we have neglected the whole variety of values which are produced by these actions and which may be political or economical, religious or scientific, etc. If, on the contrary, we compare the values produced by different actions and form, for example, the general concepts of economic or religious values, this means that we have neglected the whole variety of attitudes which are manifested in these actions. Scientific generalization must always base itself upon such characters of its data as can be considered essential to its purposes, and the essential characters of human actions are completely different when we treat them from the standpoint of attitudes and when we are interested in them as values. There is therefore no possibility of giving to attitudes and values the same importance in a methodical scientific investigation; either attitudes must be subordinated to values or the contrary.

Now in all the sciences which deal with separate domains of human culture like language, art, science, economics, it is the attitudes which are subordinated to values—a standpoint which results necessarily from the very specialization of these sciences in the study of certain classes of cultural values. For a theorician of art or an economist an attitude is important and is taken into consideration only in so far as it manifests itself in changes introduced into the sphere of aesthetic or economic values, and is defined exclusively by these changes—that is, by the pre-existing complex of objective data upon which it acted and by the objective results of this activity. But unless there is a special class of cultural values which are not the object-matter of any other science, and unless there are special reasons for assigning this class to social theory— a problem which we shall discuss presently—the latter cannot take the same standpoint and subordinate attitudes to values, for this would mean a useless duplication of existing sciences. There may be, as we shall see, some doubts whether such groups of phenomena as religion or morality should be for special reasons included in the field of social theory or should constitute the object-matter of distinct sciences; but there is no doubt that language and litera- ture, art and science, economics and technique, are already more or less adequately treated by the respective disciplines and, while needing perhaps some internal reforms, do not call for a supple- mentary treatment by sociology or "folk-psychology" (Wundt).

But there is also no doubt that a study of the social world from the opposite standpoint—that is, taking attitudes as special object- matter and subordinating values to them—is necessary, and that an exact methodology of such a study is lacking. Ethics, psychol- ogy, ethnology, sociology, have an interest in this field and each has occupied it in a fragmentary and unmethodical way. But in ethics the study of attitudes has been subordinated to the problem of ideal norms of behavior, not treated as an end in itself, and under these conditions no adequate method of a purely theoretic investi- gation can be worked out. Ethnology has contributed valuable data for the study of attitudes and values as found in the various social groups, particularly the "lower" races, but its work is mainly descriptive. Of the sociological method in the exact sense of the term we shall speak presently. Psychology is, however, the science which has been definitely identified with the study of consciousness, and the main question at this point is how far psychology has cov- ered or is capable of covering the field of attitudes.

As we have indicated above, the attitude is not a psychological datum in the sense given to this term by individual psychology, and this is true regardless of the differences between psychological schools. Concretely speaking, any method of research which takes the individual as a distinct entity and isolates him from his social environment, whether in order to determine by introspective analysis the content and form of his conscious processes, or in order to investigate the organic facts accompanying these processes, or, finally, in order to study experimentally his behavior as reaction to certain stimuli, finds necessarily only psychical, physical, or biological facts essentially and indissolubly connected with the individual as a psychical, physical, or generally biological reality. In order to reach scientific generalizations, such a method must work on the assumption of the universal permanence and identity of human nature as far as expressed in these facts; that is, its fundamental concepts must be such as to apply to all human beings, some of them even to all conscious beings, and individual differences must be reconstructed with the help of these concepts as variations of the same fundamental background, due to varying intensities, qualities, and combinations of essentially the same universal processes. Indeed, as every psychological fact is a state of the individual as fundamental reality, the uniformity of these facts depends on the permanence and uniformity of such individual realities. The central field of individual psychology is therefore constituted by the most elementary conscious phenomena, which are the only ones that can be adequately treated as essentially identical in all conscious beings; phenomena which are limited to a certain number of individuals either must be treated as complex and analyzed into elementary and universal elements, or, if this cannot be done, then their content, varying with the variation of social milieu, must be omitted and only the *form* of their occurrence reconstructed as presumably the same wherever and whenever they happen.

But psychology is not exclusively individual psychology. We find numerous monographs listed as psychological, but studying conscious phenomena which are not supposed to have their source in "human nature" in general, but in special social conditions, which can vary with the variation of these conditions and still be common to all individuals in the same conditions, and which are therefore treated, not as mere states of individual beings, but as self-sufficient data to be studied without any necessary assumptions about the psychological, physiological, or biological constitution of the individuals composing the group. To this sphere of psychology belong all investigations that concern conscious phenomena particular to races, nationalities, religious, political, professional groups, corresponding to special occupations and interests, provoked by special influences of a social milieu, developed by educational activities and legal measures, etc. The term "social psychology" has become current for this type of investigations. The distinction of social from individual psychology and the methodological unity of social psychology as a separate science have not been sufficiently discussed, but we shall attempt to show that social psychology is precisely the science of attitudes and that, while its methods are essentially different from the methods of individual psychology, its field is as wide as conscious life.

Indeed, every manifestation of conscious life, however simple or complex, general or particular, can be treated as an attitude, because every one involves a tendency to action, whether this action is a process of mechanical activity producing physical changes in the material world, or an attempt to influence the attitudes of others by speech and gesture, or a mental activity which does not at the given moment find a social expression, or even a mere process of sensual apperception. And all the objects of these actions can be treated as *social* values, for they all have some content which is or may be accessible to other individuals—even a personal "idea" can be communicated to others—and a meaning by which they may become the objects of the activity of others. And thus social psychology, when it undertakes to study the conscious phenomena found in a given social group, has no reasons a priori which force it to limit itself to a certain class of such phenomena to the exclusion of others; any manifestation of the conscious life of any member of the group is an attitude when taken in connection with the values which constitute the sphere of experience of this group, and this sphere includes data of the natural environment as well as artistic works or religious beliefs, technical products and economic relations as well as scientific theories. If, therefore, monographs in social psychology limit themselves to such special problems as, for example, the study of general conscious phenomena produced in a social group by certain physical, biological, economic, political influences, by common occupation, common religious beliefs, etc., the limitation may be justified by the social importance of these phenomena or even by only a particular interest of the author, but it is not necessitated by the nature of social psychology, which can study among the conscious phenomena occurring within the given social group, not only such as are peculiar to this group as a whole, but also, on the one hand, such as individual psychology assumes to be common to all conscious beings, and, on the other hand, such as may be peculiar to only one individual member of the group.

But of course not all the attitudes found in the conscious life of a social group have the same importance for the purposes of social psychology at a given moment, or even for its general purposes as a science of the social world. On the one hand, the task of every science in describing and generalizing the data is to reduce as far as possible the limitless complexity of experience to a limited number of concepts, and therefore those elements of reality are the most important which are most generally found in that part of experience which constitutes the object-matter of a science. And thus for social psychology the importance of an attitude is proportionate to the number and variety of actions in which this attitude is manifested. The more generally an attitude is shared by the members of the given social group and the greater the part which it plays in the life of every member, the stronger the interest which it provokes in the social psychologist, while attitudes which are either peculiar to a few members of the group or which manifest themselves only on rare occasions have as such a relatively secondary significance, but may become significant through some connection with more general and fundamental attitudes.[2]

On the other hand, scientific generalizations are productive and valuable only in so far as they help to discover certain relations between various classes of the generalized data and to establish a

[2]   In connection, indeed, with the problems of both the creation and the destruction of social values, the most exceptional and divergent attitudes may prove the most important ones, because they may introduce a crisis and an element of disorder. And to the social theorist and technician the disorderly individual is of peculiar interest as a destroyer of values, as in the case of the anti-social individual, and as a creator of values, as in the case of the man of genius.

systematic classification by a logical subordination and co-ordi-
nation of concepts; a generalization which bears no relation to
others is useless. Now, as the main body of the materials of social
psychology is constituted by *cultural* attitudes, corresponding to
variable and multiform *cultural* values, such elementary *natural* attitudes as correspond to stable and uniform *physical* conditions—
for example, attitudes manifested in sensual perception or in the action of eating—in spite of their generality and practical importance for the human race, can be usefully investigated within the
limits of this science only if a connection can be found between
them and the cultural attitudes—if, for example, it can be shown
that sensual perception or the organic attitude of disgust varies
within certain limits with the variation of social conditions. As
long as there is no possibility of an actual subordination or co-
ordination as between the cultural and the natural attitudes, the
natural attitudes have no immediate interest for social psychology,
and their investigation remains a task of individual psychology.
In other words, those conscious phenomena corresponding to the
physical world can be introduced into social psychology only if
it can be shown that they are not purely "natural"—independent
of social conditions—but also in some measures cultural—influenced by social values.

Thus, the field of social psychology practically comprises first
of all the attitudes which are more or less generally found among
the members of a social group, have a real importance in the life-
organization of the individuals who have developed them, and
manifest themselves in social activities of these individuals. This
field can be indefinitely enlarged in two directions if the concrete
problems of social psychology demand it. It may include attitudes
which are particular to certain members of the social group or
appear in the group only on rare occasions, as soon as they acquire
for some reason a social importance; thus, some personal sexual
idiosyncrasy will interest social psychology only if it becomes an
object of imitation or of indignation to other members of the group
or if it helps to an understanding of more general sexual attitudes.
On the other hand, the field of social psychology may be extended
to such attitudes as manifest themselves with regard, not to the

social, but to the physical, environment of the individual, as soon
as they show themselves affected by the social culture; for example,
the perception of colors would become a socio-psychological problem if it proved to have evolved during the cultural evolution
under the influence of decorative arts.

Social psychology has thus to perform the part of a general
science of the subjective side of social culture which we have heretofore usually ascribed to individual psychology or to "psychology in general." It may claim to be *the* science of consciousness
as manifested in culture, and its function is to render service, as a
general auxiliary science, to all the special sciences dealing with
various spheres of social values. This does not mean that social
psychology can ever supplant individual psychology; the methods
and standpoints of these two sciences are too different to permit
either of them to fulfil the function of the other, and, if it were not
for the traditional use of the term "psychology" for both types
of research, it would be even advisable to emphasize this difference
by a distinct terminology.

But when we study the life of a concrete social group we find
a certain very important side of this life which social psychology
cannot adequately take into account, which none of the special
sciences of culture treats as its proper object-matter, and which
during the last fifty years has constituted the central sphere of
interest of the various researches called *sociology*. Among the
attitudes prevailing within a group some express themselves only
in individual actions—uniform or multiform, isolated or combined
—but only in actions. But there are other attitudes—usually,
though not always, the most general ones—which, besides expressing themselves directly, like the first, in actions, find also an indirect manifestation in more or less explicit and formal *rules* of behavior by which the group tends to maintain, to regulate, and to
make more general and more frequent the corresponding type of
actions among its members. These rules—customs and rituals, legal and educational norms, obligatory beliefs and aims, etc.—
arouse a twofold interest. We may treat them, like actions, as manifestations of attitudes, as indices showing that, since the group
demands a certain kind of actions, the attitude which is supposed

to manifest itself in these actions is shared by all those who uphold the rule. But, on the other hand, the very existence of a rule shows that there are some, even if only weak and isolated, attitudes which do not fully harmonize with the one expressed in the rule, and that the group feels the necessity of preventing these attitudes from passing into action. Precisely as far as the rule is consciously realized as binding by individual members of the group from whom it demands a certain adaptation, it has for every individual a certain content and a certain meaning and is a value. Furthermore, the action of an individual viewed by the group, by another individual, or even by himself in reflection, with regard to this action's agreement or disagreement with the rule, becomes also a value to which a certain attitude of appreciation or depreciation is attached in various forms. In this way rules and actions, taken, not with regard to the attitudes *expressed* in them, but with regard to the attitudes *provoked* by them, are quite analogous to any other values—economic, artistic, scientific, religious, etc. There may be many various attitudes corresponding to a rule or action as objects of individual reflection and appreciation, and a certain attitude—such as, for example, the desire for personal freedom or the feeling of social righteousness—may bear positively or negatively upon many rules and actions, varying from group to group and from individual to individual. These values cannot, therefore, be the object-matter of social psychology; they constitute a special group of objective cultural data alongside the special domains of other cultural sciences like economics, theory of art, philology, etc: The rules of behavior, and the actions viewed as conforming or not conforming with these rules, constitute with regard to their objective significance a certain number of more or less connected and harmonious systems which can be generally called *social institutions*, and the totality of institutions found in a concrete social group constitutes the *social organization* of this group. And when studying the social organization as such we must subordinate attitudes to values as we do in other special cultural sciences; that is, attitudes count for us only as influencing and modifying rules of behavior and social institutions.

Sociology, as theory of social organization, is thus a special

science of culture like economics or philology, and is in so far
opposed to social psychology as the general science of the subjective side of culture. But at the same time it has this in common
with social psychology: that the values which it studies draw all
their reality, all their power to influence human life, from the
social attitudes which are expressed or supposedly expressed in
them; if the individual in his behavior is so largely determined
by the rules prevailing in his social group, it is certainly due neither to the rationality of these rules nor to the physical consequences which their following or breaking may have, but to his consciousness that these rules represent attitudes of his group and to
his realization of the *social* sonsequences which will ensue for him
if he follows or breaks the rules. And therefore both social psychology and sociology can be embraced under the general term of
social theory, as they are both concerned with the relation between
the individual and the concrete social group, though their standpoints on this common ground are quite opposite, and though
their fields are not equally wide, social psychology comprising
the attitudes of the individual toward *all* cultural values of the
given social group, while sociology can study only one type of
these values—social rules—in their relation to individual attitudes.

We have seen that social psychology has a central field of interest including the most general and fundamental cultural attitudes
found within concrete societies. In the same manner there is a certain domain which constitutes the methodological center of sociological interest. It includes those rules of behavior which concern
more especially the active relations between individual members of
the group and between each member and the group as a whole. It
is these rules, indeed, manifested as mores, laws, and group-ideals
and systematized in such institutions as the family, the tribe, the
community, the free association, the state, etc., which constitute
the central part of social organization and provide through this
organization the essential conditions of the existence of a group
as a distinct cultural entity and not a mere agglomeration of individuals; and hence all other rules which a given group may develop
and treat as obligatory have a secondary sociological importance

as compared with these. But this does not mean that sociology should not extend its field of investigation beyond this methodological center of interest. Every social group, particularly on lower stages of cultural evolution, is inclined to control all individual activities, not alone those which attain directly its fundamental institutions. Thus we find social regulations of economic, religious, scientific, artistic activities, even of technique and speech, and the break of these regulations is often treated as affecting the very existence of the group. And we must concede that, though the effect of these regulations on cultural productivity is often more than doubtful, they do contribute as long as they last to the unity of the group, while, on the other hand, the close association which has been formed between these rules and the fundamental social institutions without which the group cannot exist has often the consequence that cultural evolution which destroys the influence of these secondary regulations may actually disorganize the group. Precisely as far as these social rules concerning special cultural activities are in the above-determined way connected with the rules which bear on social relations they acquire an interest for sociology. Of course it can be determined only a posteriori how far the field of sociology should be extended beyond the investigation of fundamental social institutions, and the situation varies from group to group and from period to period. In all civilized societies some part of every cultural activity—religious, economic, scientific, artistic, etc.—is left outside of social regulation, and another, perhaps even larger, part, though still subjected to social rules, is no longer supposed to affect directly the existence or coherence of society and actually does not affect it. It is therefore a grave methodological error to attempt to include generally in the field of sociology such cultural domains as religion or economics on the ground that in certain social groups religious or economic norms are considered—and in some measures even really are— a part of social organization, for even there the respective values have a content which cannot be completely reduced to social rules of behavior, and their importance for social organization may be very small or even none in other societies or at other periods of evolution.

The fundamental distinction between social psychology and sociology appears clearly when we undertake the comparative study of special problems in various societies, for these problems naturally divide themselves into two classes. We may attempt to explain certain attitudes by tracing their origin and trying to determine the laws of their appearance under various social circumstances, as, for example, when we investigate sexual love or feeling of group-solidarity, bashfulness or showing off, the mystical emotion or the aesthetic amateur attitude, etc. Or we may attempt to give an explanation of social institutions and try to subject to laws their appearance under various socio-psychological conditions, as when our object-matter is marriage or family, criminal legislation or censorship of scientific opinions, militarism or parliamentarism, etc. But when we study monographically a concrete social group with all its fundamental attitudes and values, it is difficult to make a thoroughgoing separation of socio-psychological and sociological problems, for any concrete body of material contains both. Consequently, since the present work, and particularly its first two volumes, is precisely a monograph of a concrete social group, we cannot go into a detailed analysis of methodological questions concerning exclusively the socio-psychological or sociological investigation in particular, but must limit ourselves to such general methodological indications as concern both. Later, in connection with problems treated in subsequent volumes, more special methodological discussions may be necessary and will be introduced in their proper place.

The chief problems of modern science are problems of causal explanation. The determination and systematization of data is only the first step in scientific investigation. If a science wishes to lay the foundation of a technique, it must attempt to understand and to control the process of *becoming*. Social theory cannot avoid this task, and there is only one way of fulfilling it. Social becoming, like natural becoming, must be analyzed into a plurality of facts, each of which represents a succession of cause and effect. The idea of social theory is the analysis of the totality of social becoming into such casual processes and a systematization permitting us to understand the connections between these processes. No argu-

ments a priori trying to demonstrate the impossibility of application of the principle of causality to conscious human life in
general can or should halt social theory in tending to this idea, whatever difficulties there may be in the way, because as a matter of
fact we continually do apply the principle of causality to the social
world in our activity and in our thought, and we shall always do
this as long as we try to control social becoming in any form. So,
instead of fruitlessly discussing the justification of this application
in the abstract, social theory must simply strive to make it more
methodical and perfect in the concrete—by the actual process of
investigation.

But if the general philosophical problem of free will and determinism is negligible, the particular problem of the best possible
method of causal explanation is very real. Indeed, its solution is the
fundamental and inevitable introductory task of a science which,
like social theory, is still in the period of formation. The great and
most usual illusion of the scientist is that he simply takes the facts
as they are, without any methodological prepossessions, and gets
his explanation entirely a posteriori from pure experience. A fact
by itself is already an abstraction; we isolate a certain limited
aspect of the concrete process of becoming, rejecting, at least provisionally, all its indefinite complexity. The question is only
whether we perform this abstraction methodically or not, whether
we know what and why we accept and reject, or simply take uncritically the old abstractions of "common sense." If we want to
reach scientific explanations, we must keep in mind that our facts
must be determined in such a way as to permit of their subordination to general laws. A fact which cannot be treated as a manifestation of one or several laws is inexplicable causally. When, for
example, the historian speaks of the causes of the present war, he
must assume that the war is a combination of the effects of many
causes, each of which may repeat itself many times in history and
must have always the same effect, although such a combination
of these causes as has produced the present war may never happen
again. And only if social theory succeeds in determining causal laws
can it become a basis of social technique, for technique demands
the possibility of foreseeing and calculating the effects of given

causes, and this demand is realizable only if we know that certain causes will always and everywhere produce certain effects.

Now, the chief error of both social practice and social theory has been that they determined, consciously or unconsciously, social facts in a way which excluded in advance the possibility of their subordination to any laws. The implicit or explicit assumption was that a social fact is composed of two elements, a cause which is either a social phenomenon or an individual act, and an effect which is either an individual act or a social phenomenon. Following uncritically the example of the physical sciences, which always tend to find the one determined phenomenon which is the necessary and sufficient condition of another phenomenon, social theory and social practice have forgotten to take into account one essential difference between physical and social reality, which is that, while the effect of a physical phenomenon depends exclusively on the objective nature of this phenomenon and can be calculated on the ground of the latter's empirical content, the effect of a social phenomenon depends in addition on the subjective standpoint taken by the individual or the group toward this phenomenon and can be calculated only if we know, not only the objective content of the assumed cause, but also the meaning which it has at the given moment for the given conscious beings. This simple consideration should have shown to the social theorist or technician that a social cause cannot be simple, like a physical cause, but is compound, and must include both an objective and a subjective element, a value *and* an attitude. Otherwise the effect will appear accidental and incalculable, because we shall have to search in every particular case for the reasons why this particular individual or this particular society reacted to the given phenomenon in this way and not in any other way.

In fact, a social value, acting upon individual members of the group, produces a more or less different effect on every one of them; even when acting upon the same individual at various moments it does not influence him uniformly. The influence of a work of art is a typical example. And such uniformities as exist here are quite irrelevant, for they are not absolute. If we once suppose that a social phenomenon is the cause—which means a neces-

sary and sufficient cause, for there are no "insufficient" causes—
of an individual reaction, then our statement of this causal dependence has the logical claim of being a scientific law from which
there can be no exceptions; that is, every seeming exception must
be explained by the action of some other cause, an action whose
formulation becomes another scientific law. But to explain why
in a concrete case a work of art or a legal prescription which,
according to our supposed law, should provoke in the individual
a certain reaction *A* provokes instead a reaction *B*, we should
have to investigate the whole past of this individual and repeat
this investigation in every case, with regard to every individual
whose reaction is not *A*, without hoping ever to subordinate those
exceptions to a new law, for the life-history of every individual is
different. Consequently social theory tries to avoid this methodological absurdity by closing its eyes to the problem itself. It is
either satisfied with statements of causal influences which hold
true "on the average," "in the majority of cases"—a flat self-
contradiction, for, if something *is a cause*, it must have by its very
definition, always and necessarily *the same effect*, otherwise it is
not a cause at all. Or it tries to analyze phenomena acting upon
individuals and individual reactions to them into simpler elements,
hoping thus to find simple facts, while the trouble is not with the
complexity of data, but with the complexity of the context on
which these data act or in which they are embodied—that is, of
the human personality. Thus, as far as the complexity of social data
is concerned, the principle of gravitation and the smile of Mona
Lisa are simple in their objective content, while their influence on
human attitudes has been indefinitely varied; the complex system
of a graphomaniac or the elaborate picture of a talentless and skil-
less man provokes much more uniform reactions. And, on the individual side, the simple attitude of anger can be provoked by an
indefinite variety of social phenomena, while the very complicated attitude of militant patriotism appears usually only in very
definite social conditions.

But more than this. Far from obviating the problem of individual variations, such uniformities of reaction to social influences
as can be found constitute a problem in themselves. For with the

exception of the elementary reactions to purely physical stimuli, which may be treated as identical because of the identity of "human nature" and as such belong to individual psychology, all uniformities with which social psychology has to deal are the product of social conditions. If the members of a certain group react in an identical way to certain values, it is because they have been socially trained to react thus, because the traditional rules of behavior predominant in the given group impose upon every member certain ways of defining and solving the practical situations which he meets in his life. But the very success of this social training, the very fact that individual members do accept such definitions and act in accordance with them, is no less a problem than the opposite fact—the frequent insuccess of the training, the growing assertion of the personality, the growing variation of reaction to social rules, the search for personal definitions—which characterizes civilized societies. And thus, even if we find that all the members of a social group react in the same way to a certain value, still we cannot assume that this value alone is the cause of this reaction, for the latter is also conditioned by the uniformity of attitudes prevailing in the group; and this uniformity itself cannot be taken as granted and omitted—as we omit the uniformity of environing conditions in a physical fact—because it is the particular effect of certain social rules acting upon the members of the group who, because of certain predispositions, have accepted these rules, and this effect may be at any moment counterbalanced by the action of different causes, and is in fact counterbalanced more and more frequently with the progress of civilization.

In short, when social theory assumes that a certain social value is of itself the cause of a certain individual reaction, it is then forced to ask: "But why did this value produce this particular effect when acting on this particular individual or group at this particular moment?" Certainly no scientific answer to such a question is possible, since in order to explain this "why" we should have to know the whole past of the individual, of the society, and of the universe.

Analogous methodological difficulties arise when social theory attempts to explain a change in social organization as a result of the activity of the members of the group. If we treat individual activity as a *cause* of social changes, every change appears as inexplicable, particularly when it is "original," presents many new features. Necessarily this point is one of degree, for every product of individual activity is in a sense a new value and in so far original as it has not existed before this activity, but in certain cases the importance of the change brought by the individual makes its incalculable and inexplicable character particularly striking. We have therefore almost despaired of extending consistently the principle of causality to the activities of "great men," while it still seems to us that we do understand the everyday productive activity of the average human individual or of the "masses." From the methodological standpoint, however, it is neither more nor less difficult to explain the greatest changes brought into the social world by a Charles the Great, a Napoleon, a Marx, or a Bismarck than to explain a small change brought by a peasant who starts a lawsuit against his relatives or buys a piece of land to increase his farm. The work of the great man, like that of the ordinary man, is the result of his tendency to modify the existing conditions, of his attitude toward his social environment which makes him reject certain existing values and produce certain new values. The difference is in the values which are the object of the activity, in the nature, importance, complexity, of the social problems put and solved. The change in social organization produced by a great man may be thus equivalent to an accumulation of small changes brought by millions of ordinary men, but the idea that a creative process is more explicable when it lasts for several generations than when it is performed in a few months or days, or that by dividing a creative process into a million small parts we destroy its irrationality, is equivalent to the conception that by a proper combination of mechanical elements in a machine we can produce a *perpetuum mobile*.

The simple and well-known fact is that the social results of individual activity depend, not only on the action itself, but also on the social conditions in which it is performed; and therefore the cause of a social change must include both individual and social elements. By ignoring this, social theory faces an infinite task whenever it wants to explain the simplest social change. For the same action in different social conditions produces quite different results. It is true that if social conditions are sufficiently stable the results of certain individual actions are more or less determinable, at least in a sufficient majority of cases to permit an approximate practical calculation. We know that the result of the activity of a factory-workman will be a certain technical product, that the result of the peasant's starting a lawsuit against a member of his family will be a dissolution of family bonds between him and this member, that the result of a judge's activity in a criminal case will be the condemnation and incarceration of the offender if he is convicted. But all this holds true only if social conditions remain stable. In case of a strike in the factory, the workman will not be allowed to finish his product; assuming that the idea of family solidarity has ceased to prevail in a peasant group, the lawsuit will not provoke moral indignation; if the action upon which the judge has to pronounce this verdict ceases to be treated as a crime because of a change of political conditions or of public opinion, the offender, even if convicted, will be set free. A method which permits us to determine only cases of stereotyped activity and leaves us helpless in face of changed conditions is not a scientific method at all, and becomes even less and less practically useful with the continual increase of fluidity in modern social life.

Moreover, social theory forgets also that the uniformity of results of certain actions is itself a problem and demands explanation exactly as much as do the variations. For the stability of social conditions upon which the uniformity of results of individual activity depends is itself a product of former activities, not an original natural status which might be assumed as granted. Both its character and its degree vary from group to group and from epoch to epoch. A certain action may have indeed determined and calculable effects in a certain society and at a certain period, but will have completely different effects in other societies and at other periods.

And thus social theory is again confronted by a scientifically absurd question. Assuming that individual activity in itself is the cause of social effects, it must then ask: "Why does a certain action produce this particular effect at this particular moment in this particular society?" The answer to this question would demand a complete explanation of the whole status of the given society at the given moment, and thus force us to investigate the entire past of the universe.

The fundamental methodological principle of both social psychology and sociology—the principle without which they can never reach scientific explanation—is therefore the following one:

The cause of a social or individual phenomenon is never another social or individual phenomenon alone, but always a combination of a social and an individual phenomenon.

Or, in more exact terms:

The cause of a value or of an attitude is never an attitude or a value alone, but always a combination of an attitude and a value.[3]

It is only by the application of this principle that we can remove the difficulties with which social theory and social practice have struggled. If we wish to explain the appearance of a new attitude—whether in one individual or in a whole group—we know that this attitude appeared as a consequence of the influence of a social value upon the individual or the group, but we know also that this influence itself would have been impossible unless there had been some pre-existing attitude, some wish, emotional habit, or intellectual tendency, to which this value has in some way appealed, favoring it, contradicting it, giving it a new direction, or stabilizing its hesitating expressions. Our problem is therefore to find both the value and the pre-existing attitude upon

---

[3]   It may be objected that we have neglected to criticize the conception according to which the cause of a social phenomenon is to be sought, not in an individual, but exclusively in another social phenomenon (Durkheim). But a criticism of this conception is implied in the previous discussion of the data of social theory. As these data are both values and attitudes, a fact must include both, and a succession of values alone cannot constitute a fact. Of course much depends also on what we call a "social" phenomenon. An attitude may be treated as a social phenomenon as opposed to the "state of consciousness" of individual psychology; but it is individual, even if common to all members of a group, when we oppose it to a value.

which it has acted and get in their combination the necessary and sufficient cause of the new attitude. We shall not be forced then to ask: "Why did this value provoke in this case such a reaction?" because the answer will be included in the fact—in the pre-existing attitude to which this value appealed. Our fact will bear its explanation in itself, just as the physical fact of the movement of an elastic body B when struck by another elastic moving body A bears its explanation in itself. We may, if we wish, ask for a more detailed explanation, not only of the appearance of the new attitude, but also for certain specific characters of this attitude, in the same way as we may ask for an explanation, not only of the movement of the body B in general, but also of the rapidity and direction of this movement; but the problem always remains limited, and the explanation is within the fact, in the character of the pre-existing attitude and of the influencing value, or in the masses of the bodies A and B and the rapidity and direction of their movements previous to their meeting. We can indeed pass from the given fact to the new one—ask, for example, "How did it happen that this attitude to which the value appealed was there?" or, "How did it happen that the body A moved toward B until they met?" But this question again will find its limited and definite answer if we search in the same way for the cause of the pre-existing attitude in some other attitude and value, or of the movement in some other movement.

Let us take some examples from the following volumes. Two individuals, under the influence of a tyrannical behavior in their fathers, develop completely different attitudes. One shows submission, the other secret revolt and resentment. If the father's tyranny is supposed to be the cause of these opposite attitudes, we must know the whole character of these individuals and their whole past in order to explain the difference of effect. But if we realize that the tyranny is not the sole cause of both facts, but only a common element which enters into the composition of two different causes, our simple task will be to find the other elements of these causes. We can find them, if our materials are sufficient, in certain persisting attitudes of these individuals as expressed in words or actions. We form hypotheses which acquire more and more cer-

tainty as we compare many similar cases. We thus reach the
conclusion that the other element of the cause is, in the first case,
the attitude of familial solidarity, in the second case, the individualistic tendency to assert one's own personal desires. We have thus
two completely different facts, and we do not need to search
farther. The difference of effects is obviously explained by the
difference of causes and is necessarily what it is. The cause of the
attitude of submission is the attitude of familial solidarity plus
the tyranny of the father; the cause of the attitude of revolt is
the tendency to self-assertion plus the tyranny of the father.

As another example—this time a mass-phenomenon—we take
the case of the Polish peasants from certain western communities
who go to Germany for season-work and show there uniformly a
desire to do as much piece-work as possible and work as hard as
they can in order to increase their earnings, while peasants of these
same communities and even the same individual peasants when
they stay at home and work during the season on the Polish
estates accept only day-work and refuse piece-work under the most
ridiculous pretexts. We should be inclined to ascribe this difference of attitudes to the difference of conditions, and in fact both
the peasants and the Polish estate-owners give this explanation,
though they differ as to the nature of causes. The peasants say that
the conditions of piece-work are less favorable in Poland than in
Germany; the estate-owners claim that the peasants in Germany are
more laborious because intimidated by the despotism of German
estate-owners and farm-managers. Both contentions are wrong.
The conditions of piece-work as compared with day-work are
certainly not less favorable in Poland than in Germany, and the
peasants are more laborious in Germany on their own account,
regardless of the very real despotism which they find there. To be
sure, the conditions are different; the whole social environment
differs. The environment, however, is not the sufficient cause of
the attitudes. The point is that the peasant who goes to Germany
is led there by the desire of economic advance, and this attitude
predominates during the whole period of season-work, not on account of the conditions themselves, but through the feeling of being
in definite new conditions, and produces the desire to earn more

by piece-work. On the contrary, the peasant who stays at home preserves for the time being his old attitude toward work as a "necessary evil," and this attitude, under the influence of traditional ideas about the conditions of work on an estate, produces the unwillingness to accept piece-work. Here both components of the cause—pre-existing attitude and value-idea—differ, and evidently the effects must be different.

If now we have to explain the appearance of a social value, we know that this value is a product of the activity of an individual or a number of individuals, and in so far dependent on the attitude of which this activity is the expression. But we know also that this result is inexplicable unless we take into consideration the value (or complex of values) which was the starting-point and the social material of activity and which has conditioned the result as much as did the attitude itself. The new value is the result of the solution of a problem set by the pre-existing value and the active attitude together; it is the common effect of both of them. The product of an activity—even of a mechanical activity, such as a manufactured thing—acquires its full social reality only when it enters into social life, becomes the object of the attitudes of the group, is socially valued. And we can understand this meaning, which is an essential part of the effect, only if we know what was the social situation when the activity started, what was the social value upon which the individual (or individuals) specially acted and which might have been quite different from the one upon which he intended to act and imagined that he acted. If we once introduce this pre-existing value into the fact as the necessary component of the cause, the effect—the new value—will be completely explicable and we shall not be forced to ask: "Why is it that this activity has brought in these conditions this particular effect instead of the effect it was intended to bring?" any more than physics is forced to ask: "Why is it that an elastic body struck by another elastic body changes the direction and rapidity of its movement instead of changing merely its rapidity or merely its direction?"

To take some further examples, the American social institutions try, by a continuous supervision and interference, to develop a strong marriage-group organization among the Polish immigrants who begin to show certain signs of decay of family life or among whom the relation between husband and wife and children does not come up to the American standards in certain respects. The results of this activity are quite baffling. Far from being constructive of new values, the interference proves rather destructive in a great majority of cases, in spite of the best efforts of the most intelligent social workers. In a few cases it does not seem to affect much the existing state of things; sometimes, indeed, though very seldom, it does bring good results. This very variation makes the problem still more complicated and difficult. To explain the effects, the social workers try to take into consideration the whole life-history and character of the individuals with whom they deal, but without progressing much in their efforts. The whole misunderstanding comes from the lack of realization that the Polish immigrants here, though scattered and losing most of their social coherence, are still not entirely devoid of this coherence and constitute vague and changing but as yet, in some measure, real communities, and that these communities have brought from the old country several social institutions, among which the most important is the family institution. In new conditions these institutions gradually dissolve, and we shall study this process in later volumes. But the dissolution is not sudden or universal, and thus the American social worker in his activity meets, without realizing it, a set of social values which are completely strange to him, and which his activity derectly affects without his knowing it. As far as the family organization is concerned, any interference of external powers—political or social authorities—must act dissolvingly upon it, because it affects the fundamental principle of the family as a social institution —the principle of solidarity. An individual who accepts external interference in his favor against a family member sins against this principle, and a break of family relations must be thus the natural consequence of the well-intentioned but insufficiently enlightened external activities. The effect is brought, not by these activities alone, but by the combination of these activities and the pre-existing peasant family organization. Of course, if the family organization is different—if, for example, in a given case the marriage-group has already taken the place of the large family—the effect will be different because the total cause is different. Or, if instead of the protective and for the peasant incomprehensible attitude of the social worker or court officer a different attitude is brought into action—if, for example, the family is surrounded by a strong and solidary community of equals who, from the standpoint of communal solidarity, interfere with family relations, just as they do in the old country—again the effect will be different because the other component of the cause—the attitude as expressed in action—is no longer the same.

Another interesting example is the result of the national persecution of the Poles in Prussia, the aim of which was to destroy Polish national cohesion. Following all the efforts which the powerful Prussian state could bring against the Poles, national cohesion has in a very large measure increased, and the national organization has included such elements as were before the persecution quite indifferent to national problems—the majority of the peasants and of the lower city classes. The Prussian government had not realized the existence and strength of the communal solidarity principle in the lower classes of Polish society, and by attacking certain vital interests of these classes, religious and economic, it contributed more than the positive efforts of the intelligent Polish class could have done to the development of this principle and to its extension over the whole Polish society in Posen, Silesia, and West Prussia.

These examples of the result of the violation of our methodological rule could be multiplied indefinitely from the field of social reform. The common tendency of reformers is to construct a rational scheme of the social institution they wish to see produced or abolished, and then to formulate an ideal plan of social activities which would perhaps lead to a realization of their scheme if social life were merely a sum of individual actions, every one of them starting afresh without any regard for tradition, every one having its source exclusively in the psychological nature of the individual and capable of being completely directed, by well-selected motives, toward definite social aims. But as social reality contains, not only individual acts, but also social institutions, not only attitudes, but also values fixed by tradition and conditioning the attitudes, these values cooperate in the production of the final effect quite independently, and often in spite of the intentions of the social reformer. Thus the socialist, if he presupposes that a solidary and well-directed action of the masses will realize the scheme of a perfect socialistic organization, ignores completely the influence of the whole existing social organization which will co-operate with the revolutionary attitudes of the masses in producing the new organization, and this, not only because of the opposition of those who will hold to the traditional values, but also because many of those values, as socially sanctioned rules for defining situations, will continue to condition many attitudes of the masses themselves and will thus be an integral part of the causes of the final effect.

Of course we do not assert that the proper way of formulating social facts is never used by social theory or reflective social practice. On the contrary, we very frequently find it applied in the study of particular cases, and it is naïvely used in everyday business and personal relations. We use it in all cases involving argument and persuasion. The business man, the shopkeeper, and the politician use it very subtly. We have been compelled in the case of our juvenile delinquents to allow the judges to waive the formal and incorrect conception of social facts and to substitute in the case of the child the proper formula. But the point is that this formula has never been applied with any consistency and systematic development, while the wrong formula has been used very thoroughly and has led to such imposing systems as, in reflective practice, the whole enormous and continually growing complexity of positive law, and in social theory to the more recent and limited, but rapidly growing, accumulation of works on political science, philosophy of law, ethics, and sociology. At every step we try to enforce certain attitudes upon other individuals without stopping to consider what are their dominant attitudes in general or their prevailing attitudes at the given moment; at every step we try to produce certain social values without taking into account the values which are already there and upon which the result of our efforts will depend as much as upon our intention and persistence.

The chief source of this great methodological mistake, whose various consequences we have shown in the first part of this note, lay probably in the fact that social theory and reflective practice started with problems of political and legal organization. Having thus to deal with the relatively uniform attitudes and relatively permanent conditions which characterized civilized societies several thousand years ago, and relying besides upon physical force as a supposedly infallible instrument for the production of social uniformity and stability whenever the desirable attitudes were absent, social theory and reflective practice have been capable of holding and of developing, without remarking its absurdity, a standpoint which would be scientifically and technically justifiable only if human attitudes were absolutely and universally uniform and social conditions absolutely and universally stable.

A systematic application and development of the methodological rules stated above would necessarily lead in a completely different direction. Its final result would not be a system of definitions, like law and special parts of political science, nor a system of the philosophical determination of the essence of certain data, like philosophy of law, the general part of political science, ethics, and many sociological works, nor a general outline of social evolution, like the sociology of the Spencerian school or the philosophies of history, but a system of laws of social becoming, in which definitions, philosophical determinations of essence, and outlines of evolution would play the same part as they do in physical science—that is, would constitute either instruments helping to analyze reality and to find laws, or conclusions helping to understand the general scientific meaning and the connection of laws.

It is evident that such a result can be attained only by a long and persistent co-operation of social theoricians. It took almost four centuries to constitute physical science in its present form, and, though the work of the social scientist is incalculably facilitated by the long training in scientific thinking in general which has been acquired by mankind since the period of renaissance, it is on the other hand made more difficult by certain characters of the social world as compared with the natural world. We do not include among these difficulties the complexity of the social world which has been so often and unreflectively emphasized. Complexity is a relative characteristic; it depends on the method and the purpose of analysis. Neither the social nor the natural world presents any ready and absolutely simple elements, and in this sense they are both equally complex, because they are both infinitely complex. But this complexity is a metaphysical, not a scientific, problem. In science we treat any datum as a simple element if it behaves as such in all the combinations in which we find it, and any fact is a simple fact which can indefinitely repeat itself—that is, in which the relation between cause and effect can be assumed to be permanent and necessary. And in this respect it is still a problem whether the social world will not prove much less complex than the natural world if only we analyze its data and determine its facts by proper methods. The prepossession of complexity is due to the naturalistic way of treating the social reality. If it is maintained that the social world has to be treated as an expression or a product of the psychological, physiological, or biological nature of human beings, then, of course, it appears as incomparably more complex than the natural world, because to the already inexhaustibly complex conscious human organism as a part of nature is added the fact that in a social group there are numerous and various human beings interacting in the most various ways. But if we study the social world, without any naturalistic prepossessions, simply as a plurality of specifica data, causally interconnected in a process of becoming, the question of complexity is no more baffling for social theory, and may even prove less so, than it is for physical science.

The search for laws does not actually present any special difficulties if our facts have been adequately determined. When we have found that a certain effect is produced by a certain cause, the formulation of this causal dependence has in itself the character of a law; that is, we assume that whenever this cause repeats itself the effect will necessarily follow. The further need is to explain apparent exceptions. But this need of explanation, which is the stumbling-block of a theory that has defined its facts inadequately, becomes, on the contrary, a factor of progress when the proper method is employed. For when we know that a certain cause can have only one determined effect, when we have assumed, for example, that the attitude A plus the value B is the cause of the attitude C, then if the presumed cause $A + B$ is there and the expected effect C does not appear, this means either that we have been mistaken in assuming that $A + B$ was the cause of C, or that the action of $A + B$ was interfered with by the action of some other cause $A + Y$ or $X + B$ or $X + Y$. In the first case the exception gives us the possibility of correcting our error; in the second case it permits us to extend our knowledge by finding a new causal connection, by determining the partly or totally unknown cause $A + Y$ or $X + B$ or $X + Y$ which has interfered with the action of our known case $A + B$ and brought a complex effect $D = C + Z$, instead of the expected C. And thus the exception from a law becomes the starting-point for the discovery of a new law.

This explanation of apparent exceptions being the only logical demand that can be put upon a law, it is evident that the difference between particular and general laws is only a difference of the field of application, not one of logical validity. Suppose we find in the present work some laws concerning the social life of Polish peasants showing that whenever there is a pre-existing attitude A and the influence of a value B, another attitude C appears, or whenever there is a value D and an activity directed by an attitude E, a new value F is the effect. If the causes $A + B$ and $D + E$ are found only in the social life of the Polish peasants and nowhere else, because some of their components—the attitudes or values involved—are peculiar to the Polish peasants, then, of course, the laws $A + B = C$ and $D + E = F$ will be particular laws applicable only to the Polish peasant society, but within these limits as objectively valid as others which social theory may eventually find of applicability to humanity in general. We cannot extend them beyond these limits and do not need to extend them. But the situation will be different if the attitudes A and E and the values B and D are not peculiar to the Polish peasant society, and thus the causes $A + B$ and $D + E$ can be found also in other societies. Then the laws $A + B = C$ and $D + E = F$, based on facts discovered among Polish peasants, will have quite a different meaning. But we cannot be sure whether they are valid for other societies until we have found that in other societies the causes $A + B$ and $D + E$

produce the same respective effects C and F. And since we cannot know whether these values and attitudes will be found or not in other societies until we have investigated these societies, the character of our laws must remain until then undetermined; we cannot say definitely whether they are absolutely valid though applicable only to the Polish peasants or only hypothetically valid although applicable to all societies.

The problem of laws being the most important one of methodology, we shall illustrate it in detail from two concrete examples. Of course we do not really assert that the supposed laws which we use in these illustrations are already established; some of them are still hypotheses, others even mere fictions. The purpose is to give an insight into the mechanism of the research.

Let us take as the first example the evolution of the economic life of the Polish peasant as described in the introduction to the first and second volumes of this work. We find there, first, a system of familial economic organization with a thoroughly social and qualitative character of economic social values, succeeded by an individualistic system with a quantification of the values. This succession as such does not determine any social fact; we obtain the formula of facts only if we find the attitude that constructs the second system out of the first. Now, this attitude is the tendency to economic advance, and thus our empirical facts are subsumed to the formula: familial system—tendency to advance—individualistic system. The same facts being found generally among Polish peasants of various localities, we can assume that this formula expresses a law, but whether it is a law applicable only to the Polish peasants or to all societies depends on whether such a familial economic organization associated with a tendency to advance results always and everywhere in an individualistic system. We may further determine that if we find the familial system, but instead of the tendency to economic advance another attitude—for example, the desire to concentrate political power in the family—the result will be different—for example, the feudal system of hereditary estate. Or we may find that if the tendency to economic advance acts upon a different system—for example, a fully developed economic individualism—it will also lead to a different social formation—for example, to the constitution of trusts. These other classes of facts may become in turn the bases of social hypotheses if they prove sufficiently general and uniform. But certainly, whether the law is particular or general, we must always be able to explain every seeming exception. For example, we find the familial system and the tendency to advance in a Polish peasant family group, but no formation of the individualistic system—the family tends to advance as a whole. In this case we must suppose that the evolution has been hindered by some factors which change the expected results. There may be, for example, a very strong attitude of family pride developed traditionally in all the members, as in families of peasant nobility who had particular privileges during the period of Poland's independence. In this case familial pride co-operating with the tendency to advance will produce a mixed system of economic organization, with quantification of values but without individualism. And if our law does not stand all these tests we have to drop it. But even then we may still suppose that its formulation was too general, that within the range of facts covered by these concepts a more limited and particular law could be discovered—for example, that the system of "work for living," under the influence of the tendency to advance, becomes a system of "work for wages."

As another type of example we select a particular case of legal practice and attempt to show what assumptions are implicitly involved in it, what social laws are uncritically assumed, and try to indicate in what way the assumptions of common sense could be verified, modified, complemented, or rejected, so as to make them objectively valid. For, if science is only developed, systematized, and perfected common sense, the work required to rectify common sense before it becomes science is incomparably greater than is usually supposed.

The case is simple. A Polish woman (K) has loaned to another (T) $300 at various times. After some years she claims her money back; the other refuses to pay. K goes to court. Both bring witnesses. The witnesses are examined. First assumption of legal practice, which we may put into the form of a social law, is: "A witness who has sworn to tell the truth will tell the truth, unless there are reasons for exception."[4] But according to our definition there can be no such law where only two elements are given. There might be a law if we had (1) the oath (a social value); (2) an individual attitude *x*, still to be determined; (3) a true testimony. But here the second element is lacking; nobody has determined the attitude which, in connection with the oath, results in a true testimony, and therefore, of course, nobody knows how to produce such an attitude. It is supposed that the necessary attitude—whatever it is—appears automatically when the oath is taken. Naturally in many, if not in the majority of cases, the supposition proves false, and if it proves true, nobody knows why. In our case it proved mainly false. Not only the witnesses of the defense, but some of the witnesses of the plaintiff, were lying. What explanation is possible? We could, of course, if we knew what attitude is necessary for true testimony, determine why it was not there or what were the influences that hindered its action. But, not knowing it, we have simply to use some other common-sense generalization, such as: "If the witnesses are lying in spite of the oath, there is some interest involved—personal, familial, friendly." And this was the generalization admitted in this case, and it has no validity whatever because it cannot be converted into a law; we cannot say that interest is the cause making people lie, but we must have again the *tertium quid*—the attitude upon which the interest must act in order to produce a lie. And, on the other hand, a lie can be the result of other factors acting upon certain pre-existing attitudes, and this was precisely the case in the example we are discussing. The Polish peasants lie in court because they bring into court a fighting attitude. Once the suit is started, it becomes a fight where considerations of honesty or altruism are no longer of any weight, and the only problem is—not to be beaten. Here we have, indeed, a formula that may become, if sufficiently verified, a sociological

---

4   It is the formal side of this assumption, not the sphere of its application, that is important. Whether we admit few or many exceptions, whether we say, "The witness often [or sometimes] tells the truth," has not the slightest bearing on the problem of method. There is a general statement and a limitation of this statement, and both statement and limitation are groundless—cannot be explained causally.

law—the lawsuit and a radical fighting attitude result in false testimonies. Apparent exceptions will then be explained by influences changing either the situation of the lawsuit or the attitude. Thus, in the actual case, the essence of most testimonies for the plaintiff was true, namely, the claim was real. But the claim preceded the lawsuit; the peasant woman would probably not have started the lawsuit without a just claim, for as long as the suit was not started considerations of communal solidarity were accepted as binding, and a false claim would have been considered the worst possible offense. The situation preceding the suit was, in short: law permitting the recovery of money that the debtor refused to pay—creditor's feeling of being wronged and desire of redress—legal complaint. There was no cause making a false claim possible, for the law, subjectively for the peasant, can be here only a means of redress, not a means of illicit wrong, since he does not master it sufficiently to use it in a wrong way, and the desire of redress is the only attitude not offset by the feeling of communal solidarity.

It would lead us too far if we analyzed all the assumptions made by legal practice in this particular case, but we mention one other. The attorney for the defense treated as absurd the claim of the plaintiff that she had loaned money without any determined interest, while she could have invested it at good interest and in a more secure way. The assumption was that, being given various possibilities of investing money, the subject will always select the one that is most economically profitable. We see here again the formal error of stating a law of two terms. The law can be binding only if the third missing term is inserted, namely, an attitude of the subject which can express approximately: desire to increase fortune or income. Now, in the actual case, this attitude, if existing at all, was offset by the attitude of communal solidarity, and among the various possibilities of investing money, not the one that was economically profitable, but the one that gave satisfaction to the attitude of solidarity was selected.

The form of legal generalization is typical for all generalizations which assume only one datum instead of two as sufficient to determine the effect. It then becomes necessary to add as many new generalizations of the same type as the current practice requires in order to explain the exceptions. These new generalizations limit the fundamental one without increasing positively the store of our knowledge, and the task is inexhaustible. Thus, we may enumerate indefinitely the possible reasons for a witness not telling the truth in spite of the oath, and still this will not help us to understand why he tells the truth when he tells it. And with any one of these reasons of exception the case is the same. If we say that the witness does not tell the truth when it is contrary to his interest, we must again add indefinitely reasons of exception from this rule without learning why the witness lies when the truth is not contrary to his interest if he does. And so on. If in practice this process of accounting for exceptions, then for exceptions from these exceptions, etc., does not go on indefinitely, it is simply because, in a given situation, we can stop at a certain point with sufficient approximation to make our error not too harmful practically.

It is evident that the only way of verifying, correcting, and complementing the generalizations of common sense is to add in every case the missing third element. We cannot, of course, say in advance how much will remain of these generalizations after such a conversion into exact sociological laws; probably, as far as social theory is concerned, it will be more economical to disregard almost completely the results of common sense and to investigate along quite new and independent lines. But for the sake of an immediate improvement of social practice it may sometimes prove useful to take different domains of practical activity and subject them to criticism.

In view of the prevalent tendency of common-sense generalizations to neglect the differences of values and attitudes prevailing in various social groups—a tendency well manifested in the foregoing example—the chief danger of sociology in searching for laws is rather to overestimate than to underestimate the generality of the laws which it may discover. We must therefore remember that there is less risk in assuming that a certain law applies exclusively in the given social conditions than in supposing that it may be extended over all societies.

The ideal of social theory, as of every other nomothetic science, is to interpret as many facts as possible by as few laws as possible, that is, not only to explain casually the life of particular societies at particular periods, but to subordinate these particular laws to general laws applicable to all societies at all times—taking into account the historical evolution of mankind which continually brings new data and new facts and thus forces us to search for new laws in addition to those already discovered. But the fact that social theory as such cannot test its results by the laboratory method, but must rely entirely on the logical perfection of its abstract analysis and synthesis, makes the problem of control of the validity of its generalizations particularly important. The insufficient realization of the character of this control has been the chief reason why so many sociological works bear a character of compositions, intermediary between philosophy and science and fulfilling the demands of neither.

We have mentioned above the fact that social theory as nomothetic science must be clearly distinguished from any philosophy of social life which attempts to determine the essence of social reality or to outline the unique process of social evolution. This distinction becomes particularly marked when we reach the problem of testing the generalizations. Every scientific law bears upon the empirical facts themselves in their whole variety, not upon their underlying common essence, and hence every new discovery in the domain which it embraces affects it directly and immdiately, either by corroborating it or by invalidating it. And, as scientific laws concern facts which repeat themselves, they automatically apply to the future as well as to the past, and new happenings in the domain embraced by the law must be taken into consideration as either justifying or contradicting the generalization based upon past happenings, or demanding that this generalization be supplemented by a new one.

And thus the essential criterion of social science as against social philosophy is the direct dependence of its generalizations on new discoveries and new happenings. If a social generalization is not permanently qualified by the assumption that at any moment a single new experience may contradict it, forcing us either to reject it or to supplement it by other generalizations, it is not scientific and has no place in social theory, unless as a general principle helping to systematize the properly scientific generalizations. The physicist, the chemist, and the biologist have learned by the use of experiment that their generalizations are scientifically fruitful only if they are subject to the check of a possible experimental failure, and thus the use of experiment has helped them to pass from the mediaeval *philosophia naturalis* to the modern natural science. The social theorician must follow their example and methodically search only for such generalizations as are subject to the check of a possible contradiction by new facts and should leave the empirically unapproachable essences and meanings where they properly belong, and where they have a real though different importance and validity—in philosophy.

The ultimate test of social theory, as we have emphasized throughout the present note, will be its application in practice, and thus its generalizations will be also subject in the last resort to the check of a possible failure. However, practical application is not experimentation. The results of the physical sciences are also ultimately tested by their application in industry, but this does not alter the fact that the test is made on the basis of laboratory experiments. The difference between experiment and application is twofold : (1) The problems themselves usually differ in complexity. The experiment by which we test a scientific law is artificially simplified in view of the special theoretic problem, whereas in applying scientific results to attain a practical purpose we have a much more complex situation to deal with, necessitating the use of several scientific laws and the calculation of their interference. This is a question with which we shall deal presently. (2) In laboratory experiments the question of the immediate practical value of success or failure is essentially excluded for the sake of their theoretical value. Whether the chemist in trying a new combination will spoil his materials and have to buy a new supply, whether the new combination will be worth more or less money than the elements used, are from the standpoint of science completely irrelevant questions; and even a failure if it puts the scientist on the trail of a new law will be more valuable than a success if it merely corroborates once more an old and well-established law. But in applying scientific results in practice we have essentially the practical value of success or failure in view. It is unthinkable that a chemist asked to direct the production of a new kind of soap in a factory should test his theory by direct application and risk the destruction of a hundred thousand dollars worth of material, instead of testing it previously on a small scale by laboratory experiments. Now in all so-called social experiments, on however small a scale, the question of practical value is involved, because the objects of these experiments are men; the social scientist cannot exclude the question of the bearing of his "experiments" on the future of those who are affected by them. He is therefore seldom or never justified in risking a failure for the sake of testing his theory. Of course he does and can take risks, not as a scientist, but as a practical man; that is, he is justified in taking the risk of bringing some harm if there are more chances of benefit than of harm to those on whom he operates. His risk is then the practical risk involved in every application of an idea, not the special theoretic risk involved in the mere testing of the idea. And, in order to diminish this practical risk, he must try to make his theory as certain and applicable as possible before trying to apply it in fact, and he can secure this result and hand over to the social practitioner generalizations at least approximately as applicable as those of physical science, only if he uses the check of contradiction by new experience. This means that besides using only such generalizations as can be contradicted by new experiences he must not wait till new experiences impose themselves on him by accident, but must search for them, must institute a systematic method of *observation*. And, while it is only natural that a scientist in order to form a hypothesis and to give it some amount of probability has to search first of all for such experiences as may corroborate it, his hypothesis cannot be considered fully tested until he has made subsequently a systematic search for such experiences as may contradict it, and proved those contradictions to be only seeming, explicable by the interference of definite factors.

Assuming now that social theory fulfils its task satisfactorily and goes on discovering new laws which can be applied to regulate social becoming, what will be the effect of this on social practice?

First of all, the limitations with which social practice has struggled up to the present will be gradually removed. Since it is theoretically possible to find what social influences should be applied to certain already existing attitudes in order to produce certain new attitudes, and what attitudes should be developed with regard to certain already existing social values in order to make the individual or the group produce certain new social values, there is not a single phenomenon within the whole sphere of human life that conscious control cannot reach sooner or later. There are no objective obstacles in the nature of the social world or in the nature of the human mind which would essentially prevent social practice from attaining gradually the same degree of efficiency as that of industrial practice. The only obstacles are of a subjective kind.

There is, first, the traditional appreciation of social activity as meritorious in itself, for the sake of its intentions alone. There must, indeed, be some results in order to make the good intentions count, but, since anything done is regarded as meritorious, the standards by which the results are appreciated are astonishingly low. Social practice must cease to be a matter of merit and be treated as a necessity. If the theorician is asked to be sure of his generalizations before trying to apply them in practice, it is at least strange that persons of merely good will are permitted to try out on society indefinitely and irresponsibly their vague and perhaps sentimental ideas.

The second obstacle to the development of a perfect social practice is the well-known unwillingness of the common-sense man to accept the control of scientific technique. Against this unwillingness there is only one weapon—success. This is what the history of industrial technique shows. There is perhaps not a single case where the first application of science to any field of practice held by common sense and tradition did not provoke the opposition of the practitioner. It is still within the memory of man that the old farmer with his common-sense methods laughed at the idea that the city chap could teach him anything about farming, and was more than skeptical about the application of the results of soil-analysis to the growing of crops. The fear of new things is still strong even among cultivated persons, and the social technician has to expect that he will meet at almost every step this old typical hostility of common sense to science. He can only accept it and interpret it as a demand to show the superiority of his methods by their results.

But the most important difficulty which social practice has to overcome before reaching a level of efficiency comparable to that of industrial practice lies in the difficulty of applying scientific generalizations. The laws of science are abstract, while the practical situations are concrete, and it requires a special intellectual activity to find what are the practical questions which a given law may help to solve, or what are the scientific laws which may be used to solve a given practical question. In the physical sphere this intellectual activity has been embodied in technology, and it is only since the technologist has intervened between the scientist and the practitioner that material practice has acquired definitely the character of a self-conscious and planfully developing technique and ceased to be dependent on irrational and often unreasonable traditional rules. And if material practice needs a technology in spite of the fact that the generalizations which physical science hands over to it have been already experimentally tested, this need is much more urgent in social practice where the application of scientific generalizations is their first and only experimental test.

We cannot enter here into detailed indications of what social technology should be, but we must take into account the chief point of its method—the general form which every concrete problem of social technique assumes. Whatever may be the aim of social practice—modification of individual attitudes or of social institutions—in trying to attain this aim we never find the elements whch we want to use or to modify isolated and passively waiting for our activity, but always embodied in active practical *situations*, which have been formed independently of us and with which our activity has to comply.

The situation is the set of values and attitudes with which the individual or the group has to deal in a process of activity and with regard to which this activity is planned and its results appreciated. Every concrete activity is the solution of a situation. The situation involves three kinds of data: (1) The objective conditions under which the individual or society has to act, that is, the totality of values—economic, social, religious, intellectual, etc.—which at the given moment affect directly or indirectly the conscious status of the individual or the group. (2) The pre-existing attitudes of the individual or the group which at the given moment have an actual influence upon his behavior. (3) The definition of the situation, that is, the more or less clear conception of the conditions and consciousness of the attitudes. And the definition of the situation is a necessary preliminary to any act of the will, for in given conditions and with a given set of attitudes an indefinite plurality of actions is possible, and one definite action can appear only if these conditions are selected, interpreted, and combined in a determined way and if a certain systematization of these attitudes is reached, so that one of them becomes predominant and subordinates the others. It happens, indeed, that a certain value imposes itself immediately and unreflectively and leads at once to action, or that an attitude as soon as it appears excludes the others and expresses itself unhesitatingly in an active process. In these cases, whose most radical examples are found in reflex and instinctive actions, the definition is already given to the individual by external conditions or by his own tendencies. But usually there is a process of reflection, after which either a ready social definition is applied or a new personal definition worked out.

Let us take a typical example out of the fifth volume of the present work concerning the family life of the immigrants in America. A husband, learning of his wife's infidelity, deserts her. The objective conditions were: (1) the social institution of marriage with all the rules involved; (2) the wife, the other man, the children, the neighbors, and in general all the individuals constituting the habitual environment of the husband and, in a sense, given to him as values; (3) certain economic conditions: (4) the fact of the wife's infidelity. Toward all these values the husband had certain attitudes, some of them traditional, others recently developed. Now, perhaps under the influence of the discovery of his wife's infidelity, perhaps after having developed some new attitude toward the sexual or economic side of marriage, perhaps simply influenced by the advice of a friend in the form of a rudimentary scheme of the situation helping him to "see the point," he defines the situation for himself. He takes certain conditions into account, ignores or neglects others, or gives them a certain interpretation in view of some chief value, which may be his wife's infidelity, or the economic burdens of family life of which this infidelity gives him the pretext to rid himself, or perhaps some other woman, or the half-ironical pity of his neighbors, etc. And in this definition some one attitude—sexual jealousy, or desire for economic freedom, or love for the other woman, or offended desire for recognition—or a complex of these attitudes, or a new attitude (hate, disgust) subordinates to itself the others and manifests itself chiefly in the subsequent action, which is evidently a solution of the situation, and fully determined both in its social and in its individual components by the whole set of values, attitudes, and reflective schemes which the situation included. When a situation is solved, the result of the activity becomes an element of a new situation, and this is most clearly evidenced in cases where the activity brings a change of a social institution whose unsatisfactory functioning was the chief element of the first situation.

Now, while the task of science is to analyze by a comparative study the whole process of activity into elementary facts, and it must therefore ignore the variety of concrete situations in order to be able to find laws of causal dependence of abstractly isolated attitudes or values on other attitudes and values, the task of technique is to provide the means of a rational control of concrete situations. The situation can evidently be controlled either by a change of conditions or by a change of attitudes, or by both, and in this respect the rôle of technique as application of science is easily characterized. By comparing situations of a certain type, the social technician must find what are the predominant values or the predominant attitudes which determine the situation more than others, and then the question is to modify these values or these attitudes in the desired way by using the knowledge of social causation given by social theory. Thus, we may find that some of the situations among the Polish immigrants in America resulting in the husband's desertion are chiefly determined by the wife's infidelity, others by her quarrelsomeness, others by bad economic conditions, still others by the husband's desire for freedom, etc. And, if in a given case we know what influences to apply in order to modify these dominating factors, we can modify the situation accordingly, and ideally we can provoke in the individual a behavior in conformity with any given scheme of attitudes and values.

To be sure, it may happen that, in spite of an adequate scientific knowledge of the social laws permitting the modification of those factors which we want to change, our efforts will fail to influence the situation or will produce a situation more undesirable than the one we wished to avoid. The fault is then with our technical knowledge. That is, either we have failed in determining the relative importance of the various factors, or we have failed to foresee the influence of other causes which, interfering with our activity, produce a quite unexpected and undesired effect. And since it is impossible to expect from every practitioner a complete scientific training and still more impossible to have him work out a scientifically justified and detailed plan of action for every concrete case in particular, the special task of the social technician is to prepare, with the help of both science and practical observation, thorough schemes and plans of action for all the various *types* of situations which may be found in a given line of social activity, and leave to the practitioner the subordination of the given concrete situation to its proper type. This is actually the rôle which all the organizers of social institutions have played, but the technique itself must become more conscious and methodically perfect, and every field of social activity should have its professional technicians. The evolution of social life makes necessary continual modifications and developments of social technique, and we can hope that the evolution of social theory will continually put new and useful scientific generalizations within the reach of the social technician; the latter must therefore remain in permanent touch with both social life and social theory, and this requires a more far-going specialization than we actually find.

But, however efficient this type of social technique may become, its application will always have certain limits beyond which a different type of technique will be more useful. Indeed, the form of social control outlined above presupposes that the individual—

or the group—is treated as a passive object of our activity and that we change the situations for him, from case to case, in accordance with our plans and intentions. But the application of this method becomes more and more difficult as the situations grow more complex, more new and unexpected from case to case, and more influenced by the individual's own reflection. And, indeed, from both the moral and the hedonistic standpoints and also from the standpoint of the level of efficiency of the individual and of the group, it is desirable to develop in the individuals the ability to control spontaneously their own activities by conscious reflection. To use a biological comparison, the type of control where the practitioner prescribes for the individual a scheme of activity appropriate to every crisis as it arises corresponds to the tropic or reflex type of control in animal life, where the activity of the individual is controlled mechanically by stimulations from without, while the reflective and individualistic control corresponds to the type of activity characteristic of the higher conscious organism, where the control is exercised from within by the selective mechanism of the nervous system. While, in the early tribal, communal, kinship, and religious groups, and to a large extent in the historic state, the society itself provided a rigoristic and particularistic set of definitions in the form of "customs" or "mores," the tendency to advance is associated with the liberty of the individual to make his own definitions.

We have assumed throughout this argument that if an adequate technique is developed it is possible to produce any desirable attitudes and values, but this assumption is practically justified only if we find in the individual attitudes which cannot avoid response to the class of stimulations which society is able to apply to him. And apparently we do find this disposition. Every individual has a vast variety of wishes which can be satisfied only by his incorporation in a society. Among his general patterns of wishes we may enumerate: (1) the desire for new experience, for fresh stimulations; (2) the desire for recognition, including, for example, sexual response and general social appreciation, and secured by devices ranging from the display of ornament to the demonstration of worth through scientific attainment; (3) the desire for mastery, or the "will to power," exemplified by ownership, domestic tyranny, political despotism, based on the instinct of hate, but capable of being sublimated to laudable ambition; (4) the desire for security, based on the instinct of fear and exemplified negatively by the wretchedness of the individual in perpetual solitude or under social taboo. Society is, indeed, an agent for the repression of many of the wishes in the individual; it demands that he shall be moral by repressing at least the wishes which are irreconcilable with the welfare of the group, but nevertheless it provides the only medium within which any of his schemes or wishes can be gratified. And it would be superfluous to point out by examples the degree to which society has in the past been able to impose its schemes of attitudes and values on the individual. Professor Sumner's volume, *Folkways*, is practically a collection of such examples, and, far from discouraging us as they discourage Professor Sumner, they should be regarded as proofs of the ability of the individual to conform to any definition, to accept any attitude, provided it is an expression of the public will or represents the appreciation of even a limited group. To take a single example from the present, to be a bastard or the mother of a bastard has been regarded heretofore as anything but desirable, but we have at this moment reports that one of the warring European nations is officially impregnating its unmarried women and girls and even married women whose husbands are at the front. If this is true (which we do not assume) we have a new definition and a new evaluation of motherhood arising from the struggle of this society against death, and we may anticipate a new attitude—that the resulting children and their mothers will be the objects of extraordinary social appreciation. And even if we find that the attitudes are not so tractable as we have assumed, that it is not possible to provoke all the desirable ones, we shall still be in the same situation as, let us say, physics and mechanics: we shall have the problem of securing the highest degree of control possible in view of the nature of our materials.

As to the present work, it evidently cannot in any sense pretend to establish social theory on a definitely scientific basis. It is clear from the preceding discussion that many workers and much time will be needed before we free ourselves from the traditional ways of thinking, develop a completely efficient and exact working method, and reach a system of scientifically correct generalizations. Our present very limited task is the preparation of a certain body of materials, even if we occasionally go beyond it and attempt to reach some generalizations.

Our object-matter is one class of a modern society in the whole concrete complexity of its life. The selection of the Polish peasant society, motivated at first by somewhat incidental reasons, such as the intensity of the Polish immigration and the facility of getting materials concerning the Polish peasant, has proved during the investigation to be a fortunate one. The Polish peasant finds himself now in a period of transition from the old forms of social organization that had been in force, with only insignificant changes, for many centuries, to a modern form of life. He has preserved enough of the old attitudes to make their sociological reconstruction possible, and he is sufficiently advanced upon the new way to make a study of the development of modern attitudes particularly fruitful. He has been invited by the upper classes to collaborate in the construction of Polish national life, and in certain lines his development is due to the conscious educational efforts of his leaders—the nobility, the clergy, the middle class. In this respect, he has the value of an experiment in social technique; the successes, as well as the failures, of this educational activity of the upper classes are very significant for social work. These efforts of the upper classes themselves have a particular sociological importance in view of the conditions in which Polish society has lived during the last century. As a society without a state, divided among three states and constantly hampered in all its efforts to preserve and develop a distinct and unique cultural life, it faced a dilemma— either to disappear or to create such substitutes for a state organization as would enable it to resist the destructive action of the oppressing states; or, more generally, to exist without the framework of a state. The substitutes were created, and they are interesting in two respects. First, they show, in an exceptionally intensified and to a large extent isolated form, the action of certain factors of social unity which exist in every society but in normal conditions are subordinated to the state organization and seldom sufficiently accounted for in sociological reflection. Secondly, the lack of permanence of every social institution and the insecurity of every social value in general, resulting from the destructive tendencies of the dominating foreign states, bring with them a necessity of developing and keeping constantly alive all the activities needed to reconstruct again and again every value that had been destroyed. The whole mechanism of social creation is therefore here particularly transparent and easy to understand, and in general the rôle of human attitudes in social life becomes much more evident than in a society not living under the same strain, but able to rely to a large extent upon the inherited formal organization for the preservation of its culture and unity.

We use in this work the inductive method in a form which gives the least possible place for any arbitrary statements. The basis of the work is concrete materials, and only in the selection of these materials some necessary discrimination has been used. But even here we have tried to proceed in the most cautious way possible. The private letters constituting the first two volumes have needed relatively little selection, particularly as they are arranged in family series. Our task has been limited to the exclusion of such letters from among the whole collection as contained nothing but a repetition of situations and attitudes more completely represented in the materials which we publish here. In later volumes the selection can be more severe, as far as the conclusions of the preceding volumes can be used for guidance.

The analysis of the attitudes and characters given in notes to particular letters and in introductions to particular series contains nothing not essentially contained in the materials themselves; its task is only to isolate single attitudes, to show their analogies and dependencies, and to interpret them in relation to the social background upon which they appear. Our acquaintance with the Polish society simply helps us in noting data and relations which would perhaps not be noticed so easily by one not immediately acquainted with the life of the group.

Finally, the synthesis constituting the introductions to particular volumes is also based upon the materials, with a few exceptions where it was thought necessary to draw some data from Polish ethnological publications or systematic studies. The sources are always quoted.

The general character of the work is mainly that of a systematization and classification of attitudes and values prevailing in a concrete group. Every attitude and every value, as we have said above, can be really understood only in connection with the whole social life of which it is an element, and therefore this method is the only one that gives us a full and systematic acquaintance with all the complexity of social life. But it is evident that this monograph must be followed by many others if we want our acquaintance with social reality to be complete. Other Slavic groups, particularly the Russians; the French and the Germans, as representing different types of more efficient societies; the Americans, as the most conspicuous experiment in individualism; the Jews, as representing particular social adaptations under peculiar social pressures; the Oriental, with his widely divergent attitudes and values; the Negro, with his lower cultural level and unique social position—these and other social groups should be included in a series of monographs, which in its totality will give for the first time a wide and secure basis for any sociological generalizations whatever. Naturally the value of every monograph will increase with the development of the work, for not only will the method continually improve, but every social group will help to understand every other.

In selecting the monographic method for the present work and in urging the desirability of the further preparation of large bodies of materials representing the total life of different social groups, we do not ignore the other method of approaching a scientific social theory and practice—the study of special problems, of isolated aspects of social life. And we are not obliged even to wait until all the societies have been studied monographically, in their whole concrete reality, before beginning the comparative study of particular problems. Indeed, the study of a single society, as we have undertaken it here, is often enough to show what rôle is played by a particular class of phenomena in the total life of a group and to give us in this way sufficient indications for the isolation of this class from its social context without omitting any important inter-action that may exist between phenomena of this class and others, and we can then use these indications in taking the corresponding kinds of phenomena in other societies as objects of comparative research.

By way of examples, we point out here certain problems sug-gested to us by the study of the Polish peasants for which this study affords a good starting-point:[5]

1. *The problem of individualism.*—How far is individualiza-tion compatible with social cohesion? What are the forms of indi-vidualization that can be considered socially useful or socially harmful? What are the forms of social organization that allow for the greatest amount of individualism?

We have been led to the suppositions that, generally speaking, individualization is the intermediary stage between one form of social organization and another; that its social usefulness depends on its more or less constructive character—that is, upon the ques-tion whether it does really lead to a new organization and whether the latter makes the social group more capable of resisting disinte-grating influences; and that, finally, an organization based upon a conscious co-operation in view of a common aim is the most compatible with individualism. The verification of these supposi-tions and their application to concrete problems of such a society as the American would constitute a grateful work.

2. *The problem of efficiency.*—Relation between individual and social efficiency. Dependence of efficiency upon various indi-vidual attitudes and upon various forms of social organization.

The Polish society shows in most lines of activity a particularly large range of variation of individual efficiency with a relatively low scale of social efficiency. We have come to the conclusion that both phenomena are due to the lack of a sufficiently persistent and detailed frame of social organization, resulting from the loss of state-independence. Under these conditions individual efficiency depends upon individual attitudes much more than upon social

[5]   Points 2 and 8 following are more directly connected with ma-terials on the middle and upper classes of Polish society which do not appear in the present work.

conditions. An individual may be very efficient because there is little to hinder his activity in any line he selects, but he may also be very inefficient because there is little to push him or to help him. The total social result of individual activities under these conditions is relatively small, because social efficiency depends, not only on the average efficiency of the individuals that constitute the group, but also on the more or less perfect organization of individual efforts. Here again, the application of these conclusions to other societies can open the way to important discoveries in this particular sphere by showing what is the way of conciliating the highest individual with the highest social efficiency.

3. *The problem of abnormality—crime, vagabondage, prostitution, alcoholism, etc.*—How far is abnormality the unavoidable manifestation of inborn tendencies of the individual, and how far is it due to social conditions?

The priests in Poland have a theory with regard to their peasant parishioners that there are no incorrigible individuals, provided that the influence exercised upon them is skillful and steady and draws into play all of the social factors—familial solidarity, social opinion of the community, religion and magic, economic and intellectual motives, etc. And in his recent book on *The Individual Delinquent*, Dr. William Healy touches the problem on the same side in the following remark: "Frequently one wonders what might have been accomplished with this or that individual if he had received a more adequate discipline during his childhood." By our investigation of abnormal attitudes in connection with normal attitudes instead of treating them isolately, and by the recognition that the individual can be fully understood and controlled only if all the influences of his environment are properly taken into account, we could hardly avoid the suggestion that abnormality is mainly, if not exclusively, a matter of deficient social organization. There is hardly any human attitude which, if properly controlled and directed, could not be used in a socially productive way. Of course there must always remain a quantitative difference of efficiency between individuals, often a very far-going one, but we can see no reason for a permanent qualitative difference between socially normal and antisocial actions. And from this standpoint the question of the antisocial individual assumes no longer the form of the right of society to protection, but that of the right of the antisocial individual to be made useful.

4. *The occupational problem.*—The modern division and organization of labor brings an enormous and continually growing quantitative prevalence of occupations which are almost completely devoid of stimulation and therefore present little interest for the workman. This fact necessarily affects human happiness profoundly, and, if only for this reason, the restoration of stimulation to labor is among the most important problems confronting society. The present industrial organization tends also to develop a type of human being as abnormal in its way as the opposite type of individual who gets the full amount of occupational stimulation by taking a line of interest destructive of social order—the criminal or vagabond. If the latter type of abnormality is immediately dangerous for the present state of society, the former is more menacing for the future, as leading to a gradual but certain degeneration of the human type—whether we regard this degeneration as congenital or acquired.

The analysis of this problem discloses very profound and general causes of the evil, but also the way of an eventual remedy. It is a fact too well known to be emphasized that modern organization of labor is based on an almost absolute prevalence of economic interests—more exactly, on the tendency to produce or acquire the highest possible amount of economic values—either because these interests are actually so universal and predominant or because they express themselves in social organization more easily than others—a point to be investigated. The moralist complains of the materialization of men and expects a change of the social organization to be brought about by moral or religious preaching; the economic determinist considers the whole social organization as conditioned fundamentally and necessarily by economic factors and expects an improvement exclusively from a possible historically necessary modification of the economic organization itself. From the sociological viewpoint the problem looks much more serious and objective than the moralist conceives it, but much less limited and determined than it appears to the economic determinist. The economic interests are only one class of human attitudes among others, and every attitude can be modified by an adequate social technique. The interest in the nature of work is frequently as strong as, or stronger than, the interest in the economic results of the work, and often finds an objective expression in spite of the fact that actual social organization has little place for it. The protests, in fact, represented by William Morris mean that a certain class of work has visibly passed from the stage where it was stimulating to a stage where it is not—that the handicrafts formerly expressed an interest in the work itself rather than in the economic returns from the work. Since every attitude tends to influence social institutions, we may expect that, with the help of social technique, an organization and a division of labor based on occupational interests may gradually replace the present organization based on demands of economic productivity. In other words, with the appropriate change of attitudes and values all work may become artistic work.

5. *The relation of the sexes.*—Among the many problems falling under this head two seem to us of fundamental importance, the first mainly socio-psychological, the second mainly sociological: (1) In the relation between the sexes how can a maximum of reciprocal response be obtained with the minimum of interference with personal interests? (2) How is the general social efficiency of a group affected by the various systems of relations between man and woman?

We do not advance at this point any definite theories. A number of interesting concrete points will appear in the later volumes of our materials. But a few suggestions of a general character arise in connection with the study of a concrete society. In matters of reciprocal response we find among the Polish peasants the sexes equally dependent on each other, though their demands are of a rather limited and unromantic character, while at the same time this response is secured at the cost of a complete subordination of their personalities to a common sphere of group-interests. When the development of personal interests begins, this original harmony is disturbed, and the disharmony is particularly marked among the immigrants in America, where it often leads to a complete and radical disorganization of family life. There does not seem to be as yet any real solution in view. In this respect the situation of the Polish peasants may throw an interesting light upon the general situation of the cultivated classes of modern society. The difference between these two situations lies in the fact that among the peasants both man and woman begin almost simultaneously to develop personal claims, whereas in the cultivated classes the personal claims of the man have been developed and in a large measure satisfied long ago, and the present problem is almost exclusively limited to the woman. The situations are analogous, however, in so far as the difficulty of solution is concerned.

With regard to social efficiency, our Polish materials tend to show that, under conditions in which the activities of the woman can attain an objective importance more or less equal to those of the man, the greatest social efficiency is attained by a systematic collaboration of man and woman in external fields rather than by a division of tasks which limits the woman to "home and children." The line along which the peasant class of Polish society is particularly efficient is economic development and co-operation; and precisely in this line the collaboration of women has been particularly wide and successful. As far as a division of labor based upon differences of the sexes is concerned, there seems to be at least one point at which a certain differentiation of tasks would be at present in accordance with the demands of social efficiency. The woman shows a particular aptitude of mediation between the formalism, uniformity, and performance of social organization and the concrete, various, and changing individualities. And, whether this ability of the woman is congenital or produced by cultural conditions, it could certainly be made socially very useful, for it is precisely the ability required to diminish the innumerable and continually growing frictions resulting from the misadaptations of individual attitudes to social organization, and to avoid the incalculable waste of human energy which contrasts so deplorably in our modern society with our increasingly efficient use of natural energies.

6. *The problem of social happiness.*—With regard to this problem we can hardly make any positive suggestions. It is certain

that both the relation of the sexes and the economic situation are among the fundamental conditions of human happiness, in the sense of making it and of spoiling it. But the striking point is that, aside from abstract philosophical discussion and some popular psychological analysis, the problem of happiness has never been seriously studied since the epoch of Greek hedonism, and of course the conclusions reached by the Greeks, even if they were more scientific than they really are, could hardly be applied to the present time, with its completely changed social conditions. Has this problem been so much neglected because of its difficulty or because, under the influence of certain tendencies immanent in Christianity, happiness is still half-instinctively regarded as more or less sinful, and pain as meritorious? However that may be, the fact is that no things of real significance have been said up to the present about happiness, particularly if we compare them with the enormous material that has been collected and the innumerable important ideas that have been expressed concerning unhappiness. Moreover, we believe that the problem merits a very particular consideration, both from the theoretical and from the practical point of view, and that the sociological method outlined above gives the most reliable way of studying it.

7. *The problem of the fight of races (nationalities) and cultures.*—Probably in this respect no study of any other society can give so interesting sociological indications as the study of the Poles. Surrounded by peoples of various degrees of cultural development—Germans, Austrians, Bohemians, Ruthenians, Russians, Lithuanians—having on her own territory the highest percentage of the most unassimilable of races, the Jews, Poland is fighting at every moment for the preservation of her racial and cultural status. Moreover, the fight assumes the most various forms: self-defense against oppressive measures promulgated by Russia and Germany in the interest of their respective races and cultures; self-defense against the peaceful intrusion of the Austrian culture in Galicia; the problem of the assimilation of foreign colonists— German or Russian; the political fight against the Ruthenians in Eastern Galicia; peaceful propaganda and efforts to maintain the supremacy of Polish culture on the vast territory between the

Baltic and the Black Seas (populated mainly by Lithuanians, White Ruthenians, and Ukrainians), where the Poles constitute the cultivated minority of estate-owners and intellectual bourgeoisie; various methods of dealing with the Jews—passive toleration, efforts to assimilate them nationally (not religiously), social and economic boycott. All these ways of fighting develop the greatest possible variety of attitudes.

And the problem itself assumes a particular actual importance if we remember that the present war is a fight of races and cultures, which has assumed the form of war because races and cultures have expressed themselves in the modern state-organization. The fight of races and cultures is the predominant fact of modern historical life, and it must assume the form of war when it uses the present form of state-organization as its means. To stop wars one must either stop the fight of races and cultures by the introduction of new schemes of attitudes and values or substitute for the isolated national state as instrument of cultural expansion some other type of organization.

8. Closely connected with the foregoing is *the problem of an ideal organization of culture*. This is the widest and oldest sociological problem, lying on the border between theory and practice. Is there one perfect form of organization that would unify the widest individualism and the strongest social cohesion, that would exclude any abnormality by making use of all human tendencies, that would harmonize the highest efficiency with the greatest happiness? And, if one and only one such organization is possible, will it come automatically, as a result of the fight between cultures and as an expression of the law of the survival of the fittest, so that finally "the world's history will prove the world's tribunal"? Or must such an organization be brought about by a conscious and rational social technique modifying the historical conditions and subordinating all the cultural differences to one perfect system? Or is there, on the contrary, no such unique ideal possible? Perhaps there are many forms of a perfect organization of society, and, the differentiation of national cultures being impossible to overcome, every nation should simply try to bring its own system to the greatest possible perfection, profiting by the experiences of

others, but not imitating them. In this case the fight of races and cultures could be stopped, not by the destruction of historical differences, but by the recognition of their value for the world and by a growing reciprocal acquaintance and estimation. Whatever may be the ultimate solution of this problem, it is evident that the systematic sociological study of various cultures, as outlined in this note and exemplified in its beginnings in the main body of the work, is the only way to solve it.

ANALYTIC INDUCTION

1934

ENUMERATIVE INDUCTION, as we have seen, originates in the common tendency to reach quickly secure, even though superficial and inexact generalizations for the purpose of ordinary practical orientation. The same practical tendency obviously underlies the modern statistical form of enumerative induction: nearly all statistical "research" has political, economic or philanthropic aims in view. This is probably the main reason why enumerative induction has remained prevalent in the social and economic fields, where practical interest has always been paramount. "Practical" people are continually forgetting the lesson that quick results are seldom satisfactory, and that the purposes of practical control of cultural reality would be served best by a science entirely independent of these purposes,[1] a science which followed exclusively the two leads of a deep intellectual curiosity about particular data and an insatiable philosophic tendency to use acquired knowledge for the acquisition of new knowledge.

This is, indeed, how the other logical method developed which we call *analytic induction*, its development emphasizing what we believe to be its most important characteristic. We find it applied by Plato when he analyzed individual instances of figures drawn

---

From *The Method of Sociology* (New York: Farrar & Rinehart, 1934), pp. 235–245. Reprinted by permission of Eileen Markley Znaniecki.

[1] For criticism of the practical applicability of statistical results, see the author's paper, "An Analysis of Social Processes," in *Publications of the Am. Sociol. Society*, 1932.

upon sand and concluded from this analysis as to the general properties of figures of the same type—in this way laying (or perhaps only perfecting) the foundations of inductive geometry. We see Aristotle absorbed in a detailed analytic study of individual specimens of animals, and utilizing every discovery to build the first systematic zoology. We find Theophrastus, too, who had, as he says, at the age of one hundred and five learned at last how to enjoy life, settling down to observe, analyze and compare individual men, thus making the first really positive differential psychology. There is Galileo, who, after investigating thoroughly a few systematically differentiated cases of movements, drew conclusions which bear on all movements of a certain general type. And there are all those innumerable laboratory workers—some obscure, some renowned—who have made physics, chemistry and general biology, not by agglomerating large masses of superficial observations, but by inducing laws from a deep analysis of experimentally isolated instances.

Into sociology this method did not penetrate until recently. Le Play began by using it, but (being interested in practical atoms) combined it with enumerative induction, and thus lost most of its advantages. The school which centered around Durkheim tried to use it consciously and planfully, but made the mistake of believing that a self-sufficient theory can be built on one instance thoroughly analyzed. This is what Durkheim did when he defined the essence of religion on the basis of a study of Australian totemism, and Czarnowski when he drew from the study of the legend of St. Patrick conclusions about the cult of heroes in general.[2] The same mistake has been committed by the phenomenologists harking back to the Platonic Idea under the direct influence of Husserl's logical reasoning.

In fact, William I. Thomas was probably the first who based sociological research entirely on the analysis of particular cases, utilizing several *different* instances for every generalization. He developed this method chiefly in his lectures from about 1905 to

[2]   Cf. E. Durkheim, *Elementary Forms of Religious Life*, and S. Czarnowski, *Le culte des héros*.

1915 and so influenced many young sociologists. In his *Source Book for Social Origins* the method was already partly applied. We used it together on a large scale in the *Polish Peasant.* The disciples of Thomas have since spread it pretty widely.

Thomas chose this method instead of the prevalent one of enumerative induction not because of abstract methodological considerations nor yet under the influence of older sciences. He was simply led by his own vivid intellectual curiosity and interest in particular cases, coupled with an incomparable genius for the selection and interpretation of significant concrete data. New methods are always initiated in this way—and not only in the field of science. But in order to develop fully all the implications of the new method and to raise continually the level of its exactness and reliability, its further use must be accompanied for a long time by critical methodological reflection.

As a matter of fact, little methodological thought has been expended on this new method in sociology, while the adherents of enumerative induction have never ceased to discuss the statistical method, to extol its alleged merit, and to improve it within the narrow limits of its possibilities. It is high time to correct this deficiency. But before trying to outline the leading ideas of analytic induction, it will be well to mention with a warning certain intellectual traditions which in all sciences did for a time, and in sociology still do, obstruct its progress and favor the domination of the older and less efficient methodological tendencies. These traditions are: the common use of words in an indicative rather than in a descriptive sense, and the current pseudo-deductive ways of exposition and demonstration.

In common speech, a word symbolizes logical extension rather than comprehension. In general, when people use words like "criminals," "marriages," "unemployment," they are more interested in determining whether particular men are or are not criminals, whether a given couple are or are not married, how numerous the cases of unemployment are as against employment in a city or a county, than in learning exactly what a criminal, a marriage, or a case of employment or unemployment *is.* Even when they are conscious that they do not know the meaning of some unfamiliar word, they prefer to have several objects or processes indicated to which the word applies rather than to have an analytic definition of the concept given to them. This is because the primary use of words is for social communication, and it is easier to establish a community of objects indicated by the word than a community of its conceptual meaning.

Thence the common assumption that when any word *A* is used, the class A to which it applies has been already circumscribed, i.e., that any datum is already either A or non-A. Thence also the demand that when word *A* is used in discussion, it be defined in advance in such a way that everybody who participates in the discussion should include the same data under class A. But it is obvious that from a scientific point of view logical extension depends entirely on logical comprehension. Any object belongs to the Class A only if it possesses all those fundamental characters which all other objects belonging to class A possess, and which are comprehended in the concept A. The assumption that a certain word is applicable to all the objects or processes of a class, and only to the objects or processes of this class, is justified if we know already all the common and distinctive characters of this class and are using this word entirely and exclusively to symbolize this knowledge of ours. That happens only when the word is a scientific term carefully selected and defined *after* a full and thorough study of the kind of objects or processes to which we wish to apply it. Until then the use of words as indicative of classes should be purely tentative and provisional.

The traditional and common demand that terms be defined in advance and consistently used in accordance with their first definition has not originated in scientific considerations, but in the purely social needs of discussion. Verbal consistency is necessary to avoid misunderstandings and waste of time in verbal disputations; consequently, it was sublimated at the time when intellectual life centered in small groups, like ancient and mediaeval "schools," and most of it expressed itself in personal intercourse. It remains, of course, a valuable rule for the communication of knowledge already achieved: but it is decidedly harmful if applied to knowledge in the making. It hinders the progress of inductive knowledge, particularly in those fields where, as in sociology, numerous popular terms became more or less fixed by long usage prior to any scientific research. The sociologist who uses any of these terms (and no sociologist can avoid them) must be always ready to qualify it, to exclude from the sphere of its application data which he began by including in it, or to extend its application to data which at first he did not think of taking into account, or even to reject it—all depending on the results of his analytic studies. And in any case he must be sure that his final use of the term be very different from its popular use; if it is not, there is a strong presumption that his research has been as superficial as common-sense reflection.

In the course of research, the way of preserving a proper plasticity of the popular terms used is not to define them at all, but to rely on the context for any shades of meaning one wishes to convey. If sociologists kept to this rule, and made only such definitions as follow logically from their theoretic investigations, much of the present terminological chaos would be avoided; for then every difference in terms would be significant of a theoretic conflict, and would thus stimulate further research to remove it. To bring this condition about, it would be desirable if sociologists even now learned to view every terminological definition as an implicit or explicit hypothesis, and instead of granting it, demanded that it be tested. Indeed, it should not be very difficult to correct the custom of using terms dogmatically—physical and biological sciences have done it with complete success.

More important is the other impediment in the way of analytic inductive science which, though it cannot prevent its progress altogether, hinders it considerably. We mean the traditional method of exposition and demonstration which modern sciences inherit from the time when perfect science was thought to be deductive, and efforts were made to give all valid knowledge a deductive form.

It is a fact that a sociologist, just as a physicist or a biologist, as soon as he passes from actual investigation to a systematic presentation of a definite body of knowledge concerning a certain object-matter, begins to proceed in an entirely different way than before. He formulates first his most general principles as if these were unconditional, basic truths on which the validity of all that follows reposed; then he orders his theses in logical sequence, as if each subsequent one were deductively derived from the preceding ones, and its validity were due to this derivation; and he quotes particular facts as if they were mere instances illustrating the general truths. He has been taught in school and trained by reading older scientists' works thus to organize his ideas. If he does not do so, it is not because he knows a better way of organizing them, but because he has not had a sufficient training, and is either incapable or too lazy to organize them at all.

Social factors have contributed in a large measure to the strength of this tradition. Whereas the demand for terminological consistency originated in verbal disputes between scholars, the dominance of deductive systematization is closely connected with traditional methods of teaching. Since teaching became a socially organized function of school masters, every recognized science has been taught by way of communicating to the students a logically coherent set of such available results of previous research as are considered certain. And almost every scientist, when formulating in writing his knowledge of a certain field of reality viewed as a whole, has consciously or unconsciously assumed the rôle of a master teaching his science, or branch of some science, to his readers; between the exposition of a new and original system of science and a textbook the formal difference is often very slight, however widely both may differ from monographic publications.

Now, there is no doubt that the deductive form of exposition is eminently satisfactory for the purposes of authoritative communication of science. It gives the whole body of knowldege communicated an appearance of dogmatic certainty and internal coherence; and since the most general truths formally condition the rest, students who for some reason cannot assimilate all the details and developments of a science may at least learn its "principles," "fundamentals" or "elements," that is, what is considered its most (if not its only) important part. Moreover, whether intrinsically or simply by force of custom, deductive systematization certainly does seem to use a relatively easy and, so to speak, "natural" way of organizing knowledge: a survey of the total field of established special truths is best achieved if we start with the most general principles, and each new truth is best understood by being connected with other truths already known.

But this is not all. Since for twenty-two centuries logic was essentially deductive logic, and even after that theories of induction remained dependent on the latter with regard to the problem of proof, deductive systematization has had not only the force of custom and the motive of pedagogical expediency, but the power of rational justification behind it. When toward the end of the nineteenth century it became clear that scientific investigation does not follow the rules of logic, this discovery was minimized by the distinction between the "psychological" process of thinking and the "logical" order of truths.[3] To the logician it did not matter how in fact we arrived at our conclusions: there was no logical order in the psychological process in any case, even though the psychologist might find some uniformities in it. The important point was that only those conclusions were valid which, once

---

[3]   Typically, this distinction is expressed in a recent book as follows: "Psychologically, reasoning is a temporal event in an individual biography. In the logical sense, however, reason is not concerned with the manner in which ideas or propositions actually succeed each other in our consciousness, but with the weight of evidence or proof. Now, . . . it is very seldom, indeed, that in any active inquiry . . . we start from the right premises and go on from them in a definite order to the proper conclusions . . . When we first ask a question, we seldom have an adequate idea of what it is that we have assumed or that conditions our question. It is only after a great deal of intellectual work that we can see what are the proper premises and implications of our position . . . If, then, we distinguish between the premises which logically justify a conclusion and the psychological starting points from which we jump to arrive at them it becomes extremely doubtful whether there is any well-defined psychologic difference between the actual processes of reasoning in inductive sciences like experimental medicine and in deductive sciences like geometry or dynamics. Whatever difference there is must be sought elsewhere.

"But if every inductive inference can be put in the form of a syllogism, what can logically differentiate it from other syllogisms? The answer for purposes of scientific method is to be found in the character of the (generally unexpressed) premise of such inductive syllogisms." p. 117, Morris R. Cohen, *Reason and Nature*, Harcourt, Brace & Co., New York.

reached, could be deduced from valid premises in accordance with the rules of logic; and these rules remain always the same, even if the premises differ. Deductive systematization was, therefore, considered the only valid kind of systematization.

This assumption would be true only if there were no other but enumerative induction; for, indeed, the latter involves no logical principles which are not included in deductive logic. But, as we shall try to show, the logic—not merely the psychology—of analytic induction is essentially different, though its distinctive characters have attracted very little notice from logicians, owing to the very custom of organizing its results into pseudo-deductive systems for the use of students.

However, the following attempt, as the reader must be warned, will not appear very satisfactory from a logician's point of view; for this is not a general theory of science, but a mere introduction to analytic sociology. Though it is impossible to avoid the most fundamental problems of logic, we can do more than touch upon them briefly and superficially. Furthermore, though I consider the traditional form of scientific systematization very bad and see the possibility of a radically new form, more in accordance with the logic of scientific research, I still keep personally to the old form. *Video meliora proboque, deteriora sequor.* I discovered the new possibilities too late in life: the old ways had already become deeply ingrained in the functional organization of my personal knowledge. True, they might be changed, but at the cost of efforts which can be more productively used elsewhere. The new form of systematization will probably develop gradually; we already find it in many of the best scientific monographs, and it will be applied to systematic works as soon as the traditional method of teaching science undergoes a thorough and well-merited reform.

3. The Method of Sociology

THE PRINCIPLES OF SELECTION
OF CULTURAL DATA
1934

1. The Distinction between Natural and Cultural Data

A COMPARATIVE SURVEY of the closed systems with which various special sciences have to deal shows a fundamental difference between two main types of systems: the *natural* and the *cultural*. The difference concerns both the composition and the structure of the systems, and the character of the elements and of the forces which bind them together. The distinguishing features are by no means hidden from observation and to be discovered only after a long process of research: on the contrary, they are given at the outset of the study; they determine from the first moment the direction of all further research; and it is their very obviousness which, as often happens, has made many methodologists and philosophers ignore them in attempts to create an artificially monistic conception of science.

The difference concerns the part which human experience and activity play in the real world. And here we must settle once for all a much discussed point. What we know about reality, we know only by experiencing it and actively thinking about it; that being so, human experience and activity, i.e. the experience and activity of the investigating scientist, are ever present factors in the study

Chapter 2 of *The Method of Sociology* (New York: Farrar & Rinehart, 1934), pp. 34–80. Reprinted by permission of Eileen Markley Znaniecki.

of all real systems. The idealistic philosophers will say that it is the determining factor, that all reality is only what the scientist makes it; the empirical realist assumes, on the contrary, that the scientist does nothing except discover what exists independently of him, that his experience and thought do not affect in any way the reality he investigates, but merely serve to introduce him to it, as it actually is. This conflict of philosophic opinions does not interest us here. The attitude of the positive scientist, the specialist in any field, is uniformly realistic. He always means to learn as exactly as possible about reality such as it is, independently of him. Whether his object-matter be nature or culture, he eliminates himself entirely, tries to behave not as a human being who wishes reality to accord with his particular prejudices, but as an impersonal "knower." If he notices that his experience and activity do affect his data, he treats this as a source of error to be avoided. Thus the astronomer corrects his "personal equation" in observations, and the psychologist or sociologist tries not to influence personally the people whose behavior he studies. In short, all science tends alike to approach complete objectivity. The difference in question does not lie in the attitude of the scientist but exclusively in the character of reality itself as given to the scientist when it is made the object-matter of impersonal investigation.

Natural systems are objectively given to the scientist as if they existed absolutely independently of the experience and activity of men. The planetary system, the geological composition and structure of the rind of the earth, the chemical compound, the magnetic field, the plant and the animal, are such as they appear to the student, without any participation of human consciousness; scientifically speaking, they would be exactly the same if no men existed (apart, of course, from the metaphysical problem which we have already left aside). The essential characters of their elements, i.e. those characters which determine their functions in their respective systems, are such as they are apart from the question whether and how anybody experiences them; they are bound together by forces which have nothing to do with human activity. Even if a particular system has been artificially and intentionally constructed by men, as the experimental system in a physical laboratory or the ecological system of plants cultivated in a certain area, the naturalist is not interested in the experiences and activities of those who made it, but only in the natural characters of the elements which have been used for its construction, in the natural forces which hold them together after the system has been constructed, in the natural processes which occur within it. Therefore he can treat the laboratory system as a typical instance of systems existing outside, without the participation of men, but not so easily circumscribed, and consider the ecological system of cultivated plants as a particular variation of "communities" of plants growing wild.

2. The Humanistic Coefficient of Cultural Data

Very different appear such indubitably cultural systems as those dealt with by students of language and literature, art, religion, science, economics, industrial technique and social organization. Generally speaking, every cultural system is found by the investigator to exist for certain conscious and active historical subjects, i.e. within the sphere of experience and activity of some particular people, individuals and collectivities, living in a certain part of the human world during a certain historical period. Consequently, for the scientist this cultural system is really and objectively as it was (or is) given to those historical subjects themselves when they were (or are) experiencing it and actively dealing with it. In a word, the data of the cultural student are always "somebody's," never "nobody's" data. This essential character of cultural data we call the *humanistic coefficient*, because such data, as objects of the student's theoretic reflection, already belong to somebody else's active experience and are such as this active experience makes them.

If the humanistic coefficient were withdrawn and the scientist attempted to study the cultural system as he studies a natural system, i.e. as if it existed independently of human experience and activity, the system would disappear and in its stead he would find a disjointed mass of natural things and processes, without any similarity to the reality he started to investigate.

For instance languages, whether modern French or ancient Greek, exist only in so far as they are spoken and understood by the people using them, i.e., by a historical collectivity living in a certain area within a certain period, with the addition of some scattered individuals living elsewhere or at later periods; and they have for the philologist the characters they possess or possessed for that collectivity. Islam as a religious system exists only in so far as a certain wide and complex human collectivity in the East believes in it and follows its ritual; and it is viewed by the student of religion through the eyes of that collectivity, or as modified by particular sects and theological schools. The Bank of England as an economic system exists only in so far as numbers of people in England and elsewhere perform certain economic activities and have certain experiences, owing to which "the Bank" has a reality and exercises an influence upon human life; the student of economics must take it as he finds it within the sphere of experience and activity of those people, with all it means to its shareholders, directors and employees, agents, correspondents, debtors and creditors. The Platonic system of philosophy means that system as it has existed within the sphere of mental activity and experience of Plato himself and of all his disciples, readers and critics from antiquity down to the present day, and must be studied by the objective historian of philosophy and science only in so far as it has been understood by all those people.

Suppose the student eliminates the humanistic coefficient: the French language then becomes an enormous and disconnected complexity of sounds pronounced through centuries by hundreds of millions of individuals belonging to the species *Homo Sapiens*, together with a still more voluminous and chaotic complexity of physiological processes going on within the bodies of those individuals; Islam or the Bank of England will appear as a still more bewildering chaos of sounds, bodily movements, physiological processes, piles of wood, bricks and mortar, masses of inkspotted paper; and the philosophy of Plato (unless the student is prepared to treat it as a superhuman, absolute system of pure, objective "Ideas") dissolves similarly into organic processes, sounds, volumes of paper, printers' ink. Within such an inexhaustible chaos of natural things and processes, the scientist may indeed find certain kinds of natural systems relatively closed, such as typical organic responses to certain classes of external stimuli; but these are as incommensurable with the empirical reality originally found by the student of language, religion, economics, or philosophy as are the systems of chemical elements of which painters' colors are composed with a portrait by Gainsborough or a landscape by Turner.

3. Values as Cultural Objects

The humanistic coefficient concerns both the composition and the structure of cultural systems. Every element which enters into the composition of a cultural system is what it appears to be in the experience of those people who are actively dealing with it, and the student cannot know what it is unless he ascertains how it appears to them. The words used in the composition of a French poem are what they appear to be to the poet himself, to his listeners, readers, and imitators. The myths, verbal formulas, sacred implements, ritual gestures entering into the composition of a Mohammedan public ceremony exist as religious realities just as they appear to the believers who participate in this ceremony. The coin, notes, securities, bills of exchange, checks, etc., composing the assets and liabilities of a bank as an economic system are what they appear to be to the shareholders, workers and clients of the bank.

The scientist who wishes to study the poem, the ceremony, the bank, cannot approach any of their elements the way he approaches a stone or a tree, as a mere thing which is supposed to exist independently of any human being for all human beings to see who have similar sense organs: for if he tried to do so, the reality of the elements would escape him entirely and he would fail to understand the real rôle which they play within their respective systems. This rôle is determined not merely by the characters these elements possess as natural things, but also (and chiefly) by characters which they have acquired in the experience of people during their existence as cultural objects.

No natural analysis can detect these characters. The student of culture can ascertain them in two ways: by interpreting what the people whose cultural system he is studying communicate, directly or indirectly, about their experiences with these cultural objects, and by observing their outward behavior with regard to those objects. These methods supplement one another and both must be used to obtain adequate knowledge. Thus, the musical quality and particularly the significance of the words of a poem, the non-material reality of a religious myth accepted by believers, the mystical force of formulas and gestures, the sacredness of implements of religious service, the economic power attached to little pieces of gold and printed paper, are as essential characters of these objects as their physical and chemical properties, and influence at least as much not only the thoughts and desires, but also the external, naturally observable behavior of the people. Indeed, they often influence it incomparably more. The partial destruction of a temple may not prevent religious ceremonies from being performed within it, but its desecration by an iniquitous deed which does not in any way change its natural properties makes public worship impossible within its precincts. For a bank the amount of economic power inherent in a purely ideal "sum" of money is much more important practically than the obvious and marked physical difference between gold coin and bills of exchange.

It is well to express by a difference of terms this essential distinction between natural objects, elements of natural systems, and cultural objects, elements of cultural systems. We call natural objects *things*, cultural objects *values*, in view of their essential practical determination with reference to human activity.[1]

A value differs from a thing in that it possesses both a given *content*, which distinguishes it as an empirical object from other objects, and a *meaning*, by which it suggests other objects—those with which is has been actively associated in the past; whereas a thing has no meaning, but only a content, and stands only for itself. Thus, a word of some language has a sensible content—composed

---

[1]   For a general theory of cultural objects, see the author's *Cultural Reality*, University of Chicago Press, 1919. I advocated the use of the term *value* as a logical category distinct from the traditional category of *"thing"* or "substance" in my book *The Problem of Values in Philosophy* (in Polish), Warsaw, 1910.

of auditive, muscular, and (in languages which have a literature) visual data; but it has also a meaning, i.e., suggests those objects which it has been made to indicate. A "sacred" vessel, as an implement of a cult, in addition to its content (visual, tactile, etc.) has a meaning in a particular religion, owing to the fact that it has been connected with certain words, myths, ritualistic gestures, human bodies as objects of sanctification, and suggests them when experienced. A coin, by content a piece of metal, has a familiar meaning called "buying power." And so on. Whereas a stone or a drop of water, as things, have no meaning, or at least are treated by the physicist who studies them as if they had none and suggested nothing beyond thmselves. This distinction has nothing to do with any opposition of "subjective" and "objective" data. Only from the point of view of naïvely materialistic metaphysics (unhappily quite popular now in certain circles of social scientists and psychologists) does objectivity appear coextensive with sensory experience. A value is as objective as a thing in the sense that the experience of a meaning, like the experience of a content, can be indefinitely repeated by an indefinite number of people and consequently "tested." To experience a meaning, indeed, a certain preparation or "learning" is needed; the individual must be put into definite conditions and be taught how to use the given value. But the same holds true of experiencing contents: the reproduction of a sensory observation is only possible under definite conditions of the individual's organism and milieu, and requires a previous training. In another sense again we might say that things are as subjective as values, since the ultimate empirical test of the reality of both is actual individual experience which, as shown by illusions and hallucinations, is not sufficient guarantee of objectivity and in both cases must be controlled by reflection. Moreover, psychogenetically, values seem more primary and fundamental than things: we begin our life by adapting ourselves to a world full of meanings, and only much later, under the influence of certain practical and theoretic considerations, some of us learn to treat certain objects at certain moments as if they were meaningless.

When a value is taken with reference to a particular system, it may appear as "desirable" or "undesirable," "useful" or "harmful,"etc., in connection with the other values involved in it and from the point of view of its realization. We call this character of the value its positive or negative *axiological significance*. Thus, to the poet who tries to use a certain word in a sonnet the word has a positive axiological significance, if it appears aesthetically suitable, a negative significance in the opposite case. An instrument employed in a Christian religious ceremony is axiologically positive with reference to the Christian religion, but axiologically negative from the point of view of the Mohammedan cult. A sum of "money" has a positive significance for an estate, if it figures among its assets; a negative significance, if it is a part of its liabilities.

4. The Problem of Human Activities

What are, now, the factors involved in the structure of a cultural system which hold its elements together and isolate in some respects the system as a whole from the external world? The answer seems easy and obvious. It is human activity which has constructed the system by selecting its elements and combining them together to the exclusion of disturbing factors; it is human activity of a similar kind which actualizes the system again and again in a certain field of human experience and prevents it from being different each time it appears. A poem as a system of words has been built up by the poet, who selected and combined them in a certain logical and rhythmical order so as to produce a total aesthetic effect: every reader, reciter and listener reproduces this effect by repeating, either audibly or mentally, this combination; and while doing so not only tries not to drop any words or introduce any new ones, but intentionally excludes external noises and distractions as well as all psychological associations which might interfere with his rendering and enjoyment of the poem. A religious cermony is generally constructed gradually in the course of many years by a succession of religious leaders, each adding some elements, excluding others, combining and recombining them so as to obtain what seems the best religious result in the form of a certain mystical connection between the deity and the community of worshippers. Finally, the system becomes stabilized and sanctioned by tradition, and is afterwards reproduced again and again by priests and their faithful followers, with the same supposed consequences occurring whenever all the essential elements are there and no material or psychological disturbances are allowed to interfere with its reproduction. A bank is organized by the common activity of a group of capitalists and experts, the former getting together the capital stock, the latter planning and organizing the economic operations, including some things and excluding others, so as to reach the desired result in the form of a yearly dividend to the shareholders: it is maintained by the activities of the directors and employees, who systematically perform the operations as planned, utilizing the economic resources of the community by definite methods, and forestalling or counteracting all interfering external factors and even any disturbances which may possibly spring from their own private interests.

But the meaning of the term "human activity" is still rather vague and full of scientifically undesirable suggestions. We must give this concept a greater precision, since it is the pivot of all research in the domain of culture. Of course, experience is the only possible source from which scientific knowledge about any kind of human activity can be gained. The question is, how shall we utilize this source? For here, as well as in the study of empirical objects, elements of closed systems, there are two ways of approach. One is the way of the naturalist who, even while recognizing that cultural objects are human values and that cultural systems are constructed by human activity, believes that human activity can nevertheless be studied as a natural process given to him (like other natural processes) without any reference to how it appears to anybody else; and also that a human value viewed in the light of a naturalistic theory of activity can be simply analyzed into a natural thing *plus* an equally natural process which goes on in the human being as a psycho-biological entity, and corresponds to this thing. The other way of obtaining an inductive knowledge of human activity would be to use consistently the humanistic coefficient in dealing with it, and take it as it appears to the agent himself and to those who cooperate with him or counteract him.

This is not the place to describe and explain the historical evolution which has led to an almost exclusive predominance of the naturalistic approach in all attempts to reach by scientific induction a general knowledge of human activities—though it would make one of the most interesting and significant chapters in the history of science. The humanistic approach, on the other hand, is the usual approach of popular reflection dominated by practical interests, and has in fact remained current in historical interpretation and in all the special sciences of culture that study particular historical forms of literary, religious, artistic, economic, intellectual, political activity. But when it comes to a search for general principles and laws of activity, there is a powerful influence with which scientific induction has to contend in this line: the influence of traditional normative speculation. The humanistic point of view, the point of view of the active subject, has been used much oftener to establish general standards of human activities than to discover general truths about them.

Thus it came to pass that a disinterested inductive search for general truths in these fields has become associated with the naturalistic point of view, not only in the eyes of the naturalists themselves, but even in those of many humanists and philosophers. "Naturalism" has come to mean not merely a particular way of approaching empirical data as independent of conscious and active beings, but in general the objective scientific attitude toward reality as against an attitude imbued with subjective valuation, respect for facts as against speculation that bends facts to fit preconceived ideas.[2] How widely spread this identification of naturalism with objective general knowledge still is, even among scientists dealing with culture, is manifest in two striking phenomena. On the one hand, we see the pitiful attempts of many prominent specialists (chiefly in America, England and France), great authorities in their respective fields, who are trying to assimilate second and third hand knowledge of the latest results of experimental psychology and biology in order to give their general hypotheses what they

[2]   Cf. Carl Rahn, *Science and the Religious Life*, Chap. IV, for this conception of the naturalistic attitude.

believe to be a firmer scientific foundation. On the other hand, the modern reaction against this current (chiefly in Germany) and against the whole naturalistic point of view tends to reject the method of scientific induction as developed by the sciences of nature and to substitute instead some special method.

Following in the wake of many better thinkers, I have subjected the naturalistic approach to general criticism in several works. I do not mean to do so in detail again, especially as I have found that scientists with a naturalistic trend of mind "never know when they are beaten." I shall, therefore, pass over the many problems and pseudo-problems which spring from the conception of activity as a natural, psycho-biological process, leaving them to those who are positively interested in this kind of conception and its logical consequences. Only at the most important points I shall mark clearly the dividing line between the field of research circumscribed by this work and the fields of the biologist and the biological psychologist.

At the same time, and even more strictly, all connection must be avoided between sociological theory and normative speculation. Not that I wish to deny the importance of that kind of hierarchization of human activities with reference to some supreme norm or ideal with which in the social field ethics, philosophy of law, philosophy of education, and philosophy of social progress have always been concerned. Such a hierarchization will always be indispensable for the intellectual guidance of social activities in addition to that organization of knowledge for practical purposes which is the task of practical or applied sciences like political science, educational science, and the various disciplines used in social welfare and social reform. Every instance of practical organization of knowledge in any line implies the acceptance of a definite goal; and since human goals are multiple, changing, competing and often conflicting, the need for their standardization has always been patent, and always will be patent, to those interested in the practical control of human life. Normative philosophy satisfies this need.

But, while recognizing its justification, we cannot sufficiently emphasize the necessity of keeping it altogether out of the field of theoretic research, not because it is "philosophy," but because it is normative. When theoretic investigation of activities is combined with their normative standardization, there is always the danger that the former will be subordinated to the latter with results detrimental to scientific validity. The method of normative standardization is essentially deductive: having established a supreme standard in any field—be it ethics, politics, religion, or aesthetics—the thinker deduces from it a systematic hierarchy of ideals and norms. He may use induction as an auxiliary method, either before establishing his supreme standard, in order to find what standards human agents actually follow in their activities, or after having established it, in order to determine the conditions under which they would accept and put into action his normative system; but in either case his selection and organization of data is apt to be conditioned by his normative purposes rather than by the theoretic criteria of strictly objective, inductive research.[3] Thus the history of philosophy (particularly, though not exclusively, between the third century B.C. and the sixteenth century A.D.) shows how difficult it is to comply with these criteria, if normative interests are allowed to influence theoretic investigation.

This does not mean that a theoretic investigation carried on to gain auxiliary information for normative purposes never can be objective and scientifically valuable, nor yet that all studies of human activities carried on in the past and within the vast field known under the vague term of "philosophy" have been dominated by normative purposes. All we wish to emphasize is the existence of an essential, irreducible difference between the theoretic investigation of activities and their normative standardization, as well as the desirability of keeping the former completely separated from the latter, lest it should interfere with its progress, as it has so often done in the past.

[3] Of course, the criteria of scientific research are themselves normative in the logical sense; but to use standardized theoretic methods in investigating activities is a very different matter from demanding that the activities investigated should comply with the investigator's ethical, political, or even logical standards.

Having thus, let us hope, prevented any possible misunderstanding, we can now define more exactly the humanistic way of approaching human activities. It is very familiar to us all in our everyday life.

5. *Experiencing Activities*

When I wish to ascertain at first hand what a certain activity is, just as when I wish to obtain first-hand information about a certain object, I try to experience it. There is only one way of experiencing an object: it is to *observe* it personally. There is also only one way of experiencing an activity: it is to *perform* it personally. Practical men insist on this: they will tell you that you cannot fully realize what they are doing until you do it yourself. Scientists have come to recognize this: the modern student in ergology sees the need of learning how to practice himself the various techniques of lower civilizations, such as working in stone, shooting with a bow and arrow, etc.; the philogist does not believe his personal acquaintance with a language perfect unless he has learned to speak it or at least (with dead languages) to write it; the student of religion tries to obtain first-hand experiences by sharing actively in religious ceremonies; the epistemologist and the methodologist realize that first-hand acquaintance with scientific methods demands active participation in scientific research. And so on. Actual performance is the *primary* source of empirical knowledge about activity.

This statement must be explained and developed in view of certain artificial difficulties which have been raised by philosophers in connection with the traditional dualism of "mind" and "matter." A philosopher or psychologist faithful to the old idea of an individual consciousness, within which perceptions, representations, volitions, feelings, emotions, are somehow enclosed or imbedded, interprets activity as a mental, "internal" fact. From this point of view, the only activity I could experience would be an activity belonging to my subjective consciousness. Experiencing an activity performed by anybody else would be impossible. As a source of scientific knowledge about human activities in general, actual performance would be worthless; all I could do with its help would be to make a theory of my own particular activities.

However, similar objections have been raised by philosophers concerning the possibility of experiencing the same objects as somebody else experiences. According to subjective idealism, the objects I experience are only my own "ideas" or "states of consciousness." I have no certainty that you and I are experiencing the same object or even that you actually exist and are not merely my idea or my state of consciousness.[4] But positive science has gone ahead without heeding such problems about objects; nor can it be stopped now by similar speculations in its study of activities. It partly waives them aside, partly reduces them to mere methodological difficulties which can be overcome from case to case.

The scientific assumption with regard to objects is that every real object either is accessible to the experience of any person at any moment, if he puts himself into the proper conditions for experiencing it; or else can be logically inferred from objects which are empirically accessible to every person. Of course there is always the chance of mistaking experiences of separate realities for experiences of the same reality, and *vice versa*. The test for clearing up all such misunderstandings is furnished by the principle of closed systems. My experience of a tree or a religious myth may differ from yours, but this is scientifically irrelevant for the identification of this object; the tree or the myth is sure to be the same if it takes the same place as an element in a system—a forest or a religion—which we both share. Or on the contrary, my experiences of a tree or a myth may be similar to yours and yet our objects be distinct, as we shall find when we discover that your tree is located in a different part of our forest, or that your myth belongs to a different religious system than mine. This obviously presupposes that we can identify these systems, either directly by sharing them, or again by referring them to some wider system which we are sure of sharing.

[4]   This view with various modifications has been explicitly formulated by several German philosophers in the last quarter of the nineteenth century, such as Schuppe, Schubert-Soldern, Cornelius.

Can a parallel principle be applied to activities? According to dualistic psychology, this would be impossible. For the reason why the same object can be experienced by you and me is that it exists in the "outside world" whether we experience it or not: its real existence is not limited to the actual fact of its being perceived or represented here and now. Whereas an activity exists only while it is actual; in this respect it is not like an object, but like a perception or representation of an object; it is only there while it is being performed.[5] Consequently, not only is it impossible for me to experience your activity, but I cannot even experience today my own activity of yesterday.

For scientific purposes, however, this view has proved entirely inadequate. It has produced an unbridgeable gap between the psychology of individual consciousness and the sciences of the cultural world, because of which this psychology has been of very little use in humanistic studies.[6] Of course, it is a truism that an activity does not actually exist for the agent except while he performs it; no more does an object exist for him except while he is observing it. But just as he is aware from the content and meaning of this object that it exists as an element of some system within which it can be observed by many people, so he is aware while acting that his activity manifests itself objectively, is occurring within some system, and that other people can also act within the same system just as he does: his activity is not altogether and exclusively his own, even though he performs it. We can express this briefly by saying that every activity has an objective *form* and an objective *function*. Its form is the way in which it deals with objects—"pattern" is nowadays the more popular term; its function is the share it has in constructing, maintaining or changing a system.

There is nothing metaphysical about these concepts; they correspond to familiar, everyday data of practical life. The as-

5   This is the pivotal idea of the whole psychology and philosophy of Wilhelm Wundt; in a modified form it underlies also the psychology of William James.

6   Wundt tried in vain to bridge this gap with the help of the concepts of "collective will" and "folk-psyche."

sumption that activities have objective forms or patterns is tested every time somebody teaches somebody else how to perform an activity—drive a nail, spin or weave, play golf, say prayers, write words, analyze a Latin sentence, compose a story. Teaching and learning, consequently all cultural tradition, would be impossible if activities were not "communicable"; and what is communicable is obviously not the subject's present act as such, but the way objects are actively handled. Nor could cultural systems be constructed by the cooperation of several individuals and maintained by a succession of them if the function of an activity in a system were not essentially independent of the individual subject who performs it, though different individuals may perform it somewhat differently. When a workman in a factory finishes off the unfinished part of an automobile passed to him by another workman; when a scientist continues an investigation which another has dropped; when a newly appointed official steps into the place of his predecessor: the function is one and continuous, though the functioning agents change. It does not matter for the production of the automobile, for the advance of science, for the maintenance of the office who does the work, provided it is done as it ought to be done.

Thus, when you and I perform "the same" activity, it does not mean that our two "subjective acts" are one, any more than experiencing the same object means that our "subjective perceptions" are one. It may mean one of three things:

a) That our activities are formally the same, though functionally distinct: this is called *repetition*. Thus, the pupil in school repeats the teacher's activity of writing a word or analyzing a sentence; the golf amateur repeats the stroke of the professional; the ergologist repeats the savage's performance with a bow. Functionally, these actions are distinct, inasmuch as for the teacher writing the sentence is a part of his teaching function, for the pupil a part of his learning function; in golf, each man plays his own separate game; the ergologist shoots with bow and arrow as a matter of scientific experiment, while the savage does it in hunting or war.

b) That our activities are functionally united, but formally different: this is *participation*. For instance, the workers in a factory participate in the function of running it; the officials of a social group participate in the function of maintaining this group; the scientists interested in the same branch of science participate in the function of developing it. Formally, however, each worker, each official, each scientist may be doing something different, dealing with different objects in a different way.

c) That our activities are formally the same and also fulfil the same function: this may be called *reproduction*. People are reproducing over and over again the same technical patterns, going through the same ritualistic performances, playing the same musical compositions, reading the same books, teaching students the same geometrical demonstrations; though their personal purposes vary, there is a common objective function they all fulfil in such cases: it is that of perpetuating by reproduction the technical pattern, the rite, the musical composition, the contents of the book, the system of geometry.

Modern behaviorism has rejected the conception of a closed individual consciousness and concentrated on objective manifestations of activity. Unfortunately, in trying to get rid of the dualism of "mind and matter," it has simply adopted the naïve solution of age-old materialism: it preserves the "matter" side of it and ignores the "mind" side, instead of going beyond both and searching for a new approach. Consequently, it treats as objective "behavior" only those activities whose form or pattern is manifest in handling material objects, and is inclined to assume that the function of every activity is mutual adaptation between the organism and its environment. Now, much of the content of cultural reality is non-material, even though symbolized by words or other signs, and even material cultural objects have meanings which are empirically observable, but not sensually given; obviously the patterns of activities dealing with this non-material aspect of culture cannot be deduced from those of activities handling material objects. Moreover, the functions of most cultural activities at higher levels of development have nothing to do with the individual's adaptation to his environment, but only with the preservation and development of systems which transcend and sometimes conflict with the needs of each individual participant.

A student of "behavior" who refuses to recognize any but sensual patterns and biological functions cuts himself off from innumerable first-hand experiences without which cultural life becomes incomprehensible. If really consistent, he cannot repeat, participate in or reproduce the activities of people who create and maintain religion, literature, science, philosophy, moral, political and economic organization, for those people themselves perform and experience their activities as if non-material objects and systems were as real as material ones—if not more so.

The whole question is not one of metaphysics or epistemology, but of scientific method. We may waive active experience altogether as a source of knowledge, as John Watson does, and limit ourselves to outside observations of organic movements and biological experimentation. This means resigning the investigation of cultural activities altogether. But there is no reason whatever for doing it, since practical life shows that activities as experienced by the agent himself have an objective aspect which makes repetition, participation and reproduction possible. And this concerns all activities, not only handling objects of the material environment. A simple and obvious test is having several agents describe independently what they are doing when they repeat, participate in or reproduce an activity. If the meaning of the words they use is sufficiently stabilized, their descriptions will tally, just as the descriptions of a tree made independently by several observers. And this will hold true of eating, playing golf or producing an automobile as well as of reading a novel, canonizing a saint, discussing the philosophy of Kant, or demonstrating a mathematical theorem.

Thus, if we want to know what any particular activity or activity in general really is, we find that the humanistic approach is the only approach that brings us to the original source—the experience of the agent. And there is no difficulty about it, for we are all agents and each of us can experience the activities of others by repetition, participation or reproduction. But what does the agent experience when he performs an activity?

Psychologists have been trying to find this out for centuries. Many times introspection has discovered some specific experience which it believed could be considered "the experience of activity":

the *actus purus* of the scholastics; Maine de Biran's consciousness of "effort"; Schopenhauer's "Will," Bergson's *"élan vital"* are familiar instances. Always rational analysis has dissolved the supposed specific experience of activity into a series of emotionally tinted experiences of objective, chiefly organic, things and processes. And always, again, this analysis has been impeached by the claim—undoubtedly just—that, while activity is subjected to rational analysis, it is not being performed, and we can therefore no longer experience it. But the only alternative seems to be an appeal to some irrational power of experience, some kind of direct "intuition," simultaneous with and merged into activity itself—and this is the straight road to mysticism.

6. Activity, Tendency, and Attitude

Since the method of introspective psychology had thus far failed definitely to discover what the agent's experience of activity "really is," we had better waive it altogether. That is not the way for the agent to learn whether he is active or not, to find out what he is doing, or to distinguish one kind of activity from another. What is, in fact, given to him while he is acting is the same set of data (though with some differences of content and meaning) which is given to any observer of his behavior who knows the meaning of the objects this agent is dealing with: it is the dynamic objective manifestation of his activity, the gradual construction in actual empirical reality of a definite system of values—a poem or musical composition, a religious ceremony, a financial undertaking, an association. Activity is nothing but that which brings the construction of this system about: it is the primary factor of this construction. Only the construction itself is somewhat differently experienced by the agent than by the observer. There are two essentially distinctive characters of his active experience.

First, the system which is being constructed is somehow getting determined by the agent in advance, not in the sense of being "planned" or "foreseen" in its detail, but in that of being made to include some of the many possible values within the reach of the agent's experience and to have these values combined and modified in one of many possible ways. Writing a poem means selecting certain experiences to be expressed, organizing and modifying these experiences in mutual adaptation so as to produce an aesthetic unity, finding and combining symbols to express them in a way which will meet both the demands of this aesthetic organization and certain requirements of rhythmic cadence and rhyme. Organizing a store implies selecting certain economic needs of the community which it will aim to satisfy, finding some capital, renting or buying premises where the goods can be located, buying goods which are adapted to satisfying the needs, hiring and putting to work employees, selling the goods at a profit calculated in advance.

This prospective determination of the system by the agent is not experienced by him when his activity is going on uninterruptedly; he then experiences only the values as they are given to him, combined and modified by his activity. But if he begins his activity by thinking what he will do and how he will do it, or if at any later time during this activity he temporarily stops acting, the prospective determination of the system becomes a matter of actual experience. The term *defining a situation*,[7] or the equivalent terms of *defining* or *setting a practical problem* can be used to indicate this specific experience. The latter need not be accompanied by any rational reflection comparing and weighing possible choices; rationalized situations are a special variety of situations in general.

Alongside of this prospective determination of the system, a retrospective determination goes on, a readaptation of the values already selected and of the modifications already made to fit whatever new values and new modifications are taking their place in the system. This retrospective determination is also not primarily experienced as such: only the particular values and modifications effected by it are given. But at any moment the agent can become aware of it, if he stops to connect a present situation with a past situation and realizes that he is solving or failing to solve the practical problem included in the latter.

These two distinctive characters of the agent's experience

7   Thomas and Znaniecki, *The Polish Peasant,* p. 68.

of the construction which his activity "brings about" will be best expressed by stating that an activity from the point of view of the agent's own experience of it is *a tendency to construct a system of values in the course of its realization.* The term "tendency" suggests both the fact that the system is prospectively determined, "intended," and that this prospective determination may or may not be fulfilled. At the same time, it is a sufficiently general term not to bear any specifically psychological implications, since it can be used also in biological and even in physical sciences. Indeed, a cultural tendency is fundamentally characterized, just as a natural tendency, by its objective manifestations in so far as these are determined in advance and not disturbed by other factors.

However, there is an important difference between cultural and natural tendencies, due to the fact that the cultural world is a world of values, not of things. Whereas natural tendencies are only manifested in so far as they are being realized, a cultural tendency can manifest itself empirically not only in the course of its realization as activity, but also at other times as an *attitude*; and it does this when it only defines the situation without solving it.

We have seen that values have a positive or negative axiological significance when taken with reference to a cultural system, and that this significance depends on the bearing they have upon the system in connection with other values of the latter. While the system is being really constructed, this significance is empirically expressed in the very *act* of acceptance or rejection of the given values as its element; a successful or unsuccessful attempt is made by the agent to introduce the value into the system, or to prevent or counteract its interference with the system. Thus, during the performance of a public religious ceremony the positive axiological significance of an instrument of cult is expressed in the act of bringing and using this instrument at the proper moment; the negative significance of an "unbeliever" in the act of his expulsion from the sacred place.

When, however, as a matter of fact the system is not being constructed, this axiological significance of the values involved in its construction remains latent; but the original tendency, whenever it reappears without resulting in an active performance, shows itself in a specific attitude toward these values. Psychologically speaking, the attitude is a definite appreciation of a given object as desirable or undesirable; and this appreciation may range all the way from purely intellectual approval or disapproval to a most irrational emotion, and from a static "feeling" to a dynamic "wish." In objective terms, the attitude is a determination of the active treatment the given value would receive in the system which tends to be constructed, if it ever really be constructed. The attitude is, thus, a potential substitute for the act.

For example, when an instrument of cult or an "unbeliever" is given in experience to an agent who is not at the moment participating in a religious ceremony, but still tends to do so under the proper conditions, the axiological significance of those objects will show itself in the fact that the agent will experience an attitude of reverence toward the sacred instrument, an attitude of scorn (perhaps combined with fear) toward the unbeliever.

A tendency is not, however, realized in a single act dealing with one value, but in a whole series of acts—the total activity of constructing a system of values. There may also be complex systems involving each a combination of tendencies subordinated to one dominant tendency. Consequently, a single attitude only partially expresses a tendency when the latter is not active, and the whole set of attitudes toward the various values involved in a system is needed to reconstruct fully a tendency. On the other hand, a particular value may be used in many different and disconnected cultural systems in all of which the agent participates at various times; his attitude toward this value may then be a complex substitute for many virtual acts, a number of various tendencies may be partially manifested in it. Thus, a believer's attitude toward an unbeliever may embody a variety of potential active consequences, not only religious but social, if he is a foreigner, or if he belongs to a different race or class.

Nevertheless, in every attitude some tendency is manifested, and every tendency while not active manifests itself as an attitude, whenever any of the values it tends to utilize are given. In other words, values are not appreciated unless there is a potential tendency to use them in a cultural system; and there is no potential tendency to construct a cultural system, if the values belonging to this system are not appreciated. Instruments of cult collected and exposed in a museum are not the objects of an attitude of religious reverence even on the part of a person who would revere them, if he found them in a church ready to be used for worship; and if we see a man indifferent to the institutions of a social group, we know that he has no tendency to participate in the public life of this group.

In applying to empirical data this conception of the tendency, we meet two kinds of problems. First, why does a tendency manifest itself at one time as activity constructing a system of values, at another time merely as an attitude or set of attitudes toward one or several of these values? Secondly, why does a tendency when active succeed in some cases in realizing itself, solving the situation as defined and achieving the very system it started to construct, whereas in other cases it fails in its attempt at realization and its total result is different from the one intended? We must have definite guiding principles in dealing with such problems, otherwise we are apt to lose ourselves in the maze of concrete human life.

The first kind of problem refers approximately to the same facts as those covered by the traditional theories of "motivation," though viewed from a somewhat different standpoint. The leading principle of all theories of motivation is that human activity must and can be explained by human experience. The fact that a particular individual or collectivity begins to act in a certain way at a particular moment is supposed to need explanation; and the explanation is sought in some particular experience which this individual (or collectivity) has had and which has "motivated" his activity. There are two types of theories of motivation: those which ascribe the supposed stimulating influence exercised by human experience to feeling, and look for the feelings aroused in the individual by the objects which he has experienced (i.e. perceived, represented, or imagined); and those which claim the priority of will over feeling and explain activity by the desires which the objects experienced provoke in the individual. When the concept of value was introduced into philosophy and psychology, this duality expressed itself in dual conceptions of values as objects of feeling (emotion, sentiment) and values as objects of volition (conation, desire).

But, however important the theory of motivation may be for the study of concrete human individuals (or, lately, concrete collectivities of individuals), it has no significance whatsoever for the investigation of cultural systems. We cannot and need not explain why a cultural system tends to be constructed at a particular moment by a particular agent. We cannot, because such an explanation would involve the entire past of the cultural world. We need not, because no science conscious of its task ever tries to solve this kind of problem. The main reason for using the concept of the closed system is precisely to avoid this kind of insoluble problem. A tendency is simply there and must be taken as given; and since a tendency is by its very definition a tendency to construct a cultural system, the activity constructing this system is its primary and original manifestation. Consequently, far from explaining activity by the stimulation which the experience of a positive or negative value provides, we must derive the positiveness or negativeness of an attitude toward a value from the activity which uses or rejects this value in constructing its system. In other words, in cultural science, instead of asking (as psychology does) why X tends to perform a certain activity, we must ask why X, though tending to perform certain activity, does not perform it but merely feels or wishes.

And this question is answerable in every particular case, provided only we have sufficient data and use a proper technique in analyzing them. It all depends on how the agent defines the situation. If some of the values viewed as essential to the system which tends to be constructed seem inaccessible at the time when the tendency appears, the situation is defined as *impracticable* and no active solution is attempted, but the tendency manifests itself in attitudes, positively appreciative toward such values as are in harmony with the system, negatively appreciative toward those which hinder its construction.

For example, when obstacles impossible to overcome prevent two people from marrying, their tendencies to marry manifest themselves in attitudes of romantic love toward each other and indignation at the obstacles. The attitude of reverence to religious values is never as distinctly experienced as when persecution forcibly represses activities of religious cult. When a scientist is prevented by any reason from doing active research, he develops attitudes of dogmatic certainty towards the knowledge he already possesses. And so on.

Of course, the definition of a situation as practicable or not may be "mistaken" from the objective point of view, or conditions may change. What seemed an insuperable obstacle to the realization of the tendency may prove sometimes on closer observation no obstacle at all, or may be removed—in which case the situation becomes redefined as practicable, the potential tendency actualizes itself, attitudes pass into acts. Or, *vice versa*, after activity has started, unforeseen difficulties may be discovered or factors external to the situation thrust new obstacles in the way of tendency —and then the situation is redefined as impracticable and acts pass into attitudes.[8] Oftener still, activity becomes interrupted for the time being only, with the expectation of being resumed again. Most of our protracted activities occur in this way: actual performance stops and the tendency passes into the potential stage, because our organism is too tired to continue its rôle as instrument, because some artificial instrument becomes spoiled, or because we begin to collaborate with some one else—in a word, because a situation has been reached which we define as temporarily impracticable. After a time, the organism gets rested or our collaborator finishes his task: the situation appears practicable again and the tendency passes from attitudes to acts.

Taking for granted that everything that can be said about tendencies refers to tendencies as they appear in actuality "here and now," wherever and whenever an agent "has" them, and that the question why a particular agent "has" a particular tendency at a particular moment does not concern us at all, we can formulate the following leading principle: *A cultural tendency is always active unless hindered by an internal practical obstacle.*

[8]   As will be seen later on, situations impracticable for one tendency become reorganized and solved by some other active tendency; still, the original tendency remains as an attitude.

We shall refer to this principle as the *principle of spontaneity*, since it presupposes that activity needs no stimulus. An obstacle is "internal," if it has been included in the definition of the situation; and only such an obstacle prevents the tendency from being active. If it remains outside the situation as defined, that is, if the agent does not realize that because of it some essential elements of the system aimed at are inaccessible, the obstacle does not hinder the activity from going on, though it deflects its course and modifies its results.

Let us now consider our second problem. Assuming that a tendency is active does not at all mean that it will succeed in realizing itself by obtaining the results intended. Nor, on the other hand, is the fact that a tendency has been hindered from acting and manifests itself only in attitudes equivalent to a failure on its part to reach the results which constitute its realization. A situation defined as practicable may become actively solved indeed, but the solution prove entirely different from what was originally expected; whereas in defining a situation as impracticable and not trying to solve it actively, the tendency may be only biding its time and preparing for the expected solution whenever the obstacle be removed. Failure is not doing nothing, but doing something different from what was meant to be done.

Here again cultural science must take exactly the opposite stand to that which psychology has taken. For, while psychology tries to explain why the agent starts to act, and looks for explanation in emotionally or volitionally stimulating experiences of this agent, it waives entirely the problem of the objective results of his activity. Its interest is confined to the active process as a psycho-physiological process. The older psychologist views this process as confined within the body and consciousness of the individual; the behaviorist looks upon it as a process of interaction between the organism and its environment; but for both the interest centers in the agent as a psycho-biological entity, and activity is defined in terms of its results. Consequently, the problem of the results is from the psychologist's point of view theoretically unlimited and is implicitly regarded or even explicitly characterized as such. Given, indeed, activity as a psycho-biological process, the results of the activity must be defined as the total effect which this process as a cause produces in the "outside world" or in the environment of the agent. But this effect, so it seems, cannot be scientifically determined beyond the first stage of organic movement, for it combines with the effects of numerous other processes going on in the concrete reality in which the active individual lives, and these soon form an inextricable maze of facts mutually influencing one another.

For the cultural scientist, however, since he views activity not with reference to the agent, but with reference to the system which it tends to construct, the results are what matters, just as they are for the agent himself. He defines these results, of course, in the same way the agent does, in terms of the agent's values, with the humanistic coefficient, and not as natural processes; they are "products," not "effects." And having waived the psychological problem of the "motives" or "stimuli" which have made the agent act, we find the problem of results scientifically limited and capable of being solved.

Activity starts as a definite series of acts gradually constructing a certain system of values, and once we have discovered the dominant tendency which manifests itself in these acts, once we have found the system that is being constructed by them, it is easy to define the results of this activity in terms of this system, to determine whether it has succeeded in constructing the particular system it intended to construct or not; and if a different one, how different. In the first eventuality, there is no problem whatever. In the second, there is a problem indeed, and we have to explain the failure of the activity to construct the system it started to construct. This we do by finding the factors which made it deviate from its original course. For example, we find a musician starting to play a certain sonata or a religious congregation beginning to perform a certain rite. Once we know what this sonata or this rite is for the respective agents, we can easily determine at the end of the musical or religious performance whether it has ultimately become what it was originally intended to become. If so, there is no problem: matters are as we expected them to be. Suppose, however, that the musician introduces variations into the original composition or the congregation abbreviates the performance by omitting certain sections of the ritual, we naturally ask why, and look for explanation in some perturbing influences.

In a word, from the standpoint of cultural science as a theory of cultural systems, what primarily matters about human activity that is not prevented by internal obstacles from going on, is whether its results are what they were intended to be; and if not, then why not. And here, to make scientific analysis possible, we assume as the second fundamental principle of cultural research that *a tendency once active always achieves the construction of the system of values it started to construct and no other, unless deflected by perturbing factors.* We call this the *principle of achievement.*[9]

Of course, both the principle of spontaneity and the principle of achievement are heuristic assumptions which, like the fundamental principles of mechanics or of thermo-dynamics in physical science, cannot be directly proved or disproved by any particular fact of experience, but only tested by their continued application as instruments for the scientific interpretation and explanation of empirical facts.

7. The Duration and Extension of Cultural Systems

The construction of a system of values is a real dynamic occurrence which involves a definite series of facts and goes on in empirical cultural reality; it brings modifications into certain existing objects and their connections, and produces some object or connection that did not exist before as an empirical datum, at least within the sphere of experience of the agent, even if it did exist in the real world at large. When a poet recites his poem, the

[9]   I first used this principle in the study of social actions in the *Laws of Social Psychology*, Poznan-Chicago, 1925, p. 64. It was then formulated as follows: "A social action, once begun, continues to its purposed end, unless there are factors interfering with its continuation." I have since then come to the conclusion, however, that this principle is applicable to all cultural systems and that, consequently, it should be formulated somewhat differently, as here in the text.

words and phrases of this poem with their particular meanings surge up in his memory out of the mass of words and phrases in his language; a complicated series of movements of his lips, tongue, throat and lungs goes on, through the instrumentality of which these words and phrases become expressed aloud in a definite order, with a definite intonation; and the total result is a specific aesthetic experience given to himself and his hearers. A religious group constructs collectively, under the leadership of a priest, a religious ceremony as a system of sacred objects and mythical entities, handling these objects and influencing these entities in such a way as to produce a sanctification of all the participants; and though to the unbelieving observer some elements, connections and processes in this system are unreal, we must remember the humanistic coefficient and admit their reality in the religious sphere as a part of the cultural world, though not in nature. The managers, technicians, foremen and workmen in a factory, by performing innumerable bodily movements and keeping the machines of the factory running, are able to take raw material, modify it, divide it, combine it, and after a series of different partial changes, to bring out the finished product—safety pin or automobile. This series of actions they repeat indefinitely.

The whole existence of a cultural system as a system of values is essentially founded on those series of actions by means of which the system is being actively constructed. It is a "kinetic" existence, and in this respect the cultural system has a certain similarity to those natural systems which are systems of processes rather than of things. But there are important differences, obviously due to the humanistic coefficient of cultural systems. Duration in time and extension in space do not mean the same for cultural as for natural reality.[10]

A kinetic natural system is supposed to exist uninterruptedly in a continuous time. But outside of the simplest varieties of cultural actions few cultural systems have such an uninterrupted duration, and those which do are either very shortlived, or else are intentionally made to function without interruptions by means of

---

[10]   Cf. the author's *Cultural Reality*, University of Chicago Press, 1919.

a complicated social arrangement in which individual or group agents take periodical turns in performing the same activities, and these performances partly overlap. The first case may be exemplified by a mob as a social group; the second by certain mechanical factories with their changing shifts of workers and overlapping technical processes. This second instance shows that such a continuity is a minor matter for the duration of a cultural system. Some factories are run continuously, others stop once a week for thirty-six hours, others stop every night: all depends on economic considerations. When a factory is working continuously, it is usually because the organization of human activities is being adapted for economic purposes to the continuous functioning of some physical system artifically made (e.g. the thermodynamic system of a steam engine).

Now, the factory which stops every night; the association which meets at rare intervals, functioning at other times only vicariously through the persons of its officials, representatives and members, or not at all when neither officials nor members act for it; the rite which is performed at stated periods, but not otherwise the poem which is recited or the musical composition which is played from time to time: all these do not disappear altogether from the world in those intervals during which they are not actually functioning. They preserve a kind of latent existence, a potential reality. Their elements—the values which compose them—endure in their content and meaning, and can be experienced indefinitely. There are the buildings, materials and machines of the factory, sensual data whose meaning *as* buildings, materials and machines is obvious to anybody prepared to understand their use. The association has an office, symbols like a seal, a name (printed or written), a flag; the individuals who are its members live and preserve in their own experience and that of outsiders this characteristic of membership, this specific social meaning which designates them as belonging to the association. And the attitudes towards these values in which the tendency of the system manifests itself while inactive still have a real influence on human activities that shows itself whenever these values are to be used: they oppose a power of inertia to any use which conflicts with the axiological significance these values have acquired in their system. Thus, cases of so-called sabotage, i.e. attempts during a strike to spoil the machines used in a factory, though easy and effective, are relatively rare, not so much because of economic or moral considerations as because they provoke emotional opposition on the part of those skilled workers who consciously and planfully use these machines in normal times. An attitude of reverence would prevent a soldier from using the flag of his regiment for private purposes even when it is not being publicly used by the regiment as a group.

Unless, however, a cultural system is from time to time being actually made to function and brought into explicit dynamic reality, it loses gradually this latent existence which we are describing. Even if the values which enter into its composition should endure, the connection between them is loosened, and their axiological significance dwindles away. An association which does not meet and whose functionaries seldom act in its name dissolves gradually, often imperceptibly; a deserted farm or mine after a while ceases to be a farm or a mine for any purpose; a custom which has ceased to be periodically acted upon is no longer a custom and becomes forgotten; a language which is no longer used actively by anybody is not only what is commonly called a "dead language" (i.e. one which, like ancient Greek, does not exist in speech, only in writing for those who can read it, and consequently does not evolve) but a non-existing language. In short, a cultural system must be maintained in existence by human activity.

As long as a cultural system is maintained in existence, it is still in the course of its development; its construction has not been finally achieved; every case of its actualization contributes something to its composition along the lines of its structure. This may be rather difficult to understand, unless we realize that there are cultural systems which have a definite term of duration, are meant to be "finished" after a certain result has been reached, whereas others are meant to last indefinitely, unless prevented by external obstacles, and every result actually achieved leaves still an opening and a demand for further results. All actions, simple or complex, belong to the first type: writing a letter, buying a house, building a railroad, fighting a war, are dynamic systems of values organized by an activity which proceeds to a final realization, an "end." The duration of other kinds of systems may also be limited in advance by being subordinated to an ultimate result. Thus, an educational relation is intended to be finished when the educand's person has been formed in accordance with a certain model. In short, groups are constituted for the realization of explicit purposes and are not meant to last after such purposes have been achieved, whereas a social custom, a moral ideal, a scientific theory, a style of art, a religion, a corporation or a state are systems with an indefinite duration. They are being kept in existence by people performing—continuously, periodically or sporadically—activities in accordance with certain rules or leading principles, and thus introducing again and again new values into the system. The new values either replace other values which have been eliminated or dropped out, as in a factory where finished products are sent to the market and new products have to be made, in a traditionalistic religion where the faithful and their belongings continually fall out of the state of sanctity and have to be sanctified over and over; or else they are super-added to existing values, as new works of art manifesting a certain style or new data to which a scientific theory is applied. These activities may be reproductions of other activities or original functional extensions of the leading principles. But these are later problems.

The question of the existence of cultural systems "in space"—or, rather, their "extension"—though familiar to the ethnologist, historian and geographer, is seldom fully grasped in its essential implications. We speak of the "area" of a custom or the "reach" of a language; we say that myths, inventions or literary products "spread" more or less widely. Are these merely figures of speech, or do they indicate a real objective character of the system? What we obviously mean by such expressions is that a custom, a religion, an invention is practiced by the people, or some of the people, inhabiting a certain geographical territory; the traveller who reaches this territory and gets into contact with these people can observe it directly and personally. But the question is whether in discovering and expressing this fact we discover and express only something concerning these people or something concerning the custom, religion or invention as well. Does it make a difference to the cultural system itself how widely it "extends" in this sense? For we must agree that it does not make any difference to a natural thing —say, to the moon—how many people worship it or make love by its light. Here again the fundamental difference between natural and cultural data comes in.

Since the cultural system is what it is because of human experience and since the basis of its reality is its actual construction, the fact that it may be simultaneously constructed by many human agents must have a bearing on its objective existence in the cultural world as much as the fact that it may be successively constructed time after time. The trouble is that, although we can easily think of it as lasting in time through a series of actualizations, we cannot properly apply ideas of space to its simultaneous actualizations: we cannot say that a myth or a custom is located in space and occupies space as material objects and systems do. I have tried to introduce for this reason the conception of non-spacial cultural extension.[11] Assuming every human individual to be a distinct center of experience and activity, as he is, the totality of such centers at any time constitutes, so to speak, the living frame of concrete cultural extension within which all culture exists. Every cultural system extends over a part of this frame corresponding to the number of individual agents who participate in maintaining it. Since, however, the individual is a cultural center in this sense[12] only in so far as he is a conscious agent and not in so far as he is an organic body, human ecology is of little assistance in determining the extension of cultural systems. What matters for problems concerning this extension is not how individual bodies are located in geometrical space, but how individual agents are able and willing to communicate and cooperate with one another. Spacial distance

11   Cf. *Cultural Reality*, Chap. III.
12   I believe that the term "cultural center" is more strictly applicable to an individual than to a community, though it is usually employed with regard to the latter by ethnologists and historians; for, exactly speaking, a community from which culture radiates is a multiplicity of more or less productive individuals who are cooperating in some of the activities.

seems to be, indeed, a conditioning factor in cultural expansion, but even this factor must be taken not absolutely, but in relation to the technique of transportation[13] and of oral and written communication. And there are innumerable other factors facilitating or hindering the extension of any given system: identity or difference of language, social solidarity or social opposition, intellectual interest, religious taboo.

But when a system is thus maintained in existence only by multiple activities, contemporary or successive, each of which introduces into it some new values at least and often also new and original forms, what are the criteria which permit us to judge of the identity of a system in duration and extension? How can we tell whether a particular piece of music, mythical story, religious ceremony or scientific conception actualized by Agent A at the moment t^1 is, or is not, the same as the one Agent B actualizes at the moment t^2? How can we be sure whether a state or a religion found at a historical period p^1 is the same, or not the same, as the state or the religion which existed at a preceding period p, particularly if several centuries elapsed between? How do we know whether two works of art do, or do not, belong to the same style, whether two scientific studies are, or are not, parts of the same theory, whether two dialects are both variations of one language or different languages?

The common view is that the identity or non-identity of two systems is determinable by outside observation on the ground of their similarity or dissimilarity. In such fields as art and literature a sharp distinction is drawn between "creating" a new and original system and merely "copying" a system that already existed; and the special term of "plagiarism" has been invented to indicate a work that pretends to be original when it is a mere copy—judged to be so by its similarity to the original. In the history of science, religion, politics, it is also a usual procedure to judge whether a theory, a religion, a state has, or has not, remained the same through

---

[13]   Prof. Erle F. Young is working on an ecological scheme which would substitute distance measured in units of time used for transportation instead of distance measured in units of mere length.

the changes it has undergone, judging by the importance of these changes. In identifying a word, a tale, a technique, a custom in different countries, the ethnologist or "cultural anthropologist" is chiefly influenced by the similarity of the word as pronounced, the tale as told, the custom as observed in those countries.

Obviously, however, similarity is not a sufficient test of identity. From the point of view of a generalizing and objective cultural science the inherent difference between a system "created" and a system merely "reproduced" is one of degree, not of nature. Even the most original innovation can be viewed as a variation of something that existed before; even when cultural evolution is unusually rapid and progresses by leaps and bounds, there is still a certain continuity in it in the sense that every new system appears in consequence of a modification, differentiation or integration of some system or systems that are already in being. On the other hand, at every repeated construction a particular system is really somewhat different from what it was at any preceding construction, for it is being constructed in somewhat new circumstances; and whatever efforts may be made to maintain it such as it was by adapting the circumstances to it, some reciprocal adaptation of it to the circumstances is indispensable. Such adaptations may be very slight; and if there is no definite trend in the changes of the circumstances, they may be ignored. Thus, a religious rite, a social custom, a process of technical production is in effect slightly different at every actualization; but their variations are not significant as long as they do not affect subsequent actualizations.

But sometimes such slight variations agglomerate, and after a time we find that the rite, the custom and the technical process have changed as deeply as if they had been suddenly modified by some important innovation. Is it still the same rite or custom, or a new one? And if the latter, when did the old one disappear and the new one emerge? The criterion of similarity is even more difficult to apply when it comes to determining the identity of systems which coexist in extension. Take two factories: their composition and structure may be so similar as to be almost indistinguishable at first glance, and yet they are obviously separate systems, though belonging to one class. But the technical method which was invented and patented years ago and now makes possible the functioning of these factories is "the same" identical system in both cases, not two similar systems, as is best proved by the fact that it is protected by one patent only. A marriage ceremony as used in a certain country is manifestly one identical system in all its actualizations; but one of the conjugal relations that start with the performance of this ceremony is a separate relation. Why is this so?

The only key to the solution of all these difficulties is the humanistic coefficient. The construction of a cultural system is mere reproduction of a system already in existence when it is intended to be such by the agent and taken to be such by other participants, even if the copy is very different from the original; it is the creation of a new system when it is intended to be such and taken as such, even if the new system is exactly similar to another already existing. A musical performance which is meant to reproduce a certain composition is still the actualization of this composition, however dissimilar from the composer's performance; whereas a plagiarism is a separate work, however similar to the plagiarized original. A rite, a custom, even a personal "habit" remains identical as long as the agent intends to uphold it as the same, though it may change greatly in composition and structure; whereas at other times even a slight deviation from a custom may constitute a break of the custom, if it is intended to break it and judged to be a break by the community. A state after a revolution is still the same state, however changed, if its authorities and citizens treat it as such; it is not the same if they repudiate its identity—compare Germany and Russia. The marriage ceremony is the same at all weddings, because the married couples and their families want to have the same traditional ceremony sanctiond by the church or some other group; whereas the conjugal relation is a different system in each case, because each married couple considers itself unique. Similarly, whether a work of art does or does not belong to a certain style, whether a monograph is or is not part of a scientific theory, can be decided only when we know what was the intention of the artist or the scientist in this respect at the time he was producing that particular system, and how the latter is regarded by other artists, connoisseurs, scientists or critics.

The humanistic coefficient is not an infallible criterion, nor is it always easy to apply. There are often conflicts between the intentions and experiences of different agents cooperating in a cultural system: thus, an artist may view his work as belonging to a certain style, whereas his critics may deny it, or *vice versa*. Often also the agent, individual or group, may be mistaken about his own intentions when reflecting about them. But these are problems of scientific technique to which we shall return later on, and they do not affect the fundamental principles expressed in the humanistic coefficient.

THE DATA OF SOCIOLOGY

1934

1. Sociology as Theory of "Societies" or of "Communities"

SOCIOLOGY, from the time it consciously began to be constituted as a separate theoretic discipline, distinct from political science, took a peculiar position with regard to the choice and determination of its object-matter, which persisted up to the end of the nineteenth century and partly survives even yet among sociologists of a naturalistic bent. While the particular data in which it was primarily interested belong to the domain of culture, it conceived them as components of natural systems. This conception, already outlined in the seventeenth century, became fully developed in the middle of the nineteenth with Comte, Spencer and their followers. Sociology was meant to study "societies." A "society" was conceived as essentially a natural closed system of bio-psychological human individuals. There were other more or less similar systems in nature: aggregations of unicellular organisms, multicellular organisms with differentiated organs and functions, associations of multicellular organisms—homogeneous, like herds and flocks of animals, and heterogeneous, like plant communities. As every sociologist knows, the seeming analogy indicated by Comte between a "society" and a multicellular differentiated organism has been widely exploited by Spencer, Schäffle, Lilienfeld, Worms, Novicov, and many others.

Chapter 3 of *The Method of Sociology* (New York: Farrar & Rinehart, 1934), pp. 90–136. Reprinted by permission of Eileen Markley Znaniecki.

Three principles were used, in various proportions and combinations, to circumscribe this natural system. First, a "society" had to occupy more or less exclusively a geographical territory; secondly, it was expected to possess a certain degree of racial homogeneity. These two were purely naturalistic principles: geographic isolation and racial composition of a human "society" could be ascertained by the same methods of external observation as the isolation and composition of a plant or a colony of polyps.

But the third principle made a breach in the consistency of the naturalistic standpoint through which an enormous mass of cultural data was introduced into this system. A collectivity of human beings of a certain racial stock (pure or mixed) inhabiting a certain territory constituted a "society" only if they belonged as members to a social group—horde, family, tribe, gens, village, city, state—or at least to a conglomeration of interconnected groups. Now, whatever might be said of "animal societies," human groups are cultural products; membership in a group, and even the mere existence of a social group, however rudimentary its organization, cannot be ascertained without the use of the humanistic coefficient. The gens, the tribe, the state, even the family and the horde have their being only in the experience and activity of their members, who have constructed them and now maintain them.

Sociology did not deny it. On the contrary, its intention was to study not only social groups as cultural products of the human beings included in a collectivity, but all the cultural systems existing within the sphere of experience and activity of these beings, made and maintained by them. "Society" in the sense of Comte included the entire cultural life of the men belonging to it: language, art, religion, philosophy, science, technique, economic organization. Rooted in nature by their bodies, men were immersed in culture by their consciousness. And the culture of a society was common to its members; society, a mere collectivity of individuals from the natural point of view, was on its cultural side a superindividual entity, a *community* unified by sharing the same culture. All the cultural systems studied separately by special sciences were most closely intertwined in the cultural life of a "society," [and] formed, in fact, a static and dynamic unity.

The successors of Comte preserved these essential presuppositions with but slight variation. Some ascribed more, others less importance to psychic as against material factors in the formation and existence of societies; some acceded to Comte's idea that the individual as a conscious being was entirely a part of society, and had no conscious life apart from what he shared with his society by sharing its culture; whereas others treated him as a psychological entity secondarily connected with "society" by communication and cooperation. Among the particular kinds of data constituting the culture of a "society," some were thought more, others less fundamental. While Comte had given predominance to intellectual factors, most sociologists emphasized, as St. Simon had already done, the importance of economic or technical phenomena; some, influenced partly by older doctrines, partly by the philosophy of Hegel, saw in the state system the supreme and determining phenomenon of "society."

It is not our intention to subject this sociological conception to systematic criticism at this point, for it has been already judged by history. It has failed to produce a single valid and generally accepted scientific generalization concerning "societies": not one law which could be applied to the explanation and conditional prediction of the changes of "societies": no consistent classification of "societies," not even a general description of any particular class of "societies" which could be guaranteed to take into account all the essential characters common to that class and to no other. We do not mean, indeed, that sociologists working on this theory have not achieved any true, important, and exact scientific results. On the contrary, we believe that their works are greatly undervalued by the present generation of sociologists and that much useful knowledge is contained in them. But none of this knowledge concerns their main object-matter, "society": it bears upon what their authors thought minor matters, such as the structural characters and changes of specific groups or institutions, or particular socio-psychological processes.

The whole theory centered around the most striking fallacy. It identified two radically different and incommensurable concepts: "society" as a natural system of which the elements are individual animals of the species *Homo Sapiens,* and "society" as a combination of systems of which the elements are cultural values, like language, religion, technique, economic and political organizations, etc. That this obvious logical discrepancy did not attract the notice of those otherwise deep thinkers who created the great socio-philosophical "systems" of the past must be ascribed probably to the monistic current which prevailed in the scientific philosophy of the last century and carried these thinkers along.

But though the fundamental error was not discovered at once nor made explicit, even after it produced the usual result of scientific unproductivity, nevertheless the very progress of positive inductive research in neighboring fields has gradually corrected it by simply depriving that type of sociology of nearly all of what it conceived to be its proper object-matter, and dividing it—at least, as much of it as could be scientifically treated—among other disciplines.

On the one hand, indeed, all the positive and soluble problems bearing upon the natural aspect of human collectivities have been during the last sixty or seventy years appropriated by purely natural sciences, viz. human geography and physical anthropology, which are much better equipped than sociology for dealing with them efficiently. The sparation of their fields from that of sociology is perhaps still imperfectly achieved because some geographers and somatic anthropologists show a tendency to "explain" cultural phenomena, while many sociologists are interested in geographic and racial questions. Yet, if we compare in this respect Gobineau with Ripley, or Demolins with Brunhes, we may confidently look forward to the time when the line of demarcation between anthropology and anthropo-geography on the one hand, and sociology and other sciences of culture on the other hand, will be drawn clearly and unmistakably.

Of course, there are innumerable vital problems concerning the relationship between natural and cultural systems, and these must be treated notwithstanding the division of the respective sciences. But it does not follow by any means that, as some defenders of the old conception of sociology as an intermediary between natural and cultural sciences wish to conclude, these problems should, or even could, be the special privilege of one scientific discipline.[1] Far from it. These problems are so multiple and varied that it is absolutely impossible to reduce them to a common denominator. Every particular science handles different ones in the course of its research, and must deal with them on its own ground and with its own methods. The anthropo-geographic problems of mutual relationship between certain natural conditions and the formation of large cities are different and require different methods from those faced by a student of technology when, in investigating the development of a certain type of pottery, he tries to determine how much and in what way this devlopment is dependent upon the geographical distribution of potter's clay. No general science of the connection between nature and culture could solve the problems which beset the linguist when investigating changes of pronunciation, the anthropologist studying the connection between racial mixtures, marriage and the caste system, and the religionist trying to determine what, if any, mutual dependence there is between certain forms of mysticism and certain physiological processes induced by the massing of numerous human bodies in closed buildings.

Thus, while the investigation of the natural aspect of human collectivities is gradually but completely passing from the hands of sociologists into the better qualified ones of geographers and anthropologists, a parallel process has lately been affecting the other, cultural side, of the nineteenth century "societies." The self-imposed task of sociology with regard to cultural communities has proved beyond its powers and, indeed, beyond the powers of any science. For it meant nothing less than the comparative study of cultural communities, viewed in the total wealth and complexity of their civilizations, using the results of the historical and ethnographical studies which have been trying to describe in all relevant details the civilizations of particular communities, their techniques, their prevalent social and economic systems, their religion, language, literature, science, art and play. Sociology, from Comte on,

[1]   This thesis is, I believe, the weakest part of the otherwise very valuable work of Sorokin, *Contemporary Sociological Theories*, New York, 1928.

has attempted to draw generalizations concerning all cultural communities, or at least all those belonging to a certain type.

Here again the actual development of scientific research has dealt a death-blow to such an undertaking, both by showing the impossibility of realizing it, and by substituting instead a different task, which is being fulfilled by a number of special sciences. In ethnography and the history of culture, as long as sweeping synthetic statements of a half-literary type concerning the civilization of particular peoples and nations prevailed over patient, thorough and critical descriptions of facts, comparative generalizations seemed not only possible, but easy. This was particularly true with regard to "primitive societies," whose civilizations appeared very simple in the light of the older ethnographical works (which, by the way, had still lower standards of thoroughness than those already developed at that time in history). But the more actual knowledge of concrete cultural communities increased in wealth and exactness, the more difficult it proved to organize into a synthetic rational picture everything known about the civilization of any particular community, however apparently simple, and the more doubtful appeared most of the similarities on which sociologists (chiefly those of the evolutionary school) used to rely. The conclusion is inevitable that the total cultural life of any human community is much too rich and chaotic, contains too many heterogeneous cultural systems influencing one another in the most various and incalculable ways and is too ceaselessly and unexpectedly changing, to make valid scientific synthesis ever possible—which obviously precludes any comparative science of cultural communities.

There have been, indeed, some relatively limited and relatively stable combinations of various cultural systems recently discovered in the course of historical, prehistorical, and particularly ethnological research. These are the "cultural complexes" of the now predominant school of ethnology. Such a cultural complex does, indeed, contain definite technical, social, religious, aesthetic, economic systems interrelated in such a way as to make them usually appear together in the cultural life of human communities. But such a cultural complex is not coextensive with the civilization of any community, for every civilization we know contains several cultural complexes overlapping; and the ways they overlap, mix and influence one another are again most varied and incalculable. Moreover, there is no rational necessity, no static laws binding the various systems of a cultural complex together, connecting e.g. a particular religious system with a certain technical system. Nor is there any causal necessity, any universal dynamic law determining the origin and development of complexes and their expansion over certain cultural areas. The existence of any particular cultural complex and its acceptance, complete or partial, by certain cultural communities are simply historical facts which happened once and will never happen again. This is the main reason why modern ethnology is historical as opposed to the earlier evolutionary ethnology, which assumed that the various cultural systems coexisting in a human community were necessarily dependent on one another, and that there were universal laws ruling everywhere the passage from one type of civilization to another. Historical ethnology has thus taken whatever wind there was out of the sails of sociology as a general theory of cultural communities—and it proved to be a weak breeze, merely allowing a careful sailing along the shore of historical facts, not a trade wind capable of driving the vessel of cultural science across the wide ocean of universal determinism.

There are still, however, attempts to revive this conception of sociology as a science of cultural communities. The chief argument in its favor is drawn from the obvious fact that the total cultural life of a community—a tribe, a nation, even a village, or a town—even though it does not constitute a higher kind of organic unity as the old sociologists believed, still is more than a mere sum of heterogeneous data, since its technique, economics, political organization, mores, religion, science, art, literature are closely intertwined and exercise a mutual influence. If there are special cultural sciences, each separately dealing with one of these domains of culture apart from its connection with all the other domains in the cultural life of human communities, should there not be a science investigating their inter-relationships? Its task may be difficult, but perhaps its failure heretofore is merely due to the application of wrong methods of research.

But while the premises of this argument are perfectly true, the conclusion is wrong. The mere fact of mutual influence exercised by the various cultural systems upon one another is not enough to justify the existence of a distinct science studying this influence, for this task is already being performed by the several special sciences. All the technical, political, religious, scientific influences to which, say, economic systems are subjected in cultural communities must be investigated by the economists; the religionist has to take into account the modifications which a religion undergoes in consequence of economic, political and scientific processes going on in its cultural milieu, and so on. Something may, indeed, be left over after the various cultural systems composing the civilization of a human community have been taken into account. The people who share a certain set of interconnected systems (and among these systems there are usually also certain social groups—territorial, genetic or telic) may be more or less conscious of this fact, and more or less willing to influence one another for the benefit of their common civilization and to influence this civilization for their mutual benefit. This consciousness and willingness, in so far as they exist, constitute a social bond uniting these people over and above any formal social bonds which are due to the existence of regulated social relations and organized social groups. The reality of this bond is manifested in such familiar phenomena as public opinion, collective control of personalities and groups by their social milieu, development of new cultural ideals and attempts at their realization apart from organized group action. If the term "community" is limited to the humanistic reality embracing these phenomena, there is no doubt but that a "community" in this sense can be scientifically studied, and that sociology is the science to study it as one of the specifically social data. It is a matter for discussion whether such a community is a social group or not, whether it is identical with the "public," whether it should be connected—as MacIver is doing—with territorial groups and nations.

Of one thing we may be sure, however, and that is that new efforts will be made continually to revive the old synthetic conception of sociology, for a powerful intellectual and moral interest is here in play. Every thinking man wishes to obtain some understanding of the totality of the civilization to which he belongs, compare it with other civilizations, interpret their history, discover if possible some guiding lines in the apparent chaos of the whole historical evolution of mankind. These interests are as undying and as justifiable in their way as the old metaphysical interest in interpreting the world of nature as some kind of ordered and rational whole. And there is an old and well-established discipline which satisfies them: it is the *philosophy of history*. We do not mean to deny its rights nor to belittle its importance. All we object to is having sociology, which aims to be a positive inductive science, exact and objective, so far misunderstand its possibilities and impossibilities as to undertake practically the same task. It was in part sociology's own fault that Paul Barth twenty years ago was able to republish the second edition of his voluminous work trying to demonstrate with much first-hand evidence that sociology, such as it had heretofore been, was the same as philosophy of history.[2] Of course, this view was one-sided and behind the times, for it failed to realize the significance of the new movements expressed chiefly in monographic research; but it may be considered symptomatic of the persistence of traditional ideals.

2. Sociology as a General Theory of Cultural Data

The tendency to become a science of culture in general, as against the special sciences like economics, linguistics and theory of religion, has expressed itself in still another sociological current, of a more recent origin. This current started in the two schools of Tarde and Durkheim which, with all their well-known opposition, have yet much in common, and it has since spread very widely, sometimes moving with the older current, sometimes resulting in important new variations. The common theoretic purpose of both Tarde and Durkheim,[3] their followers and associates, was not to reach a general theory of "societies" (although the concept of

[2]   *Philosophie der Geschichte als Soziologie*, Vol. I, Leipzig, 1914.
[3]   The latter's first work on the *Division of Labor in Society* partly excepted.

"society" remained as a general heuristic foundation of research, particularly with Durkheim), but rather a general theory of *cultural phenomena viewed as social phenomena*. The idea that every cultural phenomenon—technical, economic, religious, intellectual, linguistic—is essentially social, was founded in Tarde's view on the fact that its historical existence as something common to many people appeared due to interaction between human individuals, whose various forms Tarde summed up in his leading concept of "imitation," supplemented by that of "opposition." For Durkheim, however, the social character of the same cultural phenomena resulted from their being accepted by social groups as their values, and imposed upon the individual by the group to which he belongs. Under either assumption, sociology became the science which, by studying this common social foundation of all cultural phenomena, became the fundamental science of all culture,[4] of which other special sciences were meant to be variations or even mere subdivisions.

But, however interesting and even apparently convincing this conception of cultural phenomena as social phenomena might have been, the striking fact is that during the fifty years or thereabouts which have gone by since the first promulgation of the works of Tarde and of Durkheim, sociologists alone have become aware of the need of basing scientific research in the various fields of culture upon sociology, with the exception of the few, very few, religionists, economists and linguists who have become converted Durkheimians. This suggests either that all students of culture have been and still remain incomprehensibly blind to the logical relationship between their science and sociology; or else that, whatever sociology has to say to them, though by no means irrelevant—there are few specialists nowadays who entirely ignore sociological problems—is nevertheless not absolutely essential to the

---

4   A similar rôle was ascribed somewhat later by Wilhelm Wundt to his "Völkerpsychologie." The latter, however, excluded those cultural systems which were primarily the products of individual activity and clearly manifested an objective, intrinsic order relatively independent of social influences—like science, philosophy, technical invention and literature.

pursuit of their proper studies. The first solution of the puzzle is unthinkable, particularly since during these fifty years great progress has been made in most of the special sciences of culture, not under the leadership of sociology and often without much assistance from it. Thus, we must presume that the second solution is the true one.

And, indeed, if we do take into account a cultural system like a factory, a bank, a work of literature, a system of religious dogmas and rites, a physical or mathematical theory, even though it is obvious that individual interaction, as emphasized by Tarde, was indispensable for its construction and remains indispensable for its maintenance; and even though it is usually accepted (as the school of Durkheim insists) by some group which sanctions its existence and in a sense vouches for its validity: nevertheless the system as such is *non-social* in its composition and structure in the sense that the individuals who work to construct it and maintain it are not its elements, nor is the group which supports it its structural basis. The factory, the bank, the religion, the work of literature, or the physical theory may remain exactly the same after all the individuals who participated in its maintenance leave or die and give place to others. The factory as a technical system does not necessarily change in its composition or structure by passing, say, from the control of a group of private capitalists to that of the state, nor a religion after a new nation has been converted to it, nor a physical theory in consequence of its being finally recognized in scientific circles, after having been for a while violently combated. There are cases, of course, when after such a change of participating individuals or supporting groups modifications of the system do follow, but these are directly due to the introduction of new technical instruments or processes, new religious dogmas or myths, new scientific concepts, for which the new men were perhaps responsible, but which might also have occurred while the system was still maintained by its former supporters.

This relative independence of the composition and structure of cultural systems from their social background makes a type of investigation possible which ignores this background entirely, and such is the type that predominates in all special sciences of culture. A language may be and often is studied without any other knowledge of the people who use it than that they do speak it and understand it. A factory can be described exclusively in terms of materials, machines, methods, products, with no mention of the social life of the men who run it except that these men furnish the active forces needed to do so. A physical theory can be fully understood even if nothing is known about the personal life of the scientist who created it, his social relationship with his original opponents, or the organization of the scientific societies or congresses where it was finally approved.

When we do try to explain either the origins of a system or its later modifications, we must indeed take social factors into consideration even as other kinds of factors, natural or cultural. But it does not follow from the fact that social factors contributed to the composition and structure of Islam, of Shakespeare's *Hamlet*, of the Ford automobile factory, or of Einstein's theory that these systems are social, any more than the indubitable influence of geographic conditions in shaping the ritual of Islam makes it a geographic system, or the fact that money is needed for physical experiments makes them financial undertakings.

Now, while we doubt all possibility of a positive science of natural "societies" or cultural communities, we are far from denying that a general positive science of cultural phenomena—or, more exactly, of cultural systems—is possible. There are even, we believe, particularly in older philosophic literature, certain germs of it which can be developed into a science. If such a general theory of culture is founded, then indeed all the special sciences will be dependent upon it, just as nowadays botany and zoology are branches of general biology. But it can be founded only by a slow process of induction in which the specific structural characters and changes of the systems constituting each particular domain of culture—technics, religion, art, economics—are investigated and compared with those of other domains. It is a tremendous task needing the cooperation of many specialists perfectly acquainted with their respective domains and at the same time able to rise above the limitations of their specialties.

3. Sociology as a Special Science

Having rejected the two main older conceptions according to which sociology should deal with all culture, either as a science of cultural "societies" or as a science of cultural phenomena in general—or rather, having simply accepted the unmistakable verdict the history of science has passed upon these conceptions—it still remains to show what the standards are that sociological research must apply in selecting its own data from the unlimited wealth and complexity of the empirical world. As a matter of fact, these standards need not be created. They are already implied in the successful, first-hand, positive investigation which has been carried on during the last forty or fifty years and whose results are embodied in thousands of monographs and systematic works. Most of this investigation bears the name of sociology in America, whereas in other countries, though the content is similar, it is often differently called; but the names are a minor matter. The essential point is that these investigations bear only on a certain portion of the material the older sociological schools claim as their own; but this is a portion which even in those older schools was the object of particular interest and—what is more important—this material is not dealt with at all or only inefficiently by the established special sciences of culture, with one or two exceptions which will be pointed out later.

Attempts have already been made to formulate explicitly these implicit standards of selection of sociological data under the same assumption as ours, viz., that sociology is a special cultural science with an empirical field of its own; and if we try to improve on them by giving our own definition it is only because most of them seem still somewhat influenced by the older schools. This refers particularly to the conception of Simmel, according to whom all cultural phenomena have a social "form," though their "content" is not social but religious, economic, linguistic. This conception, though it has had great influence on the present German methodology (see Vierkandt) is misleading. For this "social form" of cultural phenomena does not manifest itself either in the composition or in the structure of cultural systems. At the same time, as Simmel and others have shown, it is something which can be empirically ascertained and studied apart from the systems of which it is supposed to be the "form." Therefore, it is obviously not a mere "form," but a specific class of empirical data accompanying various cultural systems in much the same way as theoretic reflection accompanies most of them in higher civilizations and religious beliefs and practices in earlier stages of culture. The actual object-matter of the sociological research of Simmel was thus different from what he believed it to be.[5]

In comparing the specific data which have in fact been already appropriated by sociology to the complete or partial exclusion of other special sciences, we find that they easily fall into four main subdivisions.

4. The Theory of Social Actions

The first of these subdivisions is not only distinctly separated from various other kinds of cultural data—economic, religious, aesthetic, etc.—but investigations bearing upon it have already been in large measure systematized and constitute a particular discipline. We mean the so-called "social psychology" or, more exactly, that type of social psychology which has been officially initiated by McDougall, carried on by W. I. Thomas, Ross, Ellwood, Stoltenberg, Bogardus, Kimball Young; while others like Palante, and recently Vierkandt, treat it as an integral part of sociology. The data which furnish the material of this science can be briefly and provisionally described as actions bearing upon men as their objects and intending to provoke definite reactions on their part. They are *social actions,* clearly different from other actions which bear not upon men but upon material things, economic values, sacred objects and mystical powers, objects of aesthetic appreciation, linguistic symbols or scientific theories, and which intend to produce not human reactions but technical, economic, religious, artistic, literary, scientific results.

This difference, of course, does not prevent social actions from being often performed in a merely auxiliary function, as when

[5]   Cf. Theodore Abel, *Systematic Sociology in Germany*. New York, 1929.

men fight for economic purposes or induce others to assist them in a technical work. Equally frequent is the opposite connection, when non-social actions are subsidiary to social ones: thus technical production may serve the purposes of a war of revenge; a man may gather wealth not for economic reasons but to obtain recognition from his neighbors; or a woman may go on the stage not for the sake of art but merely to gain fame. Similar relations exist, of course, between other kinds of actions.

We are not concerned at this moment with the heuristic concepts and methods used to study social actions; their popular reduction to psychological dispositions and processes ("instincts," "wishes," "responses," etc.) is a later problem. The fact is that they are being studied separately and more or less successfully, though improvements of method are always desirable and possible. But we must mention that under the name "social psychology," in addition to the one here mentioned, several other disciplines appear, whose data are not social actions but something entirely different. Thus, the studies of mob behavior made toward the end of the last century by Sighele, Le Bon and others gave rise to the idea that all collective actions, whatever their object and intention, are essentially different from individual actions; and "social psychology," in the sense of a psychology of collective or group behavior in general, became opposed to "individual psychology," as a psychology of individual behavior in general.

There is an obvious and fundamental, though not always clearly realized, conflict between this conception and the one advanced above, for instead of defining the actions by their objective aspect, their objects, results and methods, it defines them by their subjective source—the nature of the agent. Now, undoubtedly most actions performed collectively do differ from most actions performed individually, but not so much by their intrinsic character as by the fact that they are usually accompanied by social actions in the sense defined above. While a number of individuals perform a public prayer together, lynch a criminal, or produce nails in a factory, there are facts of social interaction going on between many of them individually, and between some of them—leaders and their opponents—and the whole mass.

But apart from these facts, which can be isolated and studied as social actions and reactions, there is obviously very little that the three collective actions here instanced have in common. Praying collectively in a church is a religious action and differs less from praying individually in a chapel than it does from producing nails collectively in a factory. The latter is a technical performance and is more akin to the performance of the blacksmith who makes nails alone in his forge than to lynching, which again is a social action distinguished only by secondary characters from the behavior of one or two individuals who take justice into their own hands and kill a man they judge worthy of death.

Instead, therefore, of treating these collective actions indiscriminately as data of the same science, whether it be called "social psychology," "collective psychology," "group psychology" or something else, thus putting them in a different category from the individual actions most like them, it is much more useful scientifically to study both collective and individual prayers as data of the theory of religion, both collective and individual production of nails as data of the theory of technics, both collective and individual killing of criminals without due process of law as data of sociology. To the latter also may be left the investigation of those specifically social processes which may and usually do accompany the collective performance not only of social, but also of religious and technical actions.

The third conception of social psychology, radically diverging from both those we have discussed, is the one of Floyd Allport, Krueger, Reckless and others, in whose opinion the proper field of this science is, generally speaking, the bio-psychological human individual in so far as determined by the influence of the social milieu. We shall return to this matter presently when discussing the sociology of the personality. Obviously, however, a study of human individuals is a very different task from a study of social actions as defined above.

Finally, there is a fourth conception promulgated by Kantor,[6] who wishes "social psychology" to investigate individual "re-

6   *An Outline of Social Psychology*, Chicago, 1929.

sponses" to all kinds of cultural "stimuli" as distinct from responses to natural stimuli in which experimental psychology has been chiefly interested up to now. Social psychology in this sense becomes a naturalistic theory of cultural conduct, a part of the general psychological theory of the behavior of human individuals as bio-psychological entities.

This multiplicity of meanings which the term "social psychology" has acquired is an argument for the sociologist in favor of resigning it altogether and instead speaking simply of a "theory of social actions" as a branch of sociology. Though only lately circumscribed and systematized, this is the oldest branch of our science and indeed one of the oldest parts of human knowledge. Even putting aside the numerous generalizations scattered through the epic and dramatic literature of all ages and nations, we can trace its beginnings through philosophers and essayists like Nietzsche, Schopenhauer, Hume, Schaftesbury, La Rochefoucauld, Descartes, Montaigne, St. Thomas, Machiavelli, Theophrastus, Aristotle, as far back as the primitive reflection embodied in popular proverbs.

5. The Theory of Social Relations

More recent are the origins of the second branch of sociology, whose nucleus is a comparative theory of moral rules, i.e., norms regulating social actions. While every thinking observer has a great variety of social actions given to him for comparison in his own social milieu, he must usually go to other societies to find rules different from those he finds recognized by his own society. And even then it is difficult to reach the purely objective point of view of theoretic reflection, since he is used to regard the morality in which he has been brought up as the only valid morality, a standard by which to judge other moralities rather than a datum to be compared with them. Sociological theories of morality had to be preceded by ethnographic descriptions, from which only about the seventeenth century (if we except the first inklings scattered in the *Essays* of Montaigne) comparative ethnological generalizations began to emerge. And in these, up to the last quarter of the nineteenth century, the moral rules prevailing among various peoples are indiscriminately mixed up with all other cultural data composing the civilizations of these peoples. Even as late as 1906, in Sumner's *Folkways* we still find under the same denomination norms regulating the behavior of people with regard to other people, a number of purely technical, economic, religious rules, even principles of theoretic thought and aesthetic valuation.

Nevertheless, with the growing mass of ethnological material, specialization became imperative for monographic research. Norms regulating sexual life were the first to be studied separately, and have an enormous literature. Spencer's *Ceremonial Institutions* gives the first comparative outline of certain rules concerning the relations between the superior and the inferior. Of the latter, relations between masters and servants in their various historical forms have become the object-matter of the widest interest, owing to the growing social importance of the labor problem. The emphasis which social groups put upon particular rules of conduct was brought to light in studies concerning the treatment of offenders, of which the classical instance is Steinmetz' *Ethnologische Studien zur ersten Entwicklung der Strafe* (Leiden-Leipzig, 1894). Norms of solidarity between members of primary groups, particularly the various mutual obligations involved in kinship, have been investigated by many students of these groups, beginning with Morgan. Rules of peace and war between groups—since Grotius a matter of deep practical concern for students of politics—began to be investigated comparatively under the influence of those who, like Gumplowicz, applied to human groups the Darwinian conception of the struggle for existence.

The impulse toward separating this whole field and systematizing it has come, however, not from purely scientific interest, but from a philosophic opposition to traditional ethics. In order to show the vanity of all efforts to found rationally an absolute and universal morality, the varieties and contradictions of moral rules actually recognized at various times and in various societies had to be systematically described and if possible explained as products of "natural," i.e., empirical and causally determined evolution: an "ethology" became opposed to "ethics."[7] The most comprehensive synthetic work in this line was and still is Westermarck's *Origin and Development of the Moral Ideas*, a very conscientious, though methodically imperfect contribution. Hobhouse's *Morals in Evolution* is more systematic, but too much imbued with the philosophy of the evolutionary school.

In selecting the data for this branch of sociology, we must keep in mind the distinctive character of moral rules as compared with all other rules: religious, economic, technical, intellectual, aesthetic. A moral rule, in the eyes of the subject—individual or collectivity—who recognizes it as valid and tries to act in accordance with it, appears as a duty which binds this subject with regard to some other individual or collectivity and which the latter expects him to fulfil. Now, there is always some other duty (similar or different) which this other individual or collectivity recognizes (or is at least expected to recognize) with regard to the subject, by which it feels bound and which the subject expects it to fulfil. In other words, social duties are always reciprocated by other social duties. If there are moral norms actually regulating the behavior of a woman to a man, a servant to a master, a subject to a king, a group member to his group, a church to a state, there are other norms with which, in his own consciousness and in that of the other party, the man has to comply in his conduct to the woman, the master to the servant, the king to the subject, the group to the member, the state to the church. The duties may be very different, their actual recognition and fulfilment unequal, but in principle there are no one-sided social duties. Every norm recognized by a social agent as his duty toward somebody else is a component of a social system in which this agent and the object of his duty are bound together as partners. We call such a system a *social relation*,

[7]   For the exposition of this problem see Simmel, *Einleitung in die Wissenschaft*, Berlin, 1898, and Lévy-Bruhl, *La Morale et la science des mœurs*, Paris, Alcan.

and this whole branch of sociology dealing with moral data might be termed the *theory of social relations.*[8]

Other names have been suggested for that part of sociology which we are here discussing; *ethology* would be rather good, if the similarity of spelling to "ethnology" were not liable to produce misunderstandings. An apparent disadvantage of the use of our term is the existence of certain social norms which are recognized and followed by human agents with regard to everybody, not only to partners in social relations. But, as will be seen elsewhere, such norms are parts of personal or group ideals and presuppose another, higher level of organized social life than that which students of mores have usually investigated.

Although this field is indisputably sociology's own and no other science competes for it—ethics' interest being not theoretic, but normative—there has recently been much discussion as to the large domain which borders on the field of moral facts: the domain of law. While in earlier societies there is no difference between law and morality, their distinctness is very apparent in every civilized society. At the same time it is obvious that in a large measure they do coincide: many legal forms formulate duties actually recognized by people in their dealings with other people in their own society, and thus constitute a ready material for sociological study of social relations. Now, there is a "science of law," much older than sociology and very firmly established, and some of its prominent representatives have shown a marked disinclination to having sociologists meddle with the data they consider their exclusive property.

There is, we believe, no need for any contentions or misunderstandings here, as far as the study of positive law is concerned. The student of morality is not interested in legal ordinances and statutes as rules imposed by the state upon its members. As long as he limits himself to social relations, legal rules are to him merely more or

[8]   Many sociologists have given the term "social relation" a much wider extension; but the meaning in which it is used here is more in accordance with its established use in popular literature, from which we see no reason for departing. The matter will be discussed elsewhere.

less adequate expressions of the duties actually recognized by the people of the given society in dealing with each other, eventually as factors influencing these duties. For instance, in studying the type of conjugal relations prevailing among the people who inhabit a certain country, he will assume provisionally that some—though not all—of the essential characters of these relations are expressed in the marriage laws. If he has other sources of information, he will try to test this assumption and find out whether there are any disagreements between the marriage laws and the data of "moral conscience" of married couples and their social milieu, since it is this "moral conscience," and not the law which is the real object of his interest. If he investigates the changes which take place in conjugal relations within a certain community at a certain period, he must take into account marriage legislation as a possible factor of change, and try to follow up the effects it has had upon actual conjugal relations. Whereas the student of law, if he takes into account the connection between legal rules on the one hand, the "moral conscience" and the actual conduct of the people to whom these rules apply, on the other hand, is interested in it only from the point of view of the efficiency of these rules; law, not human conduct, is the primary object of his theoretic research.[9]

The divergence of standpoint is, of course, even more marked with those philosophic schools of jurisprudence whose primary interest, like that of ethics, is standardization and normative regulation. They are not concerned with the connection between law and human conduct as it really is; but, taking the efficiency of the law in controlling human conduct for granted, they try to determine what law is the best law for the promotion of human happiness, human progress, the welfare of the state, or whatever supreme standard of legislation they may accept. Of course, there is no

---

9   This distinction is, of course, difficult to establish wherever data on human conduct are lacking and legal rules are the only source both for theory of law and for theory of mores. But this simply means that the student of mores must try to supplement such sources by looking for instances of actual behavior, whereas the task of the student of law is to connect legal rules with the structure of the state which gives them its sanction.

possible conflict between this kind of legal doctrine and the sociological study of social relations, for there is no ground on which they can meet.

6. *The Theory of Social Persons*

The third branch of specifically sociological research is not yet circumscribed as distinctly as the preceding two, and its systematization is barely beginning. It deals, generally speaking, with the social aspect of the human personality as determined both by his social milieu and by his own activity. Every individual plays certain "social rôles," occupies certain positions and performs certain functions in his social environment, each involving definite rights and obligations, which in most cases are attached to similar positions and functions, and thus remain independent of him, although the way in which he actually realizes them and performs the social function corresponding to each position depends entirely upon himself.

Systematic theoretic investigation of social positions and functions was really started by Spencer in his "Professional Institutions"; certain parts of his "Political," "Ecclesiastical," "Industrial," and even "Domestic Institutions" have also a bearing upon this problem. Before him there were indeed many monographic studies made by historians and ethnographers of particular positions at certain periods and in certain societies, but few attempts at theoretic generalization. Most of the early generalizing reflection in this field is to be found in works of a practical, normative character outlining ideal requirements for various social positions and functions (kings, statesmen, judges, priests, warriors, philosophers, matrons, virgins), or else in criticism of the actual behavior of people functioning in certain positions.

The systematic attempt of Spencer has never been followed up; there is no general theory of social positions and functions. But since his time, monographic studies have been made in this field, such as the numerous comparative investigations concerning the shaman, or medicineman, and primitive chieftainship, the still more numerous studies on the social position of women, Frazer's famous theory of the king and the priest, Czarnowski's work on the hero, Sombart's on the bourgeois, Simmel's on the stranger and the poor. Recently much attention has been given to the position and functions of leaders, particularly political and economic leaders.

Since the individual is prepared for his social rôles in the process of education, which is specifically social in the strictest sense of the term, sociology has had to undertake the study of this process. However, the existence of an old and established discipline —the so-called educational theory or pedagogics, with its essentially practical trend—was a serious obstacle to the development of a purely theoretic and disinterested, comparative investigation of the facts of education as social data. Durkheim in his articles published posthumously under the title "Education et sociologie" outlined a program of such an investigation. Various historical studies of education and monographs on education among particular peoples have paved the way; but not until recently has the problem been taken in its fully sociological bearing. Krieck's *Menschenformung* and Lochner's *Descriptive Pädagogik* are the earliest comparative treatments of this problem; the present author's *Sociology of Education* (in Polish) is the first attempt at a complete sociological theory of educational facts. In connection, however, with the rapidly growing tendency to utilize the results of sociology for practical educational purposes, embodied in the so-called "Educational Sociology," more and more monographic work of a sociological character is being done, particularly with reference to the school and the family as educational institutions.

The sociological problem of education is the intermediary link between the problem of the social position and function and that of the individual's own personality. And in studying the personality, separation of sociological from psychological and even biological questions seems very difficult. The earliest studies in this field bore primarily upon socially supernormal and subnormal personalities, i.e. those who gained positions of unusual social prominence or became social outcasts; and their social superiority or inferiority was conceived as being a result of their hereditary endowment. Galton's studies on *Hereditary Genius* and Lombroso's anthropological theory of the criminal are the best known instances to the point. The investigation of the relationship between the psycho-biological aspect of the individual and his social rôle, in which the latter is conceived as completely or partly a function of the former, has since become extended from uncommon to common human types. However varied may be the parts ascribed to heredity, early biological influences, education and social opportunity, respectively, this functional relationship remains the pivot of what has become an enormous and continually growing branch of research. Its growth has been, of course, tremendously stimulated by practical interests embodied in the great movements of eugenics and the physical and mental hygiene of the child.

In view of the fact that sociologists are interested in this problem as much as anybody else, I fear that they will not feel much sympathy for my conviction that the dependence of the individual's social rôle on his psycho-biological characteristics is a matter which belongs fully and exclusively in the fields of psychology and human biology, and outside the reach of sociology. If sociology wants, it may try to solve the converse, but in a sense complementary problem: the dependence of the individual's psycho-biological characteristics on his social rôle. For, in my opinion, the sociologist must take the human individual not as he "really is" organically and psychologically, but as he is made by others and by himself to appear in their experience and his own in the course of his social relationships. From the sociological point of view, the primary matter about an individual is his social position and function, and this is not a manifestation of his nature, but a cultural system he constructs with the help of his milieu, seldom creating, usually copying it from ready models. The individual's organic and psychological features are from this point of view merely the material out of which his purely social personality, as characterized by the positions he fills and the way he fills them, has been formed in the course of education and self-education. Taking from Jung, and Park and Burgess, the conception that the essential point about a "person" is the idea he and others have of his social rôle, and remembering that the "idea" is not a mere mental picture, but a practical system of rights and obligations, we may thus call this entire branch of sociology the *theory of social persons*.

7. *The Theory of Social Groups*

The fourth and most developed branch of sociology is the *theory of social groups*. A group, of course, is not a "society" in the old sense of the term: it is not an entity fully including a number of bio-psychological individuals and unifying them in a community of their total cultural life. It is simply one of the many cultural systems these individuals construct and maintain by their activities. There are, e.g., many thousands of various groups maintained by the inhabitants of a big city, from the municipal group in whose maintenance all of them participate, down to the small family groups kept up by only a few individuals each; and new groups are being constructed all the time. Every individual takes a more or less active part in maintaining a dozen or more various social groups of which he is a "member," i.e., in which he occupies certain positions involving definite rights and performs certain functions with definite obligations with regard to other members, to the group as a whole and to its functionaries. But his social life is not coextensive with his group life; on the contrary, the latter is merely a part of it, though a very important part. There are innumerable social actions he performs not as a member of any group, but simply as individual agent, like courting a woman, helping a passing stranger, breaking a municipal ordinance; there are a number of social relations to which he is a party and which have nothing to do with any of the groups he or the other party belongs to, like love, friendship, business partnership, subordination to an intellectual leader; there are social positions which do not necessarily involve the participation in any social groups, such as the professional positions of physician, painter, retail merchant, farmer. And, needless to say, the entire social life of an individual is only a part of his total cultural life: his technical, economic, intellectual, artistic, religious, hedonistic interests depend in some measure, which varies widely with different men, on social contacts for their satisfaction, but are not specifically social. All the individuals agglomerated in a large city, besides participating in innumerable social groups, participate also in innumerable economic enterprises, construct and keep running innumerable technical mechanisms, help maintain a number of religious systems by accepting their dogmas and performing their rites, give the support of their understanding and appreciaton to art, literature, science and philosophy. Often they form special groups or utilize existing groups for the purposes of more efficient economic, technical, religious, aesthetic, intellectual cooperation; but much, perhaps most of their common cultural activity, is going on outside of any group organization.

Social groups as specific cultural systems have been discovered by ethnologists and historians rather than by sociologists, who were absorbed by their attempts to build up a general theory of "society." Imperceptibly however, the sociologists' "society" began (in some schools at least) to shade off into the "group" or combination of groups; and theories like those of Gumplowicz and Ward may be considered typical of this period of transition. Nowadays, investigation of various types of groups is the common ground on which the ethnologist and the historian meet the sociologist and the political scientist.

In ethnology the need of separating the study of groups from the studies of other systems composing the total culture of lower communities arose out of the necessity of specialization. Already the ethnographer who describes a particular community must classify his material into separate divisions since, as we have seen, rational synthesis of a cultural community has proved impossible. The ethnologist bent on comparative studies must specialize to some degree at least in some field of culture. Four main divisions can be distinguished in modern ethnology: one deals with material culture (often subdivided into technique and art), another with religion and magic, a third with language, a fourth with "social organization." The latter term included what we call social relations and social persons (data on social positions and a few—very few—on education), but the materials investigated in this section of ethnology bear mostly on social groups. In history special studies of particular types of groups have been increasing with the development of monographic research, though, of course, one type of groups—states—have always been the predominant object of the historians' interest. Lately some sociologists have done, on their own initiative, independently of ethnologists and historians, first-hand research in some typical groups found in their social milieu.

We shall point out the most important kinds of groups on which there already exists good literature, without making any special distinction between the works of ethnologists and historians and those of professed sociologists; for when "social ethnology" and "social history" compare and generalize, they pass gradually into sociology.

Apart from the state to which we shall return later on, of all the groups those based on real or fictitious kinship—the family, the clan, the gens, the sib—have, as everybody knows, received the largest amount of attention. From McLennan and Morgan up to Rivers, Malinowski and Briffault, there is a long line of works dealing with various forms of family and kinship organization among lower communities, many of them limited to certain ethnographic areas, but all implicitly or explicitly aiming at generalizations of a sociological character. Numerous comparisons of ethnographic and historical data like those of Morgan and Bachofen connect these studies with others made by historians. The Greek and Roman family, the German sib, the Indo-European or Aryan household have been the objects of special interest, and family life in the Middle Ages, the Renaissance and the modern period up to the French Revolution has not been neglected. Finally, there are monographs on the modern family in more recent times like Calhoun's *Social History of the American Family*, Thomas and Znaniecki's *The Polish Peasant* as well as innumerable less voluminous contributions made by sociologists working on first-hand materials. There are also comparative studies on the modern family in Western civilizations. And every synthetic work of the evolutionary school, every sociological textbook has a large section given to sociological theory of family and kinship organization in general. These groups form a practically indisputable part of the domain of sociology, though there are investigations lying on the borderland between this science and economics, like those done by Le Play and his school, who view the family as an economic, even more than a social system.

Among other groups in lower civilizations to which ethnologists and sociologists have given special attention are secret societies, age groups, and male groups: take Webster's study of *Primitive Secret Societies* and the work of H. Schurtz *Altersklassen und Männerbünde.* In so far as many secret societies have a religious character, there is some connection between these studies and others bearing more particularly upon religious groups (either on certain particular historical varieties or on the whole class). See, for instance, Sighele *Psychologie des sectes.* To historians chiefly we owe a rich and first-rate literature concerning professional, caste and class organizations. Thus, mediaeval guilds have long been the subject of thorough research, and the type of professional group has been followed back to European antiquity and the Orient; something akin has even been discovered among lower civilizations (e.g., blacksmiths among the Massai in Africa). The caste systems of India are still something of a puzzle to sociologists as far at least as their origin is concerned. The aristocracies of various ages and countries—Polynesia, Greece and Rome, mediaeval knighthood, Western aristocracy of the last centuries before the Revolution—have attracted many a student. Still stronger has been the fascination exercised since the times of Voltaire by the clergy and its powerful organization in ancient Egypt and Babylon, in Buddhist countries, in mediaeval and modern Catholicism.

Particularly numerous and extensive have been the works concerning the past and present of the working classes. Interest was here stimulated, of course, by the modern labor movement. The great mass of literature bearing on this subject, however, has little scientific value, since it is dominated by practical, political or reformatory purposes. Objective theoretic investigation was at first made for the most part by economists who, even if they were thorough students in their field, neglected or inadequately treated the purely social data involved in the processes they were studying. These social data, aside from the moral regulations of the duties of slave and owner, servant and master, employed and employer (which belong to the theory of social relations) are primarily the social groups formed by people of the working classes and the struggles between these groups and others organized or dominated by the master or employer class. Only recently has this problem been clearly and definitely stated in a number of comparative sociological studies.

Very instructive have been the investigations of children's groups, such as those of Varendonck, Puffer and Thrasher. And even though we do not agree with the general presuppositions of the older "crowd psychology," still there are many valuable observations and generalizations contained in the studies of crowds and mobs by Sighele and Le Bon, and their followers. A marked progress in these studies is noticeable in the more recent works. The crowd or mob as a specific variety of social group, only half-formed and temporary, has an important place in the comparative theory of groups, since it throws much light on other, more durable and structurally closed social systems. For the same reason studies in other "primary groups," like the "congenial group," the "society circle," and of course the roaming horde (in so far as it is still real and accessible), must be highly valued.

During the Great War, Western sociology began to discover national groups. It had long been aware, of course, of the existence of nationalities or "races," as they were, and still are, popularly called; but a nationality is not a group, only a mass of people with common culture. Under the influence of political science and political history, sociology had commonly assumed that the social unity and organization of a nationality was only achieved in and through the state. The most striking instances to the contrary, such as the Polish national group, which remained socially unified though belonging to three different states and actively struggling against all three, were but little known outside of Poland and Germany. The French and English languages do not have any terms to indicate this type of group, for the term "nation" is associated with the idea of the state. Even at the present moment, though much work has already been done on the subject, the theory of national groups is very imperfect.

With the state, we approach the most disputed part of sociological data. The enormous prominence of politics in practical reflection and the great complexity of state systems have resulted in an early development of political science as a discipline of a normative character, partly philosophy, partly technology. The existence of this discipline has deeply influenced all theory of social data for many centuries. When sociology became conscious of itself as a distinct science, it was still imbued with the idea of the uniqueness and supremacy of the state among all social systems. "Civilized society" in the sense of Saint-Simon and Comte was coextensive with the state; the only important difference in their view as compared with earlier thinkers was that they no longer ascribed the predominant rôle in "society" to political activities, but took other cultural forces into account. In Germany until quite recently the state was distinguished from "society" as a superior organization embracing in a kind of higher unity all the social systems which could be found among the population of the state territory.[10]

Gradually, however, the view began to dawn that states are merely a specific variety of social systems, more extensive and more complex than most (though there are religious groups still wider and with an organization not less involved), but not unique in a sense that would justify the traditional way of studying them apart, as if they bore no resemblance to any other social systems. They are obviously territorial groups like the village commune, the township, the neighborhood, the "local groups" of lower peoples. They are separate groups, not parts of other groups of the same kind, like most tribes, secret societies, religious groups of various denominations, national groups. They use coercion as means of social control in a larger measure than other groups—but few are the groups which entirely dispense with coercion. They influence and dominate many minor groups to which their members belong, but this is also a frequent feature of groups: the influence many a church, class organization or national group exercises upon minor groups is even more efficient. And, moreover, states in turn are often dominated by other groups—religious, professional, national. In short, since the study of social groups in

[10]   The problem of the political unification of Germany, which dominated German social activities in the past century, gave the practical impulse to this view; and Hegel's apotheosis of the state sanctioned it theoretically.

general belongs to sociology, there is no valid scientific reason whatever why states as social groups should be excluded from this study or given a position incomparable with that of other groups.

There are, however, other reasons why sociology cannot completely absorb the so-called political science. Speaking of the latter, we must first distinguish two radically different disciplines current under this name and seldom clearly differentiated. One is a practical discipline, a technology of political activities; like all practical disciplines, it needs the help of several theoretic sciences, such as economics, physical and human geography. It cannot be, therefore, identified with sociology any more than with any other theoretic science. The other is a comparative theory of states. Though such a theory logically is an integral part of sociology, it requires specialization in view of the enormous wealth of material it operates with (since this material includes all law, regarded not as a mere expression of moral norms, but as a constituent part of the state structure), and also because of its old tradition and vast literature. It is simply impossible to acquire proficiency in it without specializing extensively in this field. Similar specialization exists already in natural sciences; e.g., bacteriology has become a special division of biology. But a specialist in the theory of the state must be a sociologist, just as a bacteriologist is a biologist who has specialized in the study of bacteria.

There are as yet only a few explicit attempts to build a synthetic theory of social groups. Simmel in his *Sociology* deals with several varieties of groups and describes several characters and processes common to all; still, his work is a series of monographs rather than a general synthesis. In fact, however, nearly all recent general works bearing the title of "sociology" contain more or less systematic theories of groups, though many of them still partly confuse groups with "societies" in the sense of Comte and Spencer. This confusion can be avoided only by redefining the concept "society" from the point of view of these simpler systems with which monographic sociological resarch is dealing.[11]

---

[11]   This is what, e.g., MacIver does when he calls a society "the web of social relationships," *Society, Its Structure and Changes*, p. 6. I think that a definition in terms of social groups is preferable.

8. General Definition of Social Systems[12]

This cursory survey of some modern developments in sociological research makes it perfectly obvious that there is a separate class of empirical data constituting the special field of sociology. Of course, these data can be either taken on their concrete historical background and studied in their individual peculiarities, or else isolated from this background and investigated with regard to their typical characters and repeatable changes: history and social ethnography are more interested in their first, analytic and nomothetic sociology in their second aspect; but, as we have already shown, the two aspects are complementary, and there is no sharp line of division between the task of the social historian or "sociographer" and that of the sociologist. The same relationship binds economic history with economics, history of art with theory of art, particular philologies with general linguistics.

It is, therefore, high time for the sociologists to drop the superannuated claims of making a "synthetic" or "fundamental" science of societies and culture, and to realize that whatever positive scientific results they can show to their credit have been achieved only by concentrating on those kinds of specific data we have characterized above as social actions, social relations, social persons, and social groups.

The logical reason for uniting these data within the domain of one science and separating this domain from those of other sciences is founded on the fact that all of them as cultural systems have an essential *similarity of composition*, while they differ in composition from all other cultural systems—technical, economic, religious, linguistic.

In order to prevent misunderstanding at this point, we repeat that the sociologist has nothing to do with human beings as natural entities, as they "really" are, individually or collectively, in their

12   Cf. the author's article, "The Object-matter of Sociology," in the *American Journal of Sociology*, January, 1927. The term "social systems" (with a somewhat different significance) was used by J. Boodin in an important article under that title in *Am. Journal of Sociol.*, Vol. XXIII, pp. 705–734.

psycho-biological characters; he leaves their study to the psychologist, physiologist, anthropologist, human geographer. But in observing the *cultural world* he finds that in this world men play a double rôle. First, they are *conscious agents* or *active subjects*. An active subject as such is inaccessible to scientific observation; all we know is a center of experiences and activities. Consequently, there can be no positive science of "active subjects" or "conscious agents," but merely of their experiences and activities. Secondly, men are also empirical *objects of activity*, just as technical materials and instruments, economic values, works of art and literature, religious myths, words of language, etc. We have found that social actions differ from other actions in that they are dealing with men as objects; the same holds true of the other, more complex kinds of social systems. We should like to say in the language of the older psychology that human personalities, whatever they may be "in themselves," exist in the cultural world as "ideas" in the minds of other men, or as "representations" of other men; but it would be dangerous to use these terms, in view of their subjectivistic connotations. Therefore we prefer to say that they exist as *values* which active subjects experience and modify. We call them *social values* as distinguished from economic, technical, religious, aesthetic, and other values. Man as a social value is only "an aspect" of himself as he appears to somebody else who is actively interested in him, or even to himself, when he reflects about his own personality and tries to control it practically. The sociologist, we might say, has only to do with such "aspects" of men. But these "aspects" are realities, since they really condition human behavior as much as, and sometimes more than, natural things and processes.

We cannot analyze here in detail the composition of social systems, for this is not a problem of methodology, but of positive classification and description; a few general indications will be sufficient at this moment to illustrate our main point. It has been seen already that in a social action an individual or a group is given to the agent as the "social object" whom the action is meant to influence. In a social relation there are two individuals or two groups, or an individual and a group, given to each other as "part-

ners" of the relation, objects with regard to whom certain duties
have to be fulfilled and from whom the fulfilment of other duties
is expected. A "social person" is a center of relationships with a
number of other persons and groups, in which relationships he
appears as object of their activities and they appear as objects of
his activities. A group is composed fundamentally of individual
"members" each of whom is a social value for all the rest, the object of the collective assistance and control of the group as a whole,
and all of whom cooperate in supporting the group as their common value. These objects have a common and distinctive feature
which no other objects possess (unless they have been "anthro-
pomorphized," assimilated to men in imagination); the agent is
aware that they can experience the same data he experiences and
perform the same activities he performs.

Whatever other values enter into the composition of social systems are determined with reference to these fundamental or *primary social values*, are viewed as particular properties, forms of
behavior, relationships of those who are the chief objects of active
interest and in so far have the character of *secondary social values*.
For instance, among the duties which enter into the composition
of a social relation, there may be economic performances, as from
master to servants, or religious performances, as from priest to
layman. But within the relation both of them have a character of
social rather than of economic or religious values, in so far as they
are demanded, recognized, and appreciated as personal duties of
the master or of the priest, implied in their social character as partners to the relation. Apparently equivalent economic or religious
values coming to the servant or the layman from any other source
would really be entirely dissimilar; being irrelevant to the social
relation in question, they could not take the place of those which
are due from the master or the priest. Other instances: the real
estate owned by a municipal group, viewed apart from this group,
is an economic value; the language of a national group, apart from
its social structure, is a set of symbols, linguistic values. But in social activities bearing upon these groups, both acquire the character of social values as parts of these groups, as for instance when
the city inhabitants view certain kinds of municipal property as

an inalienable instrument necessary for the functioning of the municipal group which they are supporting, or when the members of a national group treat their language as a means for maintaining the national consciousness of this group, essential for its separate existence as against other groups (even though for purposes of linguistic expression any other language would do as well or even better).

Assuming, then, that the systems we call social are composed of social values in the sense characterized above, we shall call *social tendencies* those active tendencies which are manifested in these systems. It might be mentioned at once that, social tendencies being only a specific variety of cultural tendencies, there are innumerable and multiform facts of interaction going on between them and other varieties of cultural tendencies. For instance, the formation of a social group may be counteracted by a divergence of economic interests or religious beliefs among its prospective members, or a group already formed may be disrupted by economic and religious conflicts appearing later; and, on the contrary, we often see social organizers appealing to common economic or religious tendencies in order to facilitate the formation of new groups, or statesmen trying to maintain the existing political system in spite of opposition by utilizing the tendencies of economic or religious conservatism. It is obvious, therefore, that a science dealing with social systems, though specializing in this field, cannot be isolated from other cultural sciences.

Another important point must still be raised with regard to this matter of scientific specialization. We claim that sociology is a special science because the composition of social systems is different from that of any other cultural systems. In this, we are following the example of other sciences of culture: the distinctions between economics, the theory of religion, the theory of language and the theory of art, are also based on the fact that the composition of the respective kinds of systems differs—economic values are entirely dissimilar from religious values, the latter are distinct from linguistic and artistic values.

But are there no essential similarities of structure which might cut across the differences of composition? Thus, social actions, though dealing with different materials and instruments, reaching different results by different methods, than technical, economic, religious actions, still—being actions—seem obviously to bear a strong structural similarity to them. A moral norm regulating the social behavior of an individual with regard to another individual appears formally, i.e., structurally, very much like a norm of utility with which his economic actions comply, a religious norm which regulates his acts of worship, an aesthetic or intellectual norm to which his mental activities are subordinated. This being the case, why should our entire scientific knowledge of the cultural world not rather be subdivided along entirely different lines; why should we not have, instead of sociology, economics, the theory of religion and the rest, a general theory of actions which would include social, economic and religious actions, a general theory of norms, and so on?

The reason is clear why similarities and differences of composition rather than those of structure constitute the ground of division between particular sciences of culture. The former are empirically given to any attentive observer at the very outset of his research, whereas the latter can be discovered only gradually in the course of research, and many of them remain still unknown. Thus, there is no need of any deep analysis to notice the resemblance between the simplest and the most complex religious phenomena on the one hand, the simplest and the most complex economic phenomena on the other hand; and also to see the difference between these two classes. But the structural resemblance between a religious norm of sanctity and an economic norm of utility is much more difficult to discover, unless one sees it—as the schools of Durkheim and of Sumner do—in the purely external circumstance that both are usually sanctioned by social groups. While they are new data continually coming under scientific observation, the primary division of sciences of culture must be founded upon the character of the values composing the systems with which they deal. The investigation of structural similarities cutting across this primary division may become the task of a new group of sciences, or perhaps mere subdivisions of a new science—the general theory of culture, whose possibility we mentioned above.

4. The Boundaries of Sociology

SOCIAL ACTIONS

1936

1. The Scientific Approach to Social Actions

WHEN A SCIENTIST undertakes the task of investigating social actions, i.e., actions that bear upon people, such as greeting an
acquaintance, helping a beggar, writing a letter, proposing to a
girl, lynching a criminal, or fighting an enemy troop in battle, he
is faced with an obvious, though not easy problem. Social actions
are *actions:* they belong to the same general class as, for instance,
the actions of eating, dressing, hunting, plowing, harvesting, making a chair or a horseshoe, painting a landscape, writing a poem,
storing gold in a hoard or depositing it in a bank, praying, performing a religious sacrifice, formulating and solving a mathematical problem. On the other hand, social actions are *social:*
they belong to the same general class of data as morally or legally
regulated *social relations* (friendships, conjugal relations, parent-
child relations, relations between employer and employee), *social
persons,* i.e., specific "rôles" played by individuals in communities
(rôles of warrior, shaman, matron, society girl, engineer, merchant
or president), and *social groups* (clans, tribes, village communes,
churches, political parties, fraternities, trade unions). The problem
is, should the investigator approach social actions as a student of
actions in general or as a student of social data in general?

Chapter 1, "Psychology or Sociology?" from *Social Actions* (New York:
Farrar & Rinehart and the Polish Sociological Institute, 1936), pp. 1–34.
Reprinted by permission of the Polish Sociological Institute.

This problem is a result of the present scientific situation in the whole domain of studies concerning human life and culture, particularly in the fields of psychology and sociology. For a long time psychology has been investigating human activity in general, and recently such investigations have become the main subject-matter of psychological interest; but systematic studies of social actions, regarded as a part of sociology, are comparatively scarce. Naturally, therefore, there is a prevalent belief that psychology already possesses either a general theory of actions or—at least— the leading principles for such a theory; and that, consequently, a study of social actions, even if it be a distinct branch of knowledge (and there are psychologists who deny it), must be dependent on psychology and founded on psychological knowledge. The majority of sociologists are inclined to accept psychology's claim, particularly in view of the fact that a study of social actions has but little to expect from a general theory of social data as such. For social actions are the simplest kind of social data: they constitute the background of mores and laws, of personal rôles and of group organization; they may be said to be the stuff out of which all the more complex and elaborate social realities are made. Consequently, their study must precede other sociological studies and condition them. As a result of this situation most sociologists call the study of social actions "social psychology," and are perfectly willing to make it dependent on general psychological theories of activity.

Now, we shall question this dependence, because we do not believe that psychology has any valid general theory of human actions nor even any principles upon which such a theory could be built. In using the term "psychology," we mean all the branches of research going under this name which consider as their primary object-matter bio-psychological human individuals and which investigate all actions with reference to these individuals, as facts of their mental, organic, or psycho-organic life, as phenomena belonging to their total "consciousness" or "psyche," or else to their total " organic functioning" or "behavior." Though the name "psychology" has occasionally been used to indicate various other kinds of studies to which the above definition does not apply, yet the latter expresses the common subject-matter and method of the vast majority of contributions considered as "psychological" in modern scientific circles.

We should like to go even further and say that there is as yet no valid general theory of human actions, psychological or otherwise. There are indeed valid theories of certain specific classes of human actions; there are also some incipient heuristic concepts which may be used for a general theory of actions and, better still, a number of separate inductive hypotheses, some of them important and well tested, which could be incorporated into such a theory. But the theory itself, in our opinion, is as yet a matter of the future, whether distant or near.

In view of this, we think that an inductive study of social actions ought not to be hampered by any deductions from existing theories. Instead of trying to be a mere subordinate section of some alleged general theory of activity, it should—at least for the time being—be made into an independent discipline. Of course, though independent, it cannot be isolated, but must constitute a branch of sociology, because of the specifically social character of its object-matter. At the same time, however, this discipline should not forget that between specifically social actions and actions that are not social there may be many important similarities. While concentrating on its own social field, it should keep its eyes open for what is being done in neighboring fields. It should not only be ready to test hypotheses about actions in general, which have been evolved elsewhere, by applying them to its own particular data, but also have the ambition of eventually formulating as a result of inductive research in its particular line, hypotheses which may be applicable beyond its limits when tested by other scientists.

2. *Human Actions and Cultural Reality*

This suggestion that inductive sociological studies of social actions cease to be dependent on general psychological theories of activity, and that the very name "social psychology" as a symbol of this dependence be dropped by sociologists, is justified by the actual results of the tremendous work that has been progressing for centuries within the vast realm of data called "human actions."

For only a minor section of this work has been done by scientific psychology, though many workers have popularly called themselves psychologists, without having professional psychological training or using psychological methods. The great majority of inductive studies of human actions have, however, been carried on by specialists in the various sciences of culture.

Thus, philologists have investigated various actions of speaking and writing particular languages, and linguists have drawn more comprehensive generalizations from their results. Students of art have done important research concerning specific actions, productive and reproductive, in the fields of drawing, painting, sculpture, architecture, music, poetry, and the drama; and these have led to theories of aesthetic activity in general. Economic actions have been analyzed and compared carefully and exactly during the last two centuries, though the beginning of this analysis must be traced back to Aristotle and Xenophon. Religionists are making thorough studies of religious actions, particularly individual and collective performances of rites and ceremonies. The vast historical and ethnological variety of sexual actions has been subjected during the last sixty years to searching investigation by a number of scientists with cultural training. Studies of technical actions, long neglected, are now being carried on from several points of view at once: some investigators are chiefly concerned with technical invention; others in connection with the "scientific management" movement study repeatable industrial actions, while students of material culture are interested in technical performances of peoples in lower stages of civilization.

Nobody who has ever been even superficially acquainted with these studies can doubt that many highly valuable theoretic results have been reached simply by methodical induction from empirical data, that is, by a careful analysis of actions belonging to the various fields. And though the systematic study of social actions is comparatively recent, one cannot deny that even in this field much has been done by first-hand investigation of such data as sociologists have experienced and observed.

Now, psychological theories of activity are not based on inductive generalization of the results of studies made by various cultural specialists in their respective fields. Psychology as a distinct positive science was founded on the observation of individual human agents taken in isolation from the total objective domain of culture in which they live and act—often experimental or clinical, and always conceptual, isolation. The purpose of this observation is to determine whatever similarities and differences exist between them, irrespectively of the concrete, complex, and varied cultural situations in which they normally participate. The only activities the psychologist has thoroughly studied are those elementary and relatively uniform activities which can be analyzed and compared without regard to their objective bearing on any field of cultural reality, i.e., language, literature, art, religion, knowledge, technique, or social intercourse. Consequently, the psychologist has no more right to demand that the generalizations resulting from his research be accepted as valid with reference to the actions performed by men in those various cultural fields than, say, the economist to claim that his generalizations based on the study of economic actions are valid also for religious, aesthetic, intellectual, and social actions. Of course, religionists, sociologists, students of art or of knowledge may and sometimes ought to try whether any of the psychological or economic theories of activity can be extended beyond the specific field from which they were inductively derived; but this testing must be done from their own several points of view.

Older psychology, besides limiting its material, explicitly limited its generalizations to the subjective, "introspective" aspect of actions, which is expressed in such concepts as "volition," "desire," "impulse," "feeling," "will," and to certain physiological processes accompanying these introspective "conscious phenomena," thus producing very little that could be even hypothetically used by students of cultural actions in their various fields. Some of its results have indeed been applied by linguistics, aesthetics, ergology, and epistemology, but only in the study of a few very simple activities. The only really thorough attempt to combine the results of older scientific psychology with those of cultural sciences into one body of systematic knowledge about human activities was made by Wilhelm Wundt; and that covers more than twenty volumes of synthetic works, as well as some monographs. There is no doubt that, however valuable certain parts of it may be, as a total systematic effort it is a failure, though a grandiose failure, deserving more attention than it has received. This failure can be explained directly by Wundt's tendency to deduce the main lines of his theory of cultural activities from his psychology, and by his inclination to select and interpret empirical evidence in the various fields of culture in the light of the general psychological preconceptions which he had already formed before he started to study these fields.

Recent developments in the philosophy of culture and the methodology of cultural sciences have conclusively shown why such failures are inevitable. For culture is not a mere agglomeration of "facts of consciousness" with their material accompaniment and results. It is constituted by numerous *systems*, greater or smaller, more or less coherent, durable and changing, but all with a specific objectivity and an intrinsic order of their own: systems like the Erechtheion and the Ionic style in architecture, the Beata Beatrix and English Pre-Raphaelitism, the philosophy of Aristotle and modern mathematics, the bank of Morgan and American capitalism, the Buddhist, Mohammedan, or Catholic religion, the Roman Empire or the Third French Republic, a department store or an automobile factory. Though human activities construct and maintain such systems, these activities are not what they appear in introspective analysis: what matters about them is not their "subjective," "psychological" aspect, but how they manifest themselves in this objective cultural world, where they contribute something to the existing systematic order, and must on the other hand comply with this order.

During the last thirty years the psychological approach has undergone a considerable change in that the deficiencies of the old introspective method have been removed, in some schools at least. But the limitation of scientific psychological research to certain specific types of actions still remains; and, as before, generalizations based on these data claim a validity far beyond their original range. Two doctrines deserve particular attention here in view of the wide recognition which their claims to be general theories of human actions ("conduct" or "behavior") have received, particularly among sociologists.

One of these may be termed the *biogenetic* theory; it has reached its widest ramification and its greatest consistency in orthodox behaviorism.[1] The other theory can be called *psychogenetic*, and its most ambitious form is the Freudian school of psychoanalysis. The presuppositions of these two theories have to be discussed briefly, since their claims run counter to the "declaration of independence" made above in favor of the study of social actions apart from other actions. After a consideration of their heuristic concepts concerning the character of social or generally cultural activities, we will endeavor to substitute for them other more useful concepts.

3. The Biogenetic Theory of Actions as Exemplified by Behaviorism

The leading presuppositions of the biogenetic theory of human actions, or—to use the orthodox term—human behavior, are directly derived from the general theory of organic evolution. Since the human species has evolved from lower animals, all human actions, even those on the highest cultural level, have gradually developed from the original processes of biological adaptation of animal organisms to their natural environment. And as every man is born an animal that becomes human only by growing up under continuous cultural influences, his actions begin as processes of biological adaptation similar to those of lower animals, and change into cultural actions only in the course of a development which, though variable in particulars, in its most general outline is a truncated and greatly abbreviated recapitulation of the cultural evolution of the race.

From these more or less firmly established biogenetic generalizations the conclusion is drawn that all human actions remain essentially similar in form and function to those organic processes in which they originated, only differing from them in such sec-

[1]   The qualification is not intended to indicate specifically the Watsonians, but to exclude those who treat behaviorism rather as a method than as a doctrine and do not identify all behavior with organic behavior.

ondary, though important characters as complexity, indirectness, range of adaptability in space and time—characters mostly due to the development of speech. . . .

If this is so, the methodological conclusion seems to follow that a general theory of human behavior can best be built on the foundation of a systematic study of animal and infant behavior. The differentiation of cultural human activities can then be gradually explained by investigating partly the growth of technical training in the use of artificial instruments, but chiefly the origin and development of "symbolic behavior" as a specifically human phenomenon, keeping firmly in mind the biological form and function of all behavior as disclosed by the study of its original types. The behaviorist school admits without question that hypotheses which have been tested with regard to primary behavior, and proved to express its essential character, can be extended to all secondary variations which have developed from it, and will also express their essential character, even if it should be necessary to supplement them by additional hypotheses. In short, a theory of the biological origins of action is assumed to be the basic theory of all actions.

Now, this assumption is altogether arbitrary, and its uncritical acceptance has vitiated the whole doctrine based upon it. The task of genetic research in any field of reality, natural or cultural, is not to substitute for theories based upon inductive investigation of empirical data a theory which explains away their variety by reducing it to an original uniformity, but to supplement inductive investigation, in so far as it needs to be supplemented, by finding the source from which this whole variety has emerged. Evolution is not a metaphysical dogma, but a scientific postulate, valid so long as it works and so far as it is applicable. Genetic research, in accepting this postulate, must realize that certain conditions of its applicability are set by the qualitative empirical wealth of that part of the world to which it is applied, and that if these conditions are ignored the postulate ceases to work. These conditions have been variously formulated: evolution has been defined as a unique "historical" process, a "creative" process, and a process of "emergence." From the methodological point of view the essential matter is that, if we treat the multiform empirical variety of data in any field as having evolved gradually from some original uniformity, we must also treat this evolution as progressing by stages, every stage being characterized by the appearance of something essentially *new* and *not reducible* to what was before.

In this progressive differentiation a certain similarity naturally remains and binds the earlier with the later stages. But in a long and complex evolutionary process the thread of similarity between the earliest stage and later stages may become so slender as no longer to justify scientifically any conclusions drawn from the nature of the former about the nature of the latter. How much similarity there must be between the original stage and the final stages to make the study of their genetic connection scientifically useful, how far back we ought to go in any given field to trace the origin of a present variety of empirical data, it is for the student of these data to decide; for only he can tell, from what he knows by direct study about the character of present reality, at what stage in the past reality of this kind began to exist.

For instance, astronomers have assumed that our earth, as it now is, evolved from a primitive nebula, which was essentially a physical and at most also a rudimentary chemical complex. Suppose this is true: yet the geographer is not concerned with the physical similarities between our present earth and the original nebula. While agreeing that, within the concrete field of reality he studies, physical phenomena continually occur similar to those which took place within the original nebula and still take place in nebulae the astronomer investigates, and that all these phenomena are subjected to the same laws, he is only concerned with the empirical variety of data he observes on, above, and below the surface of the earth *as it now is*—data which did not exist in the original nebula, but are qualitatively new and irreducible to the latter, manifesting essential characteristics and laws of their own not deducible from physical laws.

The student of the organic world, while accepting the postulate that organic matter has developed from anorganic matter in a process of chemical evolution, though he knows that chemical phenomena similar to those found in anorganic matter continually occur within living organisms, and even studies their bearing on organic life, nevertheless does not include organisms under the same general class as anorganic bodies. What interests him is precisely all that enormous variety and complexity of living organisms which exists now and did not exist in the distant past, a new reality with uniformities and laws of its own, not deducible from those which the chemist discovers in studying anorganic matter.

Orthodox behaviorism does not follow here the example of those older and more firmly established sciences. Having arisen not out of studies of culture but out of biological psychology, it fails to realize that in the evolution of cultural conduct from the organic behavior of animals there has been at least as much novelty and irreducible qualitative differentiation as in the evolution of the geographer's earth from the primitive nebula, or the botanist's and zoologist's organic world from anorganic matter. And it does not realize this because it simply ignores nearly all the inductive knowledge agglomerated patiently by the historian and the ethnologist, the student of art, of literature, of language, of religion, of philosophy and science, of technique, of economics, of mores and social organization; or, rather, it looks in all this knowledge for only that which seems reducible to its own original scheme. This procedure is quite unparalleled in the older sciences, but might be compared to that of a chemist who offered a general theory of the organic world which ignored all the empirical evidence collected by natural scientists—Aristotle, Linné, Buffon, Lamarck, Darwin, Wallace, Mendel, and Weisman.

This fundamental scientific error of orthodox behaviorism is due to its having been concerned from the very first with metaphysical problems. In radical reaction against the old metaphysics of spiritualism, it accepted as its implicit foundaton the opposite, equally old, though slightly modernized, metaphysical doctrine of materialism. In doing so, it confused two entirely disconnected problems: the ontological dualism of body and mind as separate entities (which must be entirely eliminated from positive science) and the purely methodological distinction between the empirical evidence which the student of organic behavior and the student of cultural actions have at their disposal.

The primary empirical evidence about any cultural human action is the experience of the agent himself, supplemented by the experience of those who react to his action, reproduce it, or participate in it. The action of speaking a sentence, writing a poem, making a horseshoe, depositing money, proposing to a girl, electing an official, performing a religious rite, as empirical datum, is what it is in the experience of the speaker and his listeners, the poet and his readers, the blacksmith and the owner of the horse to be shod, the depositor and the banker, the proposing suitor and the courted girl, the voters and the official whom they elect, the religious believers who participate in the ritual. The scientist who wants to study these actions inductively must take them as they are in the human experience of those agents and re-agents; they are his empirical data inasmuch and because they are theirs. I have expressed this elsewhere by saying that such data possess for the student *a humanistic coefficient.* The humanistic coefficient distinguishes cultural data from natural data, which the student assumes to be independent of the experience of human agents.

Every student of culture takes his data with a humanistic coefficient. The philologist studies a language as experienced by the people who speak it and understand it; the economist studies money and the active use of money as experienced by the people who use it; the student of art investigates actions of painting, composing or playing music, writing or reading a poem, as experienced by the artists and those aesthetically interested in their work; the political scientist studies elections as actively experienced by the electors, the politicians, and the candidates. There are various well-known techniques of finding out how other people experience the data which the student investigates: the investigator himself repeats, reproduces fully or vicariously, participates, observes, and supplements the direct information thus gained by whatever other people can tell him about their experiences. His data become finally as reliable as any data can be: nobody can doubt the data which a good philologist collects about speaking a language, or a good economist's data about the functioning of a bank, or a good art student's data about the work of artists.

Now, the orthodox behaviorist rejects this primary empirical evidence as a basis for inductive research. He does this first in studying the behavior of animals and infants, for obvious reasons: as a culturally educated observer, he cannot adequately reproduce their active experiences, nor can those experiences be made secondarily accessible to him by verbal communication. Moreover, the behavior itself at this stage shows to the observer such uniformities and causal relationships as to make the evidence of the agent's experience comparatively unimportant for the establishment of a number of valid theoretic generalizations.

When, however, the behaviorist continues to neglect this evidence in his approach to human activities at later stages of evolution, in spite of its being there fully accessible to him, and in spite of the fact that there are already in the various sciences of culture numerous valid inductive generalizations based upon this evidence, his attitude can be only explained, but not justified, partly by a desire to extend his theories beyond their original range at the cost of very little effort—which can be achieved most easily by avoiding the check of this new evidence; partly by the fear of introducing with the agent's "conscious" experience the old "mind" or "soul." Behavioristic studies of "symbolic behavior" do not obviate this error of method, for they do not take the gestures and words used by the agent with reference to the agent's own empirical reality as he experiences it, but re-interpret those words and gestures with reference to the agent's environment as the behavioristic observer views it. We shall have several occasions in later chapters to see how this metaphysical bias revenges itself in obstructing the progress of scientific analysis and generalization. Here we must mention only two essential characteristics of active human experiences which the orthodox behaviorist is prevented by this bias from taking into consideration.

The first of these characteristics belongs to all the experiences of human agents: it is the intrinsic objective meaningfulness of every datum with which the agent deals. Behaviorism reduces the problem of meaning to the meaning of symbols. But for the human agent not only symbols have a meaning, but every datum of his experience in which he is actively interested; every datum stands not only for itself, but for other data which it suggests. At an early stage of mental development this meaning is connected with the possibility of organic experiences suggested by the object; thus, food suggests certain experiences of the organs used in eating and digesting. At this stage it is still possible to substitute for it the concept of "incipient behavior." But gradually the meaning expands, includes suggestions of objects outside the organism, and becomes irreducible—even indirectly—to any definite incipient behavior. Steps heard in the next room to the hungry infant may indirectly mean the approach of food and provoke definite organic responses, but to the grown-up they mean the approach of a person toward whom the possible range of attitudes is almost unlimited. A painting suggests, on the one hand, a fragment of nature or a historical event which we never have and never can experience directly; on the other hand, a multiplicity of paintings in similar or different styles, in comparison with which we define its aesthetic characters.

No object as experienced by an active human individual can be defined merely by its sensory content, for on its meaning rather than on its sensory contact depends its practical significance for human activity. Not because of what it "is" as a natural datum, but because of what it "means" as a humanistic, cultural datum, does an object of activity appear to the agent as "useful" or "harmful," "good" or "bad," "beautiful" or "ugly," "pleasant" or "unpleasant." Since all meaingful objects are potential objects of activity and have a practical significance in somebody's experience, I have for twenty-five years been using the term *values* to distinguish logically meaningful objects as given to an agent from *things*, meaningless objects investigated by a student who takes them not as they are given to agents, but as they are supposed to exist "in themselves," as parts of nature. I call the *axiological significance* of a value that practical significance which it acquires when it is appreciated positively or negatively with reference to other values as a possible object of activity.

The second essential point that behaviorism leaves out of consideration in studying human actions is the existence in the experience of human agents of objects which are not only meaningful, but partly—often almost completely—*non-material* in content and irreducible to sensory perception. Such objects are, for instance, myths and other religious entities, political institutions, contents of literary works, scientific and philosophic concepts. Many words in civilized languages are not used to indicate objects given in sensory experience, but precisely to symbolize non-material, "spiritual" objects, to stabilize and communicate their contents.

The student of actions need not engage in philosophic speculation as to the "true essence" of these objects: in fact, it will be safest for him as a scientist to refrain from such speculations, whether his inclination be toward a radical Platonic "realism," affirming the absolute priority of a non-sensual world, or an equally radical "nominalism," reducing non-sensual objects to infinitely complex combinations of sensory data, or toward a more moderate position, like the "conceptualism" prevailing from the end of the Middle Ages to the end of the last century, or the sociologism of Durkheim's "collective representations."

He must be satisfied with the simple and obvious fact that human agents accept such objects as real and meaningful, ascribe to them a positive or a negative practical significance, are influenced by them and try to influence them, produce and reproduce them, cooperate and fight about them. Indeed, many of their cultural actions would never be performed if such objects did not exist in their experience and were not regarded by them as real, though entirely different from the sensory data of their natural environment.

For the student of social actions this is a very important point. The primary objects of social actions are other human beings whom the agent tries to influence. This, as we have already said, is what distinguishes at first glance social actions from other actions such as technical production, economic consumption, aesthetic reproduction and creation, religious sanctification and purification, scientific thinking about nature—which do not bear upon human beings, but upon other objects, material or spiritual. We call therefore human beings, as objects of actions, *primary social values.* And a human being, as he appears to the agent for whom he is a social value, is not reducible to data of the agent's sensory experience. He is indeed a body, but he is also "something else" —a "conscious being," a being who has certain capacities and dispositions commonly called "psychological."

Now, it must be clearly understood that we, the sociologists, need not accept as "true" any ideas human agents may have about the "consciousness," "minds" or "souls," of those human beings with whom they deal actively as social values. From the scientific point of view, all we know and ever can know about human "consciousness" is the simple and obvious fact that other people, like ourselves, experience data and perform activities. In this limited and purely formal sense, we can say that every human individual is a "conscious subject," an "experiencing agent," provided we are aware that our task as scientists is not to speculate, as the metaphysicians with their own special methods do, about what conscious subjects "really are," whether their capacity to experience and to act is rooted in a "substance," a "mind," a "soul," an "organism," a "nervous system," or in a "function," an *"actus purus,"* a transcendental ego," a specific kind of "energy," or what not. Ours is simply and unpretentiously to investigate the data which conscious agents experience and the activities which they perform.

But a "social agent," i.e., an agent who deals with a human being as a social value, is not a scientific sociologist: he is interested in this being not theoretically, but practically. And from his practical point of view the fact that this human being can experience and perform activities, just as the agent himself, appears as an exceedingly important, real characteristic of this human being, as essential as the fact that he has a body, or even more so. For there may be human beings whom a social agent never has experienced as bodies, whose bodily characteristics do not interest him, and yet whom he tries to influence as social values, and from whom he expects reactions—as when he mails a written request to a firm, an office, or a board of directors whose very names as individuals are unknown to him.

In so far, now, as social values appear to the agent to be "conscious realities," having a mental as well as physical existence, they are to him values with a content partly material (like technical instruments) and partly non-material, spiritual (like myths, novels, or scientific concepts). This non-material content may predominate completely over the material content: thus, an institution like the treasury of a state is for the citizens primarily a number of active "minds" (if not a single "collective mind"), that may and do, if necessary, utilize human bodies, e.g., the bodies of policemen, to coerce citizens into paying taxes, but whose bodily composition is of no importance to the tax-payer as compared with their "mental" capacities and dispositions.

It is impossible to take into account the empirical variety of social actions and to explain their changes, unless we realize this fundamental character of social values as they appear to the agents who deal with them. This is what orthodox behaviorists are afraid to do lest, by admitting that human beings appear to each other as psychological entities, they be led to admit that human beings are "in themselves" psychological entities. We shall see later on how unmotivated is this fear. Studying the origin and development of the social objectivation of men by men in the course of social actions, the sociologist can eliminate once and for ever the traditional assumption that psychological reality originally and irreducibly exists as [the] foundation of cultural life, by showing it to be a product of cultural activity, like religious myths or literary heroes.

Behaviorism as a theory of actions is thus inapplicable beyond its original range of animal and infant behavior (including incipient symbolization), and particularly inapplicable to social actions. This does not mean that all the monographic work it has done outside of this original range is worthless: on the contrary, some of it is really important. It is not the first time in the history of science that a wrong theory has stimulated valuable investigations. But the positive results of these investigations can be adequately utilized for general scientific purposes only after they are separated from the theory which they were meant to prove, and reinterpreted with reference to sounder theoretic hypotheses. Thus, some studies of the "symbolic process" throw a new light on the hitherto neglected problem of the use of symbols as instruments in social actions;

but their true theoretic significance will become apparent only in connection with a better inductive theory of social actions than the one behaviorism now offers. The results of numerous investigations concerning the effects on human conduct of pathological organic changes or of environmental processes will be more valuable scientifically when the empirical characters of the original conduct itself are more thoroughly investigated, when cultural causality is better understood, and the effects of the changes are redefined more exactly than behavioristic preconceptions now permit.

Certain recent developments of behaviorism are already leading away from the narrowness of the theory of actions as organic responses to sensory stimuli. Behaviorism, as expressed by men like Read Bain, Kimball Young, L. L. Bernard, and E. Bogardus, ceases to be a particular doctrine or even a specific and exclusive method, and becomes an intellectual attitude which demands that human actions and their changes as empirical data be studied in the same spirit of scientific objectivity and inductive thoroughness and with the same elimination of useless traditions as chemical or biological data—which does not necessarily imply that they must be the same kind of data as the biologist's or the chemist's. We can but heartily agree with such an intellectual attitude, even though we believe that some of the methods in which it finds expression ought to be changed; but this is a later question.

4. *The Psychogenetic Theory of Actions as Exemplified by the Freudian School*

The psychogenetic approach does not attempt to deduce a theory of human actions from organic behavior as known by direct biological observation: it tries, instead, to explain them by certain fundamental and universal forces. These forces are supposed to be the *primary* forces at the origin of all cultural life of the human species and of every human individual, and to remain the *determining* forces all through the cultural history of mankind and the cultural biography of the person.

Such reductions of human conduct to a few original and dominant forces are very old. Various theories known already in antiquity and revived in modern times explain all human actions as derived from and founded on several universal *instincts*. Among the instincts appealed to for this purpose we find e.g., an "instinct of self-preservation," eventually subdivided into the two instinctive drives of hunger and fear; an "instinct of reproduction" or "preservation of the species," including a sexual instinct and a parental instinct; an instinct of gregariousness, a fighting instinct, an instinct of curiosity or exploration, and what not. But such reductions of human actions to instincts did not have much scientific significance until methods were devised for showing how a primary psychological force came to manifest in the later variety of actions which a student of human conduct observes.

One such method is the study of those processes of "learning" by which from an inborn instinct differentiated "habits" are formed. This method, however, has led to the gradual elimination of the conception of instinct as a permanent psychological force underlying the diversity of human actions at all stages of development; what remains is simply an inborn "behavior pattern" supposed to characterize the earliest stage, from which by a process of "conditioning" later behavior patterns evolve.

The other method, created by the psychoanalytic school, has led to very different theoretic views. The psychoanalyst did not begin by studying the earliest manifestations of instincts; he started with the investigation of adult and culturally developed individuals, and by analyzing their conduct was led to the hypothesis that much of this conduct was determined by psychological forces which could be traced back to the individual's childhood, or even farther to his infancy, if not to the prenatal period. Passing then from the study of individual conduct to the study of culture, he assumed that the same forces underlie many, perhaps most, cultural activities of mankind and can be traced back to the origins of the race.

If we take the Freudian school as representative of this scientific current, it is because the psychogenetic theory of this school is the most comprehensive and its theoretic presuppositions the most clearly and uncompromisingly formulated. As every one knows, the psychological force from which, according to this school, most cultural human activities are derived (among them nearly all social, religious, and aesthetic activities) and which still underlies them is the sexual *libido*—a concept which the Freudians use in a more abstract and general way than other students of sex. The *libido*, primarily under the influence of other cultural factors, undergoes modifications and finds outlets in a great multiplicity and variety of actions where its presence is not obvious to ordinary observation or to the conscious reflection of the agent, but can be discovered by special analytic methods. The latter prove that the given action is the manifestation of a modified *libido* by showing that the impulse or wish which brought its performance about evolved from the original *libido*.

We find here the same reasoning from past origin to present essence as in the biogenetic theory, with the difference that the psychoanalytic school does not try to reduce activities to material processes, and as a rule does not go back beyond the human species in search for origins. In both theories metaphysical doctrines underlie this reasoning; but, whereas the biogenetic theory has simply adopted the ready metaphysics of materialism, the psychoanalytic school created a metaphysical doctrine of its own, though it could perhaps be historically connected through Hartman and Schopenhauer with old Hellenistic Pantheism.

In order to claim that the real character of any conduct is not to be found in this conduct itself as the agent experiences it, but must be deduced from the agent's past, Freudianism has to assume that the past endures not potentially, but actually, as a dynamic, though unconscious power; and that this unconscious power, inaccessible to direct experience, becomes the metaphysical essence of human activity, of which actions as empirical data are mere accidents. And if the cultural evolution of mankind is explained by the modifications of this unconscious power—its sublimations, rationalizations, and ambivalent differentiations—rather than by conscious purposes of human agents, the conclusion is not far to seek, and has been already pointed out, that this metaphysical essence is one in all mankind—the great limbo of the Unconscious Absolute of Pantheistic Philosophy.

It is well known that the beginnings of this vast psychophilosophic structure were very modest. The psychoanalytic method was first used in dealing with pathological cases, more specifically with certain cases of neurosis; it was often indubitably successful in tracing the origin of pathological conduct to early sexual tendencies of the patient, distorted but not destroyed by social repression, and in handling them practically by counteracting the effects of this repression. On this safe, though narrow basis of clinical facts a theory has been built to explain most normal human activities: the builders have simply generalized and extended the traditional intellectual attitude of the psychiatrist toward his patient.

When a psychiatrist observes an action which he considers abnormal, he is not interested in the intrinsic character of this action as experienced by the agent; for the action, precisely because it is judged abnormal, is meaningless from the point of view of normal people. To the psychiatrist such an action is merely a symptom of the pathological condition of the agent as a bio-psychological entity; the action itself does not matter, except for the nature and the cause of the pathological condition which its performance denotes. This intellectual attitude differs radically from that of the student of language, literature, art, religion, economics, or social organization; the latter deals with actions which are meaningful and relevant in themselves, no matter what the psycho-biological condition of the individual who performs them is.

Take some instances to illustrate this difference of standpoint. When a sociologist investigates the actions of Beduins or Corsicans who attempt to kill their enemies in family feuds, it is most essential for him to reconstruct so far as possible their own active experiences; otherwise the bearing of their actions as objective social data is inaccessible to him. But the action of an insane patient who tries to kill somebody whom he believes to be persecuting him is regarded by the psychiatrist as a mere symptom of mind or brain disease with no sociological significance whatever. When a religionist studies an Egyptian Pharaoh, or a Roman Emperor who demanded worship as a god and was granted it by his social environment, the experiences of the Pharaoh or the Emperor as well as those of the persons in their environment were and are relevant for the knowledge of religious activities; but the action of a maniac who demands to be worshipped as a god is to the average psychiatrist not a religious action, but a mere indication of his abnormal psychological condition. The action of a scientist who draws a bold generalization from certain observations is treated as a scientific contribution which the historian investigates with regard to its influence on the advancement of science, and the methodologist judges to be valid or invalid; whereas the bold generalizations of lunatics are neither investigated historically nor weighed as to validity, but treated by physicians as psychological phenomena indicative of insanity.

Now, this traditional attitude of the psychiatrist toward the patient's action had a practical, not a theoretic origin. For the practical purpose of preventing the patient from doing harm the intrinsic character of his actions is indeed of minor importance; what chiefly matters is the fact of his "misadaptation" to normal life. And since a proof of his abnormality is the fact that his conduct cannot be permanently influenced by modifying his active experiences, as the conduct of normal people can be by education and control, it does not seem necessary to understand these experiences for the purpose of curing him: it is his total mental or nervous condition which must be diagnosed and dealt with.

From a theoretic point of view, however, abnormal actions can be understood and explained only in comparison with normal actions, by using the same approach as we use toward the latter, that is, by reconstructing the active experience of the subject himself and supplementing it with other people's experiences. The fundamental similarity between, on the one hand, the actions of an avenger trying to kill an individual of a hostile clan, those of an Egyptian ruler demanding divine worship, of a scientist drawing a bold generalization, on the other hand the murderous attempt, the self-deification, the absurd reasoning of a maniac, is that all these agents deal with certain values as they experience them, treat these values as having a certain content and meaning as well as an axiological significance, and try to influence them accordingly. The difference lies in the fact that in "normal" cases the experiences and activities of the agent fit into a certain cultural setting; in "abnormal" cases they do not. In a normal case the agent's values as he experiences them are a part of some wider *system of values* experienced by his social environment; and his activity contributes to the active maintenance of this system, be it a system of clan solidarity implying the duty of blood revenge, or a religious system centered in the cult of the ruler, or a scientific theory. Whereas in an abnormal case the individual's active experience disagrees with that of his environment; he has his own system of values not connected organically with any system of theirs, and his activity does not contribute anything to their activities, for it is culturally irrelevant.

It happens, of course, that a solitary scientific genius sometimes builds a system of values apparently unconnected with any systems of other people, and acts in what seems to others an irrelevant way; or, on the contrary, that during a "religious craze" a large number share a system of religious values and all act "abnormally" together, though in perfect harmony with this system. In the first case, however, the system of the genius has an intrinsic quality which distinguishes it from that of the maniac and later induces other scientists to share and develop it; whereas in the second instance the system of beliefs and practices accepted during a religious craze differs intrinsically from a normatively regulated and durable religion; it is therefore rejected at once by the wider, organized religious community and dropped after a while by most of its original participants.

We shall not discuss this problem further, for there are difficult and complex cultural problems involved in it. The essential point is that a student of human actions, if he investigates "abnormal" actions (which he may refuse to do, because of their slight cultural importance), must use the same humanistic approach as in studying "normal" actions, and follow the same scientific methods; he can no more understand pathological conduct in isolation from the cultural life of the agent's milieu than he can understand normal conduct, since even to judge whether it is pathological or not he must investigate its connection or lack of connection with existing cultural systems.

Now, the psychoanalysts have seen the theoretic inadequacy of the traditional radical separation between meaningless, merely symptomatic abnormal conduct and meaningful normal conduct; but they have been looking at it, so to speak, from the wrong end. Being psychiatrists by profession and method, they applied the psychiatric approach to normal actions instead of applying the cultural, humanistic approach to abnormal actions. In that they followed some older students, like Lombroso and Möbius. Their procedure, however, was in so far an advance scientifically in that they realized the need of modifying somewhat the psychiatric approach before using it for the study of normal conduct. They no longer treated the active experience of their patients as altogether meaningless and irrelevant: they searched it carefully for indications of past causes of the patient's present abnormality.

And yet they have preserved the basic psychiatric attitude: they are still incapable of taking the patient's experience as *prima facie* evidence of his present conduct. They look beyond it for something more real, more essential, more valid than this experience itself; since to them, as to all psychologists, the data to be studied are not human actions, but human beings as psychological entities, they postulate an "unconscious" psychological reality inherent in these entities, unconscious psychological complexes and wishes underlying the empirical actions of the subject, forces persisting in essence, though changed in effect, from an earlier period during which the given human being as a psychological entity was still normal. This conception is then extended from pathological to normal cases. The present active experiences of a normal person are not to be relied upon to be such as they appear to the subject, but need interpretation by the psychoanalyst in connection with the subject's past, as springing from his "unconscious." Dreams and slight deviations from the norms of every-day life constitute the bridge between the conduct of an abnormal and that of a normal individual.

It is not for us to say how much psychopathology (as a theory of abnormal human beings) has gained by this attitude. But for the theoretic study of human actions, the loss in methodological vaildity and precision has far overbalanced whatever gains there may have been in new hypotheses. The primary empirical evidence we have about the source from which an action springs, its "intention," its "motive," "wish," or whatever else we may call the force which brings about its performance, is the evidence furnished by the action itself. When a man paints a picture, kills an enemy, performs a religious ceremony, the first, obvious, and fundamental conclusion is that he intended to paint the picture, to kill the enemy, to perform the ceremony. Of course, he may have tried and failed to achieve any one of these actions because obstacles independent of him prevented him from fulfilling this "intention." This is why it is indispensable in studying human actions to distinguish between the *tendency* which determines what the action will be if not interfered with, and its realization. But unless we have explicit empirical evidence to the contrary, we must assume that the performance of the action is the realization of its tendency; in other words, we must define the tendency by the action as actually performed and empirically given, just as we define a physical force by its empirically given results.

Knowing many human actions, we need not always wait till the action is finished to define the tendency, for in experiencing and observing its beginning we can foresee enough of its final achievement to classify it in advance; this is particularly so when we are the agents, for we have better and more adequate information about any one of our actions than observers who do not participate in its performance. The painter knows even before he has touched the canvas with his brush that he tends to paint a portrait or a landscape, and how he tends to paint it; the man who lies in wait for an enemy according to the rules of *vendetta* knows whether he [in]tends to kill him.

Because the agent and, to a lesser degree, the observer know what is the tendency of the given action soon after it has started, they can also tell when something interferes with its performance and conclude after the result of the action has become patent whether the original tendency was realized or not; if not, whether the action can be regarded as merely interrupted or changed in its tendency. When the painter is dissatisfied with the progress of the portrait as he tends to make it, he changes the pose of his model, his light, his technique, perhaps his very style: his action becomes different from what it began to be, which means that not his original tendency, but a new tendency, has appeared and will be realized if nothing more interferes. The avenger may find that his proposed victim has taken another road: his tendency is not realized, but remains unchanged; and he will try to realize it some other time.

All this is very simple and obvious, but for this very reason can hardly be overemphasized. For whatever we may do about interpreting and explaining human actions, we cannot get away from this simple and obvious empirical evidence: it must remain the final test of all our theories, if these theories are to have any claim to scientific validity. We can no more say that the painter in painting a portrait does not tend to paint the portrait, but to give outlet to a sublimated *libido* than the zoologist can say that a mammal is not a mammal, but a modified protosaurian. Perhaps the painter's tendencies to paint portraits did develop from early sexual tendencies, just as mammals may have evolved from protosaurians. But such a hypothesis, to have any scientific validity, must itself be inductively confirmed by the same kind of empirical evidence as that furnished by the painter's action. That is, we must find sufficient data to conclude that in the painter's past there were sexual tendencies manifested in specific actions, completed or not, but in any case of a type known to us from other, more direct sources. We must further be able to indicate how from these sexual tendencies some other, more or less different tendencies evolved. To prove the existence of such modified tendencies there must also be evidence in the form of actions which they led to, and for the performance of which there is reliable authority in the past. In the same way the following stages of the evolution must be ascertained, until the last stage—aesthetic tendencies to portrait-painting—is genetically explained. The rule is the same as in the case of the zoologist, whose evolutionary hypothesis must be confirmed: first, by evidence of the real existence in the past of protosaurians, but also of animals representing intermediary stages between the protosaurian and the mammal; secondly, by some reliable evidence, direct or indirect, of evolutionary processes by which new species have evolved from preexisting species. . . .

There is one argument, sometimes openly formulated, oftener implicit, which gives the psychoanalytic theory (like all psychogenetic theories) a plausibility so great as to seem almost incontrovertible. An individual's actions are performed at different times; sometimes two similar actions are separated by a long period. If, now, there is a continuous connection between past and present actions; if the individual's present conduct evidently depends genetically on his conduct in the past (sometimes a distant past), is it not obvious that there must be something real which persists from the past into the present all through the longer or shorter periods of interruption of overt activity? Unless we accept the biogenetic theory that this something is simply the organism, which preserves somehow neuromuscular mechanisms, inborn or acquired, and actualizes them whenever adequately stimulated, must we not assume that it is some combination of psychological or psychobiological forces, some psychoenergetic system which remains latent, that is, unconscious, and expresses itself occasionally in conscious action under definite conditions? The majority of psychonanlysts are dissatisfied with the first alternative—justly so, we believe; for the cultural conduct of men, as will be seen in detail later on, follows patterns essentially irreducible to organic mechanisms such as can be scientifically ascertained. The Freudian school consequently accepts the second alternative, like the older psychological schools; but, unlike the latter, it assumes that the unconscious psychological forces do not remain purely potential while unconscious, but continue to be active and to evolve. Their dynamism finds an occasional conscious outlet which appears incomprehensible, unless we take into account those unconscious changes that have taken place during the intervals of outward conduct.

This doctrine is very plausible because it appeals to our metaphysical desire to find at once a final explanation and unity for everything that seems baffling and disconnected in our empirical world, without waiting for the slow progress of strictly scientific analysis and synthesis. Undoubtedly, for a psychologist who is used to treating a human individual as an ultimate entity and to regarding all actions as parts of this entity, it is baffling to observe that a present action may be dependent upon or be a repetition of an action performed a year ago, a month ago, or only yesterday, although in between the two the individual has been doing entirely different things, unconnected with either. Therefore the psychologist is inclined to postulate that there must be in the human entity some enduring part or process, organic or psychical, which binds these actions across the gulf of time.

But such a postulate is not a scientific hypothesis which helps us organize our inductive knowledge of these actions; what we know and need to know about their connection, we learn from experience and observation of the actions themselves as empirical data. We know as a simple empirical fact that, when the artist takes up today a portrait he left in dissatisfaction a week ago, his failure to realize his original aesthetic tendency last week has a manifest bearing on his present action; his aesthetic tendency today is different from what it would have been if he had not failed the first time. Whether we ascribe this empirical connection between the past action and the present action to the persistence of certain complexes and wishes in the unconscious, or to the duration of biological elements and processes in the nervous system, does not make the slightest difference, for both are inaccessible to our observation, and all we can scientifically know about the connection is what we can conclude from observing the conduct of the painter now and a week ago.

There is, however, one scientifically important point that still remains to be considered from the psychoanalytic doctrine of the unconscious: it is the conclusion, drawn from the observation of human conduct, that tendencies can be modified even while they are not actively manifested, i.e., during periods of intermission between actions. For example, it may happen that a painter apparently satisfied with the way a portrait was originally progressing, when resuming his work after an interruption, reorganizes it altogether: instead of his original tendency a different aesthetic tendency has unexpectedly appeared. Or an avenger who, failing to meet his enemy, still keeps the firm intention to kill him, may later when actually facing his enemy be unwilling to kill him and tend to effect a reconciliation instead. This obviously suggests the supposition that the tendency must have somehow existed during the interruption; otherwise, how could it be changed?

But from the point of view of inductive science founded on empirical evidence, such a supposition must be confirmed by empirical data. We may assume that a non-actual tendency, a tendency which is not manifesting itself in a practical performance, does not disappear but remains potential, if we find some empirical manifestation of its potential existence; just as a physical force may be assumed to exist potentially, though not manifested in dynamic changes of physical reality, whenever its existence can be induced from other empirical manifestations.

Now, we do find a phenomenon which can be interpreted as a manifestation of a non-actual tendency. This phenomenon is the axiological significance which the values that have been used in an action preserve afterwards, whenever they appear in experience. The painter's model and his unachieved portrait, having acquired an aesthetic significance in the course of his activity, preserve this significance whenever he sees or remembers them. The avenger's enemy, the memory of the wrong which he or his group inflicted, preserve a negative significance, and revenge as pictured in imagination a positive significance, whenever they occur to the avenger after his attempt to kill—a significance which may have been imparted to them long before, when the avenger first began to participate in the social life of his clan. This significance is an indication that the tendency to paint the portrait or to kill the enemy persists even while the portrait is not being actually painted, while no active preparations are being made to kill; and such a potential tendency may, become actualized, pass into activity, any time certain technical obstacles are removed.

The concept *attitude*, as now used in sociological research, covers precisely such potential tendencies as manifested in the axiological significance given by the agent to certain values of his experience. By changing the meaning of those values for the agent, the agent's attitude, i.e., the potential tendency, can be changed; and when it passes into activity, it proves to be a different tendency than it was before. Thus the painter, after comparing his unachieved portrait with other paintings or placing his model in a different position under a new light, sees a new aesthetic meaning in his work, and instead of being pleased becomes disgusted with it. The clansman, while separated from his enemy, may get converted to Christianity or lose interest in clan affairs. When the painter and the clansman start to act, they act differently than before.

The existence of potential tendencies as attitudes and the capacity of attitudes to be empirically modified by observable influences are all we need for a scientific study of those changes in human conduct which occur while no overt actions are being performed. There is no need and no possibility of delving under the surface in search for "unconscious" factors of those changes in conduct which must be traced to the agent's inactive periods. Only what is open and above the surface is empirical evidence of genetic processes, and all hypotheses must ultimately be referred to empirical evidence.

Of course, in a particular case neither the experience of the agent nor that of other people may furnish us with sufficient direct evidence of the existence of a tendency which from indirect indices we believe to be there, potential or even actual, but combined with other tendencies so closely that it cannot be separated. Or, in tracing the past evolution of tendencies, we may lack data about a particular change which we believe to have been there as a necessary link in the process. In such cases we have the right, as in every other science, to *conjecture* that the undiscoverable tendency did manifest itself at some time in the past. But conjecture is permissible only if well-grounded on analogy with otherwise similar instances where the undiscoverable tendency, or the missing link, was unmistakably experienced and observed.

There are two other arguments seemingly in favor of the psychoanalytic theory. One of these is the indubitable fact that between what the agent says he tends to do and what he actually tends to do there is often a marked discrepancy. But here a distinction must be clearly drawn between a case where the agent in what he says tries merely to describe his own experience of his action and a case where by what he says he tends to influence the listener socially, to provoke him verbally into making a certain active response or at least a certain valuation of his action. In the first case the description may lack precision or completeness, if the agent is untrained in reconstructing his experiences and observations theoretically; but it is not false, and can be used as evidence—though *imperfect* evidence—with reference to the action described. In the second case, it is not a mere description of the action to which it refers, but a new and distinct action: it is *prima facie* evidence of what the agent tends to achieve in trying to influence verbally his listener, but no evidence at all of what he tended to achieve in the original action which he pretends to describe. It is not a matter of the discrepancy between a tendency and its verbal formulation, but of [a] difference between two tendencies, one manifested in the original action, the other in the verbal action superadded to the first.

But the discrepancy in which psychoanalysts are mainly interested is not so much between what an agent does and what he says he is doing, as between what he does and what he believes himself to be doing when he thinks about it. They have unquestionably made important positive contributions to this problem in their studies of rationalization and sublimation, but their theoretic interpretation of these contributions are often vitiated by their metaphysics. They usually interpret what the agent thinks about his action as something superadded to this action which has no important influence on the fundamental "wish," the psychological force which underlies the action. Now, such an interpretation is only justified when the agent thinks about his conduct as a theorist, an objective student, who intentionally tries not to modify his tendency in reflecting about it. Obviously, such cases are rare. Apart from them, the agent's reflection is a practical, dynamic process which really modifies the tendency upon which it bears; and the primary and unmistakable evidence of this modification is, again, the action itself as experienced by the agent and observed by others. We shall investigate such processes later in the present work and distinguish several varieties of them: ordinary practical rationalization, righteous justification by ready standards, and sublimation of standards in an ethical hierarchy. Reflection may come in the course of an action; then we can experience and observe the change which the tendency undergoes. Or it may be there at the outset of the action; and then by comparing this action with others unaccompanied by reflection, we can determine the difference between the tendencies.

This brings us to the final argument of the psychoanalytic school in favor of the substitution of "unconscious" wishes as real driving powers instead of the "conscious" tendencies manifested in actions as empirical data. This argument is derived from the results of the psychoanalytic technique. The latter purports to bring to the subject's consciousness by ingenious devices those unconscious forces which underlie his conduct, with the result that the abnormal subject becomes cured and the normal subject confirms the validity of the psychoanalyst's conclusions by discovering in his unconscious self those very forces which the psychoanalyst assumed to be active. Now, here again the dynamic influence of reflection, particularly reflection carried on under the supervision and with the assistance of the psychoanalyst as social agent, is often either misinterpreted or undervalued. The plain empirical fact is that a patient's tendencies and emotional experiences become modified by the introduction of *new elements* into his *present* active system or by new revaluations of existing elements. That these new elements are presented to him and appear to him as having existed in his unconscious all the time is not a proof that they did so exist; indeed, such an assumption is completely gratuitous, since it can be neither proved nor disproved. What can be proved or disproved is whether such or similar elements existed in the subject's past as data of his experience. But it is not the data of his past experience, only the data of his present experience which influence his present conduct; and the way they influence it depends not on his past, but on his present tendencies. The meaning and practical significance of past data reproduced now in a very different situation is quite different from what the meaning and practical significance of the original data was.

Nor can the experiences of a normal agent who is being "psychoanalyzed" be taken as anything more than *prima facie* evidence of what he is experiencing during the psychoanalytic performance. Whether or not they have any validity with regard to his past, must be tested by comparing them with his past experiences; and unfortunately such a test is usually difficult, since there is seldom any adequate record preserved of his past experiences as they were at the time. Being subjected to psychoanalysis does not mean simply being given as a theoretic student a new scientific interpretation of objective materials; it means being influenced practically, having one's tendencies modified by their reflective interpretation. The results of having one's conduct psychoanalyzed are at least as important practically, and therefore at least as unreliable theoretically, as the results of rationalizing or sublimating one's own conduct.

We conclude that it is altogether impossible for a student of social actions to take as guide the theory of the Freudian school or of any other school using the same type of general approach. It is a theory that sacrifices the clear light of humanistic experience and observation for a will-o'-the-wisp of speculation, more and more arbitrary as it tries to embrace wider and wider fields. It preserves and develops the most undesirable feature of the old instinct theory: the substitution of a few psychological powers inaccessible to experience and defined *by their origin* as hidden mainsprings of human actions, instead of plain and multiple tendencies empirically manifested in the very performance of human actions and definable *in terms of this performance*.

But in rejecting the general theory of the Freudian school, we should not undervalue its many claims to positive scientific discoveries in the study of genetic and causal processes. These discoveries need to be more exactly tested and their theoretic significance reinterpreted; but the importance of some of them is undeniable. The very concept of the "unconscious," however unjustified scientifically, deserves a certain consideration as marking a reaction against that narrow intellectualism of the eighteenth and nineteenth centuries for which "consciousness" and "reflection" were practically synonymous. However, it would be best if the terms "conscious" and "unconscious" could be both eliminated from the theory of actions; in any case, we shall use the former not to characterize actions, but to indicate the capacity of a human agent to experience data and realize tendencies.

5. Positive Conclusions

The following seven points summarize very briefly the positive results of this chapter. . . .

a) Social actions are actions which deal practically with human beings, whom the agent experiences as conscious objects

b) Social actions ought to be studied *inductively as empirical data*, independently of any deductions from psychological theories. Since they already have been thus studied by sociologists, who need a knowledge of social actions for their investigation of other, more complex social data, this study should be the special task of sociology. Similar tasks are being performed by other sciences of culture, each of which investigates a specific variety of human actions—technical, economic, aesthetic, religious, linguistic, or intellectual actions.

c) Social actions, like any of the varieties of cultural action just mentioned, are as empirical scientific data entirely accessible only to the investigator who takes them with their *humanistic coefficient*, that is, who in studying them uses fully the primary evidence furnished by the active experience of the agent himself.

d) If the active experience of the agent himself is incomplete (as in the case of actions performed in a half-conscious state), or if the agent is incapable of expressing his experience reflectively, his evidence ought to be supplemented wherever possible by that of other agents who have had a practical experience of his action by participating in it, reproducing it, or opposing it.

e) The objects involved in human actions, when taken with their humanistic coefficient, are found to be *values*, that is, meaningful objects with a partly material (sensory), partly non-material (spiritual) content. A value has in the experience of the agent a positive or a negative axiological significance with reference to its active use.

f) Most values in human experience are found to be organized into cultural systems, constructed and maintained by active *tendencies*.

g) An active tendency manifests itself empirically by the practical results it achieves in dealing with values. A tendency may not be active, but potential; it is then called an *attitude* and manifests itself in a positive or negative appreciation of those values with which it deals when active.

5. Role Analysis

THE SOCIAL ROLE OF THE
MAN OF KNOWLEDGE

1940

1. The Emergence of a New Pattern

ALL NEW developments in the history of knowledge have been due to those scientists who did more in their social roles than their circles wanted and expected them to do.

Among the technologists some leaders took risks and compelled or enticed their followers to participate in difficult collective tasks where success was uncertain; some experts raised and solved practical problems in which the leaders who employed them were not interested; free inventors thrust upon an unwilling social environment disturbing new patterns of technical action. By such spontaneous individual exertions, technological knowledge has advanced from the Late Stone Age level to its present height.

Among the sages were a few who, instead of merely justifying the actual tendencies of their groups and combating those of their opponents, set up cultural ideals as standards of valuation and guides of action, and thus initiated human efforts to direct cultural evolution by reflective thought.

Some of the scholars, instead of merely receiving and transmitting the traditional doctrines of their schools, developed, re-

Chapter 4, "The Explorer as Creator of New Knowledge," from *The Social Role of the Man of Knowledge* (New York: Columbia University Press, 1940), pp. 164–199. Reprinted by permission of the publisher.

247

organized, expanded these doctrines or founded new schools; and in so doing made knowledge systematic and objective, with a validity independent of any extraneous demands and founded entirely on its own rational, theoretic order.

Probably in every other field of culture development occurs similarly by the agency of individuals who in their specific roles do more than is socially expected of them. Often, but not necessarily, this involves them in a conflict with their social environment: not all innovators are rebels, nor are all rebels innovators, by far.

Now we come to an extremely interesting phenomenon for which there is no precedent and no parallel, except perhaps in modern poetry and art. We find individual scientists who specialize, so to speak, in doing the unexpected. They may be metaphorically termed *explorers*, for they are seeking in the domain of knowledge new ways leading into the unknown. Originally they were for the most part aberrants from socially recognized ways. Some of them, however, have attempted to have this type of activity recognized as a regular social function and to construct a new pattern of the scientist's social role, implying a new conception of knowledge itself. So long as they remained isolated from one another, they were unsuccessful; but with the growing facilities of communication, their number slowly increased. The first initiators found followers in various intellectual centers and eventually there developed a world-wide solidarity of explorers in every scientific field.

Thus, an individual who performs this kind of activity at the present time finds understanding and recognition of his role, at least among his colleagues. In the circles of technologists and scholars, his function is usually recognized *ex post*, by a belated validation of those results of his exploration which have been found practically applicable or have remained unchallenged long enough to be considered reasonably certain and thus fit to be taught to students. In the wider society, popularizers of knowledge manage to stir interest in some of his results by surrounding them with the halo of sensational novelty, though such interest passes as quickly as all fads and most fashions.

However, only a few institutions especially organized for scientific research acknowledge his social role as different from other scientists' and grant him an independent status. Usually, unless possessed of hereditary wealth or endowed by a rich amateur, he is forced to perform the role of technologist or scholar, indulging in scientific exploration during his leisure time. Such material equipment and economic resources as are necessary in his field are given him primarily for technically useful or teaching purposes, and only after these have been attained can the surplus, if any, be used for free personal research. But even this is great progress as compared with the time not far distant when explorers were distinctly not wanted either in technological or in scholarly circles.

Still more vague than the conception of the explorer's function and status is the idea of the personal qualifications required for this new role of his. In scholarly tradition the study of scientific thinking has been limited to the intellectual activities which are manifested in deductive systematization and verbal disputation; and even these have been investigated only with reference to their conformity or conflict with the rules of deductive logic, gradually identified with symbolic logic. In modern times, inductive thinking has attracted considerable attention, but even here most studies have centered upon the logical validation of inductive studies. Logicians have drawn a sharp dividing line between the logic of science, clearly circumscribed and well ordered, and an indefinite, chaotic discipline called the psychology of knowledge, which—according to them—has nothing to do with questions of validity. Since modern logic, if concerned with thinking at all, deals only with that kind of thinking which establishes valid relationships between concepts expressed in exactly defined symbols, all other kinds of intellectual activity of human individuals, including the formation of concepts, are left to psychologists or to those philosophers who—like J. S. Mill, Ernest Naville, Wundt, Dewey, Le Roy —do not recognize this dividing line, however much their theories may otherwise differ from one another.

But psychologists and philosophers have not yet distinguished clearly between the different types of scientific thinking which are required of scientists in different social roles and methodically developed in the course of their preparation for those roles. For instance, Wundt's theory (as exposed in the three volumes of his *Logik*) is based upon the thinking of scholars, especially of systematizers and contributors; Dewey studies the kind of thinking typical of technologists, treating it as representative of all scientific thinking. Especially vague are still most studies dealing with the intellectual activity of theoretic exploration, although every important step in the progress of modern science is ascribed to it and it has therefore attracted considerable attention.[1]

The reason for this vagueness is not far to seek. Intellectual activity must be studied with reference to the objective structure of the science of which it forms a part. Explorative thinking— though scattered rudiments of it may be seen among older scholars, technologists, even sages—is actually a new type of scientific thinking, which has probably not yet reached its full development. Its essential and distinctive characteristic, as compared with other types, cannot be discovered unless it is taken in connection with the objective structure of the new kind of knowledge which the explorers are creating. And even among them, only a few are yet fully aware of all the revolutionary implications of their collective work. The very standardization of this new type of thinking is far from completed. There is no "logic" of creative thought; there are no principles of the search for new knowledge comparable to the principles of the systematization of ready knowledge. Books on methodology contain mainly technical rules of handling data, like those of comparative observation, experimentation,' or mathematical calculation. And we lack completely any educational method for preparing future explorers for their function: we are unable to answer the question of why and how some of the

[1] J. Picard, in the book mentioned above, gives perhaps the most complete analysis of the psychological processes involved in creative scientific thinking, though he does not take into account the contributions of James and Dewey. As to the social factors of scientific innovation, he quotes A. Rey: "Il n'y a rien que de très vague sur la question des facteurs sociaux de l'invention. . . . Tout travail positif sur ce point est encore à faire" (p. 54). This author, who applies to science the formula by which H. Taine tried to explain art (race, millieu, moment) has not contributed much to the latter problem.

individuals who have been taught in learned schools or trained under the guidance of technologists become original and independent theoretic explorers.

2. *The Discoverer of Facts*

The first stage in the development of scientific exploration is the search for new and unexpected facts, that is, for empirical data hitherto unknown to scientists and not anticipated in their theories. Many explorers do not go beyond this stage; they regard the discovery of new facts as the most important scientific achievement.

The term "fact-finder" could be used to designate them, if it had not a somewhat contemptuous connotation. The expression "discoverer of facts" is nonevaluative and has besides the advantage of denoting both an analogy and a contrast between this kind of scientific activity and the scholarly function of the "discoverer of truth."

In the history of every inductive science there have been periods of extensive search for unknown data, which were also periods of intellectual revolt against the stabilized technology of recognized leaders and experts, the self-assured wisdom of official sages, and doctrines taught by scholars as absolutely true.

Every one of these scientists desires "new" facts, facts he has not already observed, provided they are such as he expects them to be. Their essential character must be known to him in advance, for he wishes all the facts he has to deal with in the performance of his function to prove helpful for the achievement of his task; or, at least, he wants to be sure that none will interfere with this achievement.

The technological leader desires factual knowledge which he can utilize in making his plans and controlling their realization. If his plans were entirely undetermined, he might welcome any kind of new facts. But they are not: his social role gives a definite direction to his leadership and limits the range of his planning. His plans must follow certain patterns compatible with the social conditions under which he acts. The discovery of unforeseen facts within the range of his activity may show that the latter is not so rational as he and his followers believed it to be, that the means he chooses are wasteful, that his successes must be ascribed to favorable circumstances rather than to careful planning, or that the realization of his plans is followed by some undesirable and hitherto unsuspected aftereffects. Any such discovery is apt to undermine his status or be used by his rivals and competitors for planning more efficient than his own. As to technological experts, since their type of specialized research is determined by what men in power wish to know, it may be quite dangerous for their role to indulge in seeking for new data without knowing more or less what they will find: they may discover facts which from the point of view of men in power had better have remained unknown. Many an expert has been made to suffer for such unwelcome discoveries.

The sage, as we have seen, wants only facts that he expects to use in his arguments for his side in social conflicts or against the opposite side. Unexpected facts may, contrarywise, furnish material which his opponents will use in the arguments against his side. It is not so bad if the opponents themselves find such facts, for they are known to be partial, and their factual evidence can be invalidated on that ground. But facts discovered by impartial observers cannot be so easily swept away. Therefore, impartial seekers for unknown facts in the social field are viewed as unsafe people by both sides in a social conflict; and if either side be victorious, it bars free impartial observation almost as carefully as ideological opposition.

Scholars—especially secular scholars—are not averse to new and unexpected facts, so long as the system of the school is in the formative stage of discovery of new truths and fundamental systematization: new facts are even welcome to illustrate and exemplify new truths or to help disclose the errors of older schools; nor is there any danger that empirical evidence might prove an obstacle in building the system, for it will be interpreted in the light of rational evidence. We know, for instance, about the assiduous search for unknown biological facts which Aristotle carried on for years with the help of a large staff of assistants, who collected data in various countries. Albert the Great, the teacher of St. Thomas, was famous for his factual explorations; so was Descartes. The scientists of the nineteenth century who, even if they began as explorers, developed into founders of schools were eager for new facts, while they were building their systems: take the enormous mass of materials used by Wundt in psychology or by Herbert Spencer in sociology.

However, as the system becomes stabilized and extended by successive additions, the search for new and unexpected facts not only abates but becomes more and more unwelcome. Contributors, as we have seen, must take care that generalizations based on facts within the domain of the school's knowledge be reducible to the system. Inductive "verisimilitudes," if thus reduced, become accepted as certain truths, necessary and universal. Thus, the stabilization and progressive extension of the system means that the school is committing itself to uphold as absolutely true a growing number of generalizations about empirical facts. An unexpected new fact may disagree with such a generalization and thus invalidate it, since no exceptions are possible to a necessary and universal truth. It may be saved at the cost of necessity and universality: the judgment "Some S are P" may be substituted for "All S are P." But this means that the attempt to reduce it to the rationally evident truths of the deductive system was an error; and it breaks the chain of deductive reasoning, makes a further extension of the system in this direction impossible, whereas if the school assumes that the exception is only apparent and can be explained by some universal truth yet unknown, it risks the danger that this unknown truth, once discovered, will conflict with the system. Schools generally welcome factual exploration only if it upsets the theories of other schools.

It is thus obvious that a discoverer of facts, freely roaming in search of the unexpected, has no place in a milieu of scientists with well-regulated traditional roles. He may be a solitary, independent individual with no interest in professional traditions or else a rebel against established intellectual authority. Neither of these types is actuated merely by curiosity or by the desire for adventure. Curiosity alone does not make men search for facts objectively unknown, not yet observed by other investigators: on the contrary, it is rather stimulated by social communication in which the individual learns from other people about data unknown to him but known to them. As to the "spirit of adventure," it may indeed lead the individual into unexplored fields but in search not of objective facts to be recorded for scientific use but only of extraordinary personal experiences. Tourists, wild-game hunters, prospectors, pioneers, and colonists are not scientific explorers.

Other tendencies must be active in factual exploration. The solitary observer of nature, like Fabre or Thoreau, or of culture, like those archeologists and ethnologists who initiated intensive studies of various past or exotic civilizations, is animated by love for the factual domain which he investigates. He experiences aesthetic joy in contemplating every particular new phenomenon which his search discloses; and this joy alternates with a deeply thrilling consciousness of the inexhaustible wealth of his domain, the innumerable mysteries it conceals, and the possibilities of new discoveries which it provides. This kind of love can rise to a mystical enthusiasm, as with Giordano Bruno, who, though treated as a rebel, remained primarily a passionate lover of the infinite empirical world which to him offered marvels enough to contemplate through eternity.

Some of this aesthetic and intellectual thrill will probably be found in the lives of all discoverers of facts, though in the rebellious type social tendencies seem to predominate. The latter is mainly desirous to throw off the intellectual yoke of professional science. Often he is an unsuccessful technologist, sage, or scholar who could not or would not conform with traditional requirements, sometimes a rank outsider, a self-taught amateur. His rebellion, however, is not a mere personal problem of subjective misadaptation. It becomes depersonalized and objectified as a problem of the validity of the very knowledge cultivated in those scientific circles against which he revolts. He tries to undermine this validity by discovering facts hitherto unknown which will conflict with recognized generalizations.

This is how, for example, in preclassical Greece and again in the fifteenth century revolt against traditional theories of the universe, supported at the time by sacred schools, partly manifested itself in geographical exploration; and how later ethnographical exploration often accompanied the rebellion against the complacent ethnocentrism of religious, ethical, political thought. Historical exploration frequently had its first source in revolt against myths and legends which sublimated the origins of the existing social order; later historical doctrines, as taught in school and presenting a schematized and idealized reconstruction of the past, gave rebels a chance to undermine scholarly authority by uncovering historical facts which radically conflicted with this reconstruction. Even now "debunking" is sometimes the chief aim of historical fact-finders.

The wide interest in new and forgotten astronomical, physical, chemical, and biological facts which during the fifteenth, sixteenth, and seventeenth centuries spread over Europe was largely a manifestation of intellectual revolt against all scholastic knowledge, irrespective of the differences between schools. Learned schools were aware of this and opposed the current of factual exploration as long as they could.

Since the middle of the nineteenth century, discoverers of facts have been many and active in psychology, sociology, economics, and political theory. Psychology had always been a scholarly discipline, a part of general philosophy, and, though recently specialized, had preserved the tendency to scholarly stabilization of new theories. Sociology and economics had barely emerged from a stage when thinking in these fields was done mainly by sages. They were still struggling for recognition as branches of objective academic knowledge and sought to gain this recognition by building scholarly systems founded on rationally evident principles. Political theory, though since Plato an acknowledged and important part of scholarly tradition, was shown during the struggle for democracy and later for socialism to be dependent on political ideologies and far removed from theoretic objectivity. Every attempt at systematization in these fields was followed by an opposition which expressed itself, first of all, in a search for unknown and unexpected facts which could invalidate the system.

The rebellious discoverer of facts is not a system-builder himself; he does not tend to substitute new theories for those he upsets.

He finds, therefore, easy recognition among other searchers for unknown facts, since to him and to his fellows facts are objective empirical data, which as such do not conflict with one another. Subjective experiences of an objective datum may disagree; but discoverers of facts are not naïve empiricists of prescholarly days. Only data about which all competent observers agree constitute scientific facts that can be successfully used as objective empirical evidence against the standard of rational evidence to which scholars appealed in depreciating primitive empiricism. Discoverers of facts have been therefore greatly interested in standards of scientific observation. Indeed, the formation of such standards, including the invention of instruments with the help of which human powers of sensory observation have been multiplied and "subjective" variations of individual experiences excluded or measured, constitutes the main historical achievement of discoverers of facts.

A fact—as they view it—when properly observed remains a fact forever. New discoveries can supplement it by additional facts, results of even more precise and detailed observations, but they cannot invalidate it. Facts are all that is certain in any domain of knowledge. Opposition against old theories and unwillingness or incapacity to build new theories crystallize among the discoverers of facts into a norm which condemns all "theorizing."

But facts accumulate indefinitely at an ever-increasing rate, as searches for hitherto unknown empirical data penetrate into every field of science. These facts must somehow be ordered; otherwise man would be lost amongst their enormous mass and variety. From the point of view of radical objective empiricism, their ordering assumes a significance similar to that of the description and classification of collections in a museum: it serves to guide the observer. Such is, indeed, the conception of knowledge developed by those epistemologists to whom scientific progress, especially during the last centuries, consists essentially in the discovery of new facts. The entire objective content of knowledge is constituted of empirical data of standardized observation. Scientific systems introduce into this content a formal order which has no objective validity of its own, is entirely arbitrary in the sense that it is neither true nor false. If one system is preferable to another, it is only because it serves better the purposes of intellectual orientation, helps the observer survey a greater number and variety of facts with the same mental effort or the same number and variety of facts with less mental effort. In short, the principle of scientific systematization is purely utilitarian. E. Mach and his followers call it the principle of "economy of thinking."

3. The Discoverer of Problems (Inductive Theorist)[2]

The development of scientific exploration culminates in the social role of the scientist who, like the discoverer of facts, explores empirical reality but whose self-appointed function is not to find hitherto unknown empirical data but to discover new, hitherto unforeseen *theoretic problems* and to solve them by new theories. And new theoretic problems may concern data which have long been familiar to scientific observers as well as data which have never yet been observed.

We speak of "discovering," not of "raising," new problems. For a theoretic problem is an objective problem of science, not a subjective problem of an individual or a collectivity. Every theoretic problem originates in an application of an objective, rationally standardized theory to an objective, methodically standardized reality, and is solved by an objective modification of the original theory or by an entirely different theory, also rationally standardized.

The discoverer of problems is not a rebel against scientific rationalism as manifested in theoretic construction: what he rejects is scientific dogmatism, as expressed in the claim that a certain theory contains the only true knowledge about a certain object

[2]   There is a vast literature bearing upon the matters discussed in this and the next section; nearly all of it, however, is concerned with the sciences of nature and the scientists who have creatively participated in their development. The author has borrowed from so many methodologists, epistemologists, and historians working in this field that it would take a volume to acknowledge all his debts. He owes the most probably to Henri Poincaré.

matter. He is opposed to every kind of dogmatism: the kind which the social milieu imposes upon the theoretic conceptions of technologists and of sages in the name of practical utility; the kind with which a sacred school maintains that its doctrine is the Truth because its source is divine; and the kind which the knowledge of secular scholars derives from the rational evidence of its ontological principles and the formal necessity of its logic. For a dogmatic theory tends to close within the field of its application the way to new theoretic possibilities, whereas the explorer sees new theoretic possibilities in every field he approaches.

Of course, scientific dogmatism can never altogether prevent new theoretic problems from arising: there always have been scientists whose thinking transgressed the limits imposed by a socially immobilized theory. The technologists who went beyond the demands of their social circles in setting new practical problems and risking hazardous solutions were often led to doubt old theoretic certainties on which they were supposed to rely in practice, and they applied instead new theoretic hypotheses of which this very application was to be a test. This has been one of the factors in the gradual disappearance of magical thinking and has resulted in an agglomeration of many specific inductive generalizations, descriptive and causal, concerning inorganic and organic nature which—as recent historians have amply shown—prepared the way for modern science. However, theoretic problematization is only incidental in the performance of the technologist's ᵗfunction and subsidiary to his practical task; if consistently pursued, it would lead him away from his role. Therefore, even such theoretic problems as arise in the course of technological planning and invention are nowadays mostly taken over by theoretic explorers.

Sages also have occasionally raised new theoretic problems and proposed new hypotheses in psychology, sociology, political science, economics, theory of religion; and here also recent history is doing its best to separate such theoretic achievements from their evaluative and normative constructions. But it is not surprising that in their case theoretic problematization is scarce, for it does not merely transcend but actually conflicts with social demands. Whatever is right must be founded on truth, whatever is wrong must be based on error; and since the sage must be perfectly sure of right and wrong, problems of truth and error are solved for him in advance, though it may take a considerable effort of reflection and observation on his part to reach the "proper" solution. And, indeed, we find in the works of sages only such problems openly formulated as they are sure to have already solved in conformity with their ideologies. We often suspect a self-imposed check on new thinking, an unwillingness to face some new problem of which the thinker is probably conscious but which he fears may lead to a solution conflicting with his social philosophy. Thus, the French rationalists of the eighteenth century seem to have been well aware of the problems of irrationality in cultural life but would not study them lest the ideal of a perfectly rational new social order be thereby endangered. Only radical critics of all cultural orders do not hesitate to raise unsolved theoretic problems in this field; but as they are mostly also theoretic skeptics, they do not solve these problems and thus do little to promote positive knowledge.

The pitfall of skepticism has always made scholars afraid of treading the dangerous path of unrestrained new problematization. If truth is absolute, if any knowledge which is not true must be false, and if all the truths about the same object matter are bound together by a systematic order in accordance with the principles of logical deduction, then, after the essential truths within a definite field of knowledge have been discovered and their systematic order has been determined, no further study of this field will raise any *objectively new problems*, that is, problems which cannot be solved by deduction from those essential truths. A problem may be subjectively new to an individual scholar faced with unfamiliar data or unfamiliar aspects of familiar data; but after investigating it, he will find that it either is reducible to problems already solved by the system or is a pseudo-problem—does not concern the object matter upon which the system is bearing.

Of course, both the secularization of knowledge and the foundation of new secular schools involved raising objectively new problems which the old system could not solve, whereas the new system did so. But the basic pattern of the scholar's role made it impossible for him to persist in this innovating type of scientific investigation. Any scholar who opposed a new theory to the theories of his predecessors had to claim for it the same kind of absolute validity which they were supposed to possess and had to prove his claim by rational demonstration. His theory might be still incomplete and its completion left to his followers; but so far as it went, it had to be final. If, while rejecting other theories, he could not or would not use the standards of scholarly knowledge to establish the validity of his own theory, this meant to the scholarly world that he did not recognize those standards, and he was branded a skeptic. And skeptics were not regarded as fit members of a school where truth was taught to the younger generation.

It is therefore perfectly understandable from the sociological point of view that even the majority of the great theoretic explorers of the last three centuries have accepted the traditional roles of discoverers of absolute truths and builders of uncontrovertibly valid systems, when such roles were thrust upon them by scholarly circles of contemporaries and successors, since they had been brought up under the scholarly criteria of truth and saw no alternative to these criteria other than a skeptical denial of the objective validity of all theories either in the form of subjectivism or of critical empiricism. While discovering and solving their new problems, they looked toward the future, wandered into the unknown, sought for the unexpected. But when they had to organize systematically the results of their exploration and to justify them theoretically before the community of scientists which kept the scholarly traditions alive, they turned toward the past and accepted as guide its standards of valid theory; or, if they did not, their disciples did it for them. Only a few years ago a scientist, now dead, disciple of a famous theoretic explorer whose system he developed, during an academic celebration on his behalf, proudly said that for thirty years he had found no reason for changing his fundamental theory.[3]

It is no doubt a great honor to be recognized as founder of a

3   De Greef, a disciple of Comte, who supplemented Comte's general classification of sciences by a special classification of social sciences in which the science of economic phenomena is regarded as fundamental.

new school of scientific thought and to have one's theories accepted as finally and unconditionally true by a faithful body of followers; the very consideration for their trust may be a powerful factor inhibiting further excursions into the unknown in search of new problems—unless one is sure that one's theory will be adequate to deal with them, and then they cannot be objectively new and really unexpected. But apart from social influences, there has been another difficulty in breaking away from the scholarly conception of true knowledge. There is no other form of scientific systematization in existence except the systematization of scientific results. The theoretic explorer has a ready pattern, the old scholarly pattern, for systematizing the *solutions* of theoretic problems; there is no pattern for systematizing *problems*. We mentioned above the university textbook as the kind of work in which scholarly systematization survives. Every textbook, in every field of science, gives primarily a survey of those results of scientific investigation which are regarded as proven, presenting them—as far as possible —in a logical order modeled upon the deductive order of scholarly systems. Problems are given, indeed, for students to solve; but these are either problems which were solved by scientists long ago or else such as can be solved easily with the help of the systematic theory contained in the book; in short, they are patterned upon the kind of problem which scholarly contributors have been solving for over twenty centuries. Some explorers are aware that this type of systematization does not harmonize with their conception of knowledge, but they justify it on educational grounds; and in any case they have not developed any other type to take its place. Consequently, we notice that, in the scientific circles where the search for new problems dominates, systematization is more and more neglected and nearly all scientific work is expressed in monographs.

Under such strong and persistent pressure of the ideals and patterns of scholarship, the liberation of modern theoretic science from scholarly dogmatism is not easy to explain. It may be regarded as a continuation of that historical trend toward freedom of thought which was previously manifested in the struggle of secular against sacred scholars for the autonomy of knowledge. We saw that the struggle was won because secular scholars mustered organized Reason against organized Faith, opposed a standard of absolute truth founded on the inner rational evidence of knowledge to the standard of absolute truth founded on sacred traditions. Only after religion could no longer control rational science, came the new historical tendency: to make knowledge free to develop in unforeseen directions by breaking the bonds which rational systems constructed by great thinkers of the past laid upon all new thinking. The first step was the emphasis of discoverers of facts upon empirical reality as infinitely rich, varied, and imprevisibly changing, the source of new knowledge in contrast with the dry and rigid schematism of scholarly constructions.

The next step was due perhaps to that general exaltation of creative individualism which since the days of Humanism has gradually permeated all domains of cultural life—art, literature, religion, social and political organization, economic enterprise, material technique. Empirical reality gives the scientist inexhaustible materials for creative thinking; new theories are products of scientific creativeness. This involves a complete rejection of the deductive structure of science which in the scholarly conception of knowledge is essential to its validity. All science is inductive; deduction can serve only as an auxiliary method in raising problems for inductive research, never as the ruling method by which inductive solutions of those problems have to be validated. Inductive science is theoretic science, not mere agglomeration of facts; but its theories must be judged by its own standards of objective validity, which were unknown to scholars.

We may for this reason call the modern discoverer of new problems which he solves by new theories of empirical reality also an "inductive theorist." Nowadays, he is no longer (as his early predecessors were) socially dependent for his scientific status upon the recognition of scholars, who judged his theories by their criteria; he is a participant in a world-wide community of explorers with the same interest in untried theoretic possibilities as he has. He finds the problems he has discovered stimulating them to new research and is stimulated to new research by the problems which they discover.

But—and here lies a subjective difficulty which not every inductive theorist is able to overcome—he becomes aware after a time that his solutions of new objective problems, which he regards as perfectly valid, are not accepted by other explorers in the same spirit as scholarly disciples usually accept the truths discovered by their master. His theory may indeed stir interest, even enthusiasm, but the more important it is, the more widely known and recognized, the greater the stimulus it gives to new problematization. And sooner or later he finds his theory, often in consequence of the very influence it has had upon the thinking of other scientists, becomes superseded by a new theory.

This is a hard personal test. Will he successfully exclude from his own thought that very tendency to dogmatize which perhaps he, like other explorers, has often condemned in his predecessors? Of course, he will not surrender his theory without a struggle. But what will be the method of this struggle? Will he follow the example of sages, putting forward facts and interpretations which favor it, pushing into shadow facts which furnish arguments against it? Will he use the formal logical method of scholarly "polemics"? Or will he rather try to solve his theory by new exploration, modifying and developing it so that it will become fit to solve such new problems as neither he nor his opponents have yet been aware of?

In any case, as the same fortune or misfortune sooner or later befalls every inductive theorist, the community of creative scientists is attempting to develop those standards of theoretic validity which inductive science needs.

There are no absolute, unconditionally certain truths concerning any given object matter of knowledge. There are only truth-hypotheses, with a validity which is dependent on definite conditions. The verification of a hypothesis does not mean that the latter comes nearer to becoming absolute truth with every successful test. It only means ascertaining the range of its validity, determining what are the problems which it can solve. On the other hand, when a hypothesis fails in any particular test, this does not mean that it is false. It only means that we have reached a limit of its validity, discovered a problem which it cannot solve, and that another hypothesis is needed which will solve it, either in conjunction with the first or instead of the first. Experience cannot ultimately prove or disprove any scientific truth, for the facts which we use to test our hypotheses are not the original data of experience but data already selected, reconstructed, and standardized from the point of view of our problems.

A theory is a system of mutually supplementary hypotheses by the aid of which a set of theoretic problems concerning a certain complex of empirical data can be solved. Its validity is only relative, not subjectively relative in reference to the thinker but objectively relative in reference to other theories. It does not depend on the psychological dispositions or biological needs of man, individually or collectively, whether a certain theory furnishes the solution of a certain set of problems or not. He may be uninterested in these problems, or ignorant of the theory, or too stupid to understand it, or too prejudiced to use it: the theory once created is there, an objectively binding norm for any thinking that tries to solve those problems. But it is not the only theory possible about the given complex of empirical data. There may already be or there may be later created other theories that offer different solutions of the same problems, like the Ptolemaic and the Copernican theories in astronomy, the Lamarckian and the Darwinian theories in biology, the theory of parallel independent development and the theory of diffusion in cultural anthropology and so on.

There is no criterion, either logical or empirical, according to which, if one of such different theories be judged true, the other must be judged false. Each may be "true" in the sense that it is consistent in its inner structure and adequate to solve the problems within its range; the difference between their solutions means only that they are making a different use of the same empirical materials, that out of the inexhaustible wealth of the concrete empirical data with which they are dealing, each has selected different elements and relations as scientifically significant for the solution of its problems. But this, again, does not mean that the choice between any given theories is subjectively arbitrary. For there are objective standards by which inductive theories can be compared and their relative validity estimated. Of two theories, A and B, bearing on the same empirical field, if B solves all the problems A has solved and also other problems which A could not solve, B is superior to A in theoretic validity, both from the rational and from the empirical point of view. For, if not more consistent, it is more comprehensive as a system of truth-hypotheses; while the new problems it has raised imply that it has initiated or followed up the discovery of unknown empirical data or of unknown elements and relations among known empirical data which A did not use as scientific material.

But such a comparison between theories as to their relative scientific validity does not exhaust yet the problem of their relationship. Theories do not separately and abstractly subsist in a timeless world of Platonic ideas: they are created and they continue to exist in the course of the historical development of knowledge. The very discovery of objective problems which a certain theory cannot solve would have been impossible if it had not already solved its own previously discovered problems. Its hypotheses have shown explorers the way to new problems by their failure to work beyond the range of their applicability; this is the initial stage of a creative investigation resulting in a more valid theory. Every scientific theory is thus both an end and a beginning; it grows out of a preceding theory which it supplants and becomes the root of a subsequent theory which will supplant it.

According to this conception of scientific knowledge, the function of inductive theorists is to participate in the development of objective scientific thought by creating new systems of relative truths, founded upon less valid systems of their predecessors and serving as foundation for more valid systems of their successors.

4. Differentiation among Inductive Theorists

Not all who participate in this creative development of knowledge and reflect about it conceive in the same way the historical significance of their function. Scientists who investigate natural reality, especially those who specialize in physical science, tend to interpret this significance differently from scientist-humanists who explore the empirical realm of cultural data.

The former do not like to resign the guiding ideal of a logically perfect system of absolutely certain rational truths. For their knowledge grows in increasingly close connection with mathematics. And the development of pure mathematics is not subjected to that relativity which characterizes all inductive theoretic knowledge of empirical data. It is neither, as scholarly knowledge claimed to be, deduction of new truths from established truths nor substitution of new systems for old systems but creation of new systems to which old systems become logically reduced. This is because pure mathematics is not knowledge, either in the scholarly or in the modern inductive sense of the term; it has no reference to any object matter beyond itself. It is a growing structure of formal, logically standardized relationships between arbitrary, meaningless signs. Only when these signs are made meaningful by being defined as symbols designating scientific facts, mathematics becomes a symbolic expression of scientific theories. If these are inductive theories, as in modern physics, they are relative, like all inductive knowledge. But some physicists do not accept this distinction between mathematics and physical theories mathematically symbolized. To them mathematical formulas are not mere symbolic expressions of abstract inductive knowledge about empirical facts but constitute knowledge about empirical facts itself. Such a conception is in agreement with the doctrine of those schools discussed in the preceding chapter to whom knowledge is nothing but a system of symbols; consequently, there is a growing coöperation between these physicists and the builders of symbolic logic, who see in theoretic physics that ontological basis of absolutely true knowledge which they themselves cannot discover. According to this mathematicophysical philosophy, the universe in its very essence is a mathematically ordered universe. "God is a mathematician." Every mathematically expressed truth about physical facts is within its own range a fragment of the total absolute truth. If our present physical knowledge as a whole continually changes, showing that it is not yet absolutely certain, this is only because it is incomplete and not yet given a final mathematical systematization. But since we are all the time discovering new physicomathematical truths, the development of our knowledge gradually approaches a perfect and complete mathematical synthesis of the physical universe as an ideal limit. The theoretic explorer appears here as a member of a small and highly select group on its way to absolutely true and all-inclusive knowledge.

This is not how his role is conceived by those investigators of culture who view it historically and compare the history of knowledge with that of other domains of cultural achievement. The linguist, the historian and theorist of literature, the student of art, the religionist, the sociologist, the economist—each finds in the field of his own scientific research many and diverse cultural systems, each of which (just like a system of knowledge) lays claim to some kind of objective validity, though different *in specie* from theoretic validity. A drama, a symphony, a painting, a religious ritual, a bank, an army corps, each has a specific, standardized inner order of its own with which all those comply who participate in it directly or vicariously; this order raises it above the arbitrariness and variability of subjective psychological experiences and impulses.[4]

The scientific explorer of cultural reality overcame long ago the narrow exclusiveness of the sage, who exalts the religion in which he believes as the only really holy religion, the art of his own civilization as the only art which satisfies the supreme canons of beauty, the social structure which he helps promote as the only one that is ethically and politically right, the economic organization for which he and his class stand as the only one that is really conducive to common welfare, and so on. While at first, in reaction against this naïve dogmatism of sages, many investigators of culture went to the other extreme, identified relativity with subjectivity and attempted to reduce the vast and infinitely complex variety of cultural systems to psychological or psychobiological facts, the progress of critical exploration has shown that such an approach leaves most of the theoretic problems concerning culture not only insolvable but undiscoverable. To deny the objectivity

---

4   Perhaps the first origin of the idea that every cultural system has some objective, though only relative, validity must be traced back to the philosophy of Hegel; but, of course, its most important implications have been obscured by Hegel's metaphysical monism and its most fruitful consequences checked by the dogmatic absolutism of his own doctrine.

of all cultural systems is as naïve in its way as to affirm that only "our" systems are objective.

It is, indeed, a simple way of avoiding the difficulties which an investigator of culture must encounter when he explores the enormous and seemingly chaotic empirical wealth of culture in search not of one order already familiar from personal participation or known from some other science but of many diverse and partial orders theoretically unknown. And, of course, a way which shows how to play the role of scientist easily will always find many followers. But there are a number of leading scientists in all fields of cultural research who are fully aware of how very difficult the function of inductive theorist is in their fields and who for that very reason eagerly seek new problems. These men are trying to elaborate general heuristic principles which will enable the explorer to take into consideration the various claims to objective validity which all cultural systems have in the experience of the people who participate in them and yet make him maintain his own standards of theoretic objectivity by refraining from evaluative judgments about the data he investigates. Such principles have gradually and independently evolved in the several sciences of culture—and they are essentially similar to those which help the explorer to understand his own role as builder of theoretic systems.

Explorers, as we have seen, are freely promoting and accepting as normal in the domain of knowledge ceaseless and unexpected changes. Such changes are also found in every other cultural field, though not everywhere so rapid or so consciously realized by those who bring them about. If thoroughly and comprehensively investigated, cultural change proves to be a succession of cultural systems constructed according to different patterns, where new systems supplant old ones. And this process can be similarly explained as the succession of theoretic systems. Every cultural system—linguistic, artistic, religious, social, economic, technical—embodies a certain pattern of normatively regulated activities which people follow in solving certain problems which they meet in their lives. Systems vary as to the character and range of problems which can be solved by following their normative patterns. If a certain system proves unfit to solve new problems which arise in the course of historical duration—often in the very consequence of its own expansion—another kind of system becomes substituted instead by the people who are facing these problems.

This, however, does not mean that any one system is ever entirely reducible to another. For even if the new system solves, besides the new problems, all the problems which the old system used to solve—and this is by no means always the case—yet each system solves them differently. Each gives something to human lives which no system built according to a different pattern can give. Forgotten languages, works of art produced in periods long past, ancient religions, old forms of social organization, have been largely supplanted by modern cultural products but not fully absorbed by them; even modern machine technique, which leaves hardly any problems unsolved that hand technique used to solve, is nonetheless not a complete substitute for the latter, since the old patterns of technical action are different from the new. A proof of this irreducibility of earlier culture to later culture in any field is the fact that many old cultural patterns survive the material destruction of old cultural products and continue to be used, though less widely, along with modern patterns; evidently, the solution of certain cultural problems which they give is still satisfactory to some people.

Is it not the same in the evolution of knowledge? Among those who believe in absolute truth as the supreme goal which knowledge gradually approaches, the opinion is current that in science—in contrast to art, literature, religion, and social organization—there is a continuous and unreserved "progress" in the sense that anything that was valid in old theories becomes incorporated in new theories and only that which is worthless drops out. But the historian who is accustomed to apply the concept of relative but objective validity to all cultural systems will hardly agree with this opinion. In his view, no system of knowledge is entirely reducible in its theoretic bearing to any other system, however superior the latter may be in its capacity to solve many and various problems. While acknowledging, for instance, that present scientific theories in every branch of knowledge are much more valid relatively than those of Greek philosophers, yet he will not agree that modern thought has made the philosophy of Aristotle or that of Plato utterly insignificant, depriving them of all theoretic validity within the range of those problems which they have solved in their own ways.

Furthermore, recent explorers of cultural reality have discovered that in no field of culture does evolution proceed in one definite direction which could be indicated by some ultimate, supreme limit of the historical process. On the contrary, any cultural system may and often does become the starting point for several different lines of cultural development, each of which leads in turn to several unexpected possibilities of further evolution in different directions. In the history of knowledge this ceaseless growth of new and divergent lines of theoretic exploration is very clear. The line taken by modern mathematical physics is only one of many, and it may break up sooner or later into several new, now unexpected lines.

Thus viewed in the light of cultural exploration, the relativity of scientific theories cannot be overcome by the acceptance of the ideal of one absolutely valid system of knowledge which is being gradually approached by the double process of creating more and more valid theories and discarding less valid theories of the past. But does not relativism in the field of knowledge, like skepticism, turn against itself and undermine its own claim to be regarded as theoretically valid?

It is not our present task to defend the relativistic conception of theoretic validity but only to show how and why it explicitly underlies the theoretic explorer's social role when viewed as that of a creative participant in the historical evolution of culture. However, we can well understand that to combat this conception by the classical arguments invented against skepticism is a superficial quibble of verbal logicians. For those who believe that every theory is relatively valid do not assert that knowledge as a whole has only a relative validity. Theirs is not merely an abstract generalization of some common characters of scientific theories but a synthetic and dynamic view of knowledge as a totality of theoretic systems growing through the ages, each only relatively true, but all of them together embodying a supreme form of validity which the term "truth" in its scholarly meaning is quite unfit to express.

There is a parallel conception of art among modern historians and philosophers: each work of art as an aesthetic value is relative, since it solves only some artistic problems among many and satisfies only some aesthetic standards but no others; and yet art as a whole is not relative, for all artistic problems ever perceived find adequate solution in the course of its growth and there are works which satisfy every aesthetic standard.

Such a conception shows the only way to escape the dilemma of dogmatic certainty and skeptical doubt and makes the identification of relativism with subjectivism and objective validity with absolutism impossible. It is undeveloped as yet; indeed, only an inductive nonevaluative science of knowledge, which—as we mentioned in Chapter I—is not yet constituted, will be able to develop it fully. But we can see how, if it be accepted, the social role of the scientist will look in its light.

He is a creator whose work, a unique and irreducible link between the past and the future, enters as a dynamic component into the total, ever-increasing knowledge of mankind. We say, "knowledge of mankind," for it is the knowledge in which all men, from the forgotten beginning to the unknown end of history, have participated and will participate in various ways and degrees. But we do not say "human knowledge." For this knowledge as a whole, in the objective composition and structure of the systems which constitute it, steadily rises far above "human nature" and draws individuals and collectivities after it.

We spoke of the proud claim of the scholar who vindicated the inner dignity of that puny creature—man—asserting his ability to *discover* absolute truth by the unaided effort of his own reason. Cannot the scientist-explorer make the still prouder claim of being one of those who by their coöperative efforts *create* a superhuman world of relative truths, infinite in potential wealth, admirable in its trend to perfection—and who thus lead mankind to undreamed of heights of intellectual achievement?

And perhaps at no period of history was a vindication of the inner dignity of man more needed than in these days.

6. Society as a Cultural System

CULTURAL SCIENCES

1952

The Conception of Society as a Cultural System

WHEN COMTE introduced the concept of sociology as a new science using the same objective approach and the same methods as the older sciences, he gave it a definite place in his classification of sciences. It was to be the sixth and last positive science, following biology, which followed chemistry. Just as the reason why biology functioned as a distinct science was the existence of living organisms as complex systems irreducible to combinations of their chemical components, so the reason why sociology as a distinct science had to be formed was the existence of societies as the most complex of all systems, irreducible to combinations of individual human organisms.

Comte's idea of society was rooted in the age-old political theory of the state as an integral whole incorporating completely the people who inhabit a definite territory and are organized under a government. But, under the influence of eighteenth-century historians, economists, and cultural philosophers, he expanded it to include the entire culture presumably shared by the participants in a state. His society is, thus, a cultural system maintained by the biologically continuous population living within a geographically circumscribed area. The people who belong to it are united not by natural, but by cultural bonds: common political structure, mores,

From *Cultural Sciences* (Urbana: University of Illinois Press, 1952), pp. 380–400. Reprinted by permission of the publisher.

technology, economic organization, language, religion, knowledge, and art. Those cultural activities are distinct but interdependent functions of society; consequently, sociology as the science of society is also the inclusive science of culture, and all the special cultural sciences are its components.

This conception was not the result of objective studies of relationships between cultural phenomena within particular societies; it was due to Comte's attempt to combine his new science with his theory of the three progressive stages through which total historical civilizations passed. The inclusion of the latter theory in his outline of sociology under the term "social dynamics" led to the long-lasting confusion between sociology and philosophy of history, which culminated in Paul Barth's identification of the two.[1]

This definition of sociology as the science of *society* conditioned *a priori* the approach to cultural phenomena of the sociologists who accepted it. They all agreed that societies are separate wholes, territorially located, including biological human beings on the one hand and cultures on the other hand; and all of them conceived the culture of a society as systematically integrated. They differed as to the relative importance to be ascribed to natural and cultural factors in this integration. For instance, among the social organicists who conceived the unity of society as similar to that of an organism, Izoulet, with his strictly biological theory of the genesis and structure of society, differed greatly from Schäffle and Worms, who ascribed its unity to conscious solidarity manifested in cultural functions.[2]

Spencer's sociological theory of culture is highly important in that his general evolutionary philosophy enabled him to treat social evolution as a continuation of organic evolution, yet irreducible to it. As social evolution reaches the stage when it becomes an evo-

---

[1]   Paul Barth, *Die Philosophie der Geschichte als Soziologie*, 4th ed. (Leipzig, 1922).

[2]   Albert G. F. Schäffle, *Bau und Leben des sozialen Körpers*, 7 vols. (1875–78). René Worms, in his *Organisme et société* (Paris, 1896), used a predominantly biological conception. But his theory changed considerably later; cf. his *Philosophie des sciences sociales*, 3 vols. (Paris, 1903–07).

lution of institutions, his generalizations about it are increasingly based not on deductions from biology and biological psycholgy, but on cultural materal derived from ethnology and history. Only the general concept of society remains as the common link between human biology and cultural theory. Since society to Spencer, as to Comte, is the only system over and above individual organisms, all cultural phenomena are included in a society as integral components. Sociology as the science of society is thus the general science of culture.

Spencer's approach, however, differs from Comte's in that in his theory of institutions he attempts to establish a definite connection between social organization as such and specific cultural phenomena. An institution is primarily a subdivision of the total organzation of the society; domestic and political institutions are nothing but that. Some institutions, however, serve to maintain and develop specific classes of cultural phenomena. Thus, religion is maintained and developed by ecclesiastical institutions, i.e. organized religious associations, mostly controlled by the priesthood; music, art, literature, medicine, and science are maintained and developed by professional institutions. If we connect this concept of institutions with Spencer's basic premise, that the essential characteristic of society as a system is cooperation, and with his theory of ethics, we conclude that the primary condition of all cultural evolution is the evolution of morally regulated interaction between individual participants in cooperating groups. Unfortunately, he did not consistently apply this conception. Later sociologists who adopted his term "institution" gave it a somewhat different meaning. They applied it to *religions* rather than to organized religious groups, and included under it art and science, instead of the professional functions of artists and scientists.[3]

The French sociologists who more or less explicitly recognized

[3]   Cf. Florian Znaniecki, "Social Organization and Institutions," eds. Gurvich and Moore, in *Twentieth Century Sociology* (New York: Philosophical Library, 1945).

Talcott Parsons recently systematized, in his heuristic theory of the "institutional structure" of society, the strictly social conception of "institutions" initiated by Spencer. Cf. "The Position of Sociological Theory," *Am. Social Rev.* (April, 1948), pp. 156–64.

Durkheim as their leader accepted in principle the conception of society as a spatially located collectivity of human beings with a common integrated culture, but did not develop a systematic general theory of society, only a general methodical approach to the specific cultural phenomena which it includes.[4] This approach became altogether independent of biological premises,[5] except for Durkheim's early explanation of the division of labor by increasing density of the population (later almost ignored by his followers and by Durkheim himself) and some overemphasis on biographic factors in Mauss's concept of social morphology.[6] The unity of society is based on conscious solidarity among its members; its organization is founded on collectively recognized and supported norms, which regulate not only actions but experiences and representations of its members. From this point of view, all cultural phenomena are social since all are subjected to collectively sanctioned rules. The first task of sociologists is, of course, to investigate those rules which are formally expressed in law, less formally in mores, and to study the ways in which conformity with them is collectively enforced.[7] Objective comparative studies of laws and of their enforcement in various societies during various historical periods have been carried on by Durkheim,[8] Davy, Fauconnet,

[4]   And yet, according to the basic premise of this school, there *must* be a unity of society, even though it may be a long time before a systematic, general science of society develops. As Lapie said: "On ne peut croire à la sociologie sans croire à l'unité des faits sociaux." *L'Année sociologique*, I (1896–97), 274.

[5]   Cf. the sharp criticism of "biological sociology" by Bouglé in *L'Année sociologique*, I, (1896–97).

[6]   "Divisions et proportions des divisions de la sociologie," *L'Année sociologique*, new series, II (1927), 98–173.

[7]   In *L'Année sociologique*, the third section of critical reviews is devoted to "Sociologie juridique et morale." It includes, besides general theories of law and/or mores, property law, criminal law, studies of social and political organizations—among others, the local community, family, marriage. "Sociologie criminelle et statistique morale," in the sense of a sociological study of crimes and moral transgressions, constitutes a separate section.

[8]   This study forms a part of Durkheim's work *De la division du travail social.*

Duguit;[9] recently, Gurvitch gave a general systematic outline of sociology of law as a branch of sociology.[10] Lévy-Bruhl formulated a program for an objective, comparative science of the mores regulating interhuman relations,[11] but no systematization of studies of mores has been attempted.

But inasmuch as in all realms of culture specific representations and actions are collectively regulated, all of them must be investigated sociologically. In the course of this investigation some differences of approach developed. Thus, Durkheim's sociological conception of religion resulted in his well-known theory that religion as such does not constitute a separate and distinct cultural product. The antithesis between the sacred and the profane, found in all religions, is reducible to the antithesis between experiences and activities shared by a group as a whole and individual experiences and activities; gods are mere symbols of the group that worships them. This theory has been invalidated, but the dependence of religion as a distinct cultural product upon social organizations, already postulated by Spencer, proved valid.[12] Most original and historically important was the use of the sociological approach to

---

9   George Davy, *La Foi jurée* (Paris, 1922); and Paul Fauconnet, *La Responsabilité* (Paris, 1925). Léon Duguit, however, though influenced by Durkheim in his theory of law, has been criticized for not accepting the concepts of "realité collective" and "conscience sociale" by Davy, *L'Année sociologique*, XII (1909–12), 364.

10   Georges Gurvitch, *Sociology of Law* (New York: Philosophical Library, 1942).

11   Lucien Lévy-Bruhl, *La Morale et la science des moeurs* (Paris, 1903).

12   Sociology of religion was, from the very first, one of the branches of sociology in which Durkheim and his followers were most interested. If we survey, however, the content of the section "Sociologie religieuse," with its eleven subsections, in the "new series" of *L'Année sociologique* (started in 1925), we find that it includes critical reviews of all publications pertaining to religion. There is little in the reviews of these publications that would clarify the difference between sociology of religion and historical and ethnological studies of religions. Only in some of their generalizing works do members of this group use an original sociological approach: e.g., Hubert and Mauss, "Esquisse d'une théorie générale de la magie," *L'Année sociologique*, VII; or Stefan Czarnowski, *Le Culte des héros* (Paris, 1919).

knowledge, for it attempted to show that not merely particular theories, but basic logical principles and categories, are collective, i.e., social, products. Lévy-Bruhl tried to prove that the principles of identity and contradiction were unknown to primitive societies, and that the category of causation was not consistently used;[13] Durkheim showed that some early classifications of natural phenomena were not based on their similarities and differences, but on their presumed mystical connections with separate clans as subdivisions of a tribe;[14] Halbwachs tried to prove that memory, without which no individual awareness of time is possible, is socially determined;[15] Czarnowski, that all conceptions of space were originally developed by social groups with certain magico-religious ideologies.[16] This theory was used by Granet in his studies of Chinese civilization.[17]

While the general postulate that knowledge, like religion, forms part of the total organized life of a society, which regulates all the thinking of its members, has been invalidated, yet enough evidence has been obtained concerning the dependence of knowledge upon social organization to start the development of sociology of knowledge as a branch of general sociology. The same may be said of the results of monographic research carried on by French sociologists concerning economic systems,[18] political systems,[19] and language.[20]

[13] *Les Fonctions mentales dans les sociétés primitives* (Paris, 1923) ; *La Mentalité primitive* (Paris, 1925).

[14] Durkheim and Mauss, "De quelques formes primitives de classification," *L'Année sociologique*, Vol. VI (1901–02).

[15] *Les Cadres sociaux de la mémoire* (Paris, 1925).

[16] "La Division de l'étendue," *Revue d'histoire des religions* (Paris, 1927).

[17] Marcel Granet, *La Civilisation Chinoise* (Paris, 1929) ; *La Pensée Chinoise* (Paris, 1931).

[18] Simiand, Mauss, and Halbwachs eventually led to the study of economic groups and classes.

[19] Celestin Bouglé, *Les Idées égalitaires* (Paris, 1899) ; La Démocratie *devant la science* (Paris, 1903).

[20] Antoine Meillet, Ferdinand Brunot, and Jacques Vendryes. The relation between linguistics and sociology is well characterized by Meillet as follows: "Without doubt, linguistic facts have an autonomy . . . a well-marked specificity. . . . But they develop in well-defined social groups

The very progress of this research, however, has slowly undermined the conception of society as an integrated system within which all the culture shared by its members is included. In 1913, Durkheim and Mauss stated in *L'Année sociologique:*

One of the rules which we follow here, while studying social phenomena in themselves and for themselves, is not to leave them in the air, but to refer them always to a human group that occupies a definite portion of space and is capable of being geographically represented. And it seems that the largest of all these groups, the one which includes within it all the others and consequently frames and embraces all the forms of social activity, is the one which constitutes the political society. . . .

However, there are [social phenomena] which have no such clearly defined frames; they pass above political frontiers and extend over spaces which cannot be easily determined. . . .

Political and juridical institutions, phenomena of social morphology, are parts of the constitution belonging to each people. On the contrary, myths, stories, money, trade, fine arts, techniques, instruments, languages, words, scientific knowledge, literary forms and ideals, all these travel. . . .

There are not only isolated facts, but complex solidary systems which are not limited to a determined political organism. . . . To these systems of facts, which have their own unity, their own way of being, it is convenient to have a special name: the name *civilization* seems to us the most appropriate.

There was still another difficulty. The radical opposition of Durkheim and his followers to psychological individualism, especially as developed by Tarde, led to complete neglect of the function of the individual as innovator and imitator, leader and fol-

---

in response to certain social needs. And it is useless to pretend to explain this development without describing these groups and without studying these needs." *L'Année sociologique*, new series, I (1925), 947.

Two other categories of cultural phenomena were included within the domain of sociology: technology and art. Some original work has been done by followers of Durkheim, especially Charles Lalo, in the realm of art, but not much in technology.

lower. Consequently, many cultural processes remained inexplicable which could have been explained if the factual evidence on which Tarde based his hypotheses had been taken fully into consideration. But that would have meant redefinition of the whole concept of society, since Tarde's generalizations were mostly independent of this concept.

American sociology began with the explicit or implicit acceptance of the theory of society initiated by Comte and developed by Spencer, but without the organismic analogy. A society was considered to be a territorially and demographically circumscribed collectivity with an integrated culture. This cultural integration was conceived by most sociologists as a system of differentiated but interdependent, collective functions or institutions, each of which serves to satisfy certain basic needs or interests of the people included in the society. General sociological theories were essentially theories of society in this sense, e.g., Ward's *Pure Sociology*, Small's *General Sociology*, Sumner and Keller's *Science of Society*. And even now this approach is still used by quite a few sociologists who are unwilling to relinquish the original ambition of the founders of their science and by those authors of sociological textbooks who want to help college students overcome the separatism of specialists by giving them some idea of the interdependence between various categories of cultural phenomena.

However, the rapid growth of inductive sociological research, instead of providing new proof of the validity of general theories of society as an inclusive cultural system, has resulted in a gradual limitation of the realm of sociology. Sociologists cannot compete with economics, students of material techniques, linguists, historians and theorists of literature, art, music, philosophy, and science in their respective realms. What they actually do is to specialize in the investigation of what have been termed "social relations" or "human relations" and of the human groups within or between which such relations exist. As a result of this specialization, general sociological theories have become much less inclusive.

This new trend in sociological theory cannot be traced back to any single source. The explicit program of sociology as a *special* science was first formulated and partly applied by Simmel,[21] later reformulated with some changes and much more widely applied by von Wiese.[22] These authors definitely excluded from the realm of sociology the phenomena which other cultural scientists were already investigating. According to both, the first task of sociology is to study relations between individuals as elementary social phenomena, and then proceed to the study of more complex social systems. Simmel stopped with the comparative study of limited *social groups* composed of interacting, mutually conscious individuals; von Wiese went further and surveyed what he termed "abstract collectivities" composed of many smaller groups, such as the state and the church.[23] A somewhat similar approach was initiated independently by Cooley,[24] who began with the study of personal relations between individuals, continued with a survey of combinations of these relations in primary groups, and extended tentatively the realm of sociology to wider groups. Several other sociological theorists also gradually limited their generalizations to this category of phenomena.[25]

Sociologists who participate in this trend, even when they still

[21]   Georg Simmel, *Soziologie: Untersuchungen über die Formen der Vergesellschaftung* (Berlin, 1908), a collection of special studies.

[22]   Leopold von Wiese, *Allgemeine Soziologie:* Vol. I, *Beziehungslehre* (Munich, 1924); Vol. II, *Gebildelehre* (Munich, 1929). Howard Becker amplified and adapted this work to certain American trends, and it was published in English under the title *Systematic Sociology* (New York: Wiley, 1932).

[23]   We must mention here also Max Weber, who ascribed to sociology the specific task of investigating social actions. He defined a social action as "an action carried on . . . with reference to the behavior of others and oriented toward the behavior of those others throughout its course," quoted in von Wiese-Becker, *op. cit.*, p. 894. Unlike von Wiese, however, Weber did not develop a general theory of facts of *interaction* between social agents.

[24]   Charles Horton Cooley, *Human Nature and the Social Order* (New York: Scribner, 1902); and *Social Organization* (New York: Scribner, 1909).

[25]   I did this in the *Introduction to Sociology* (Warsaw, 1922), in Polish.

use the term "society," give it a new meaning. Thus, according to MacIver: "Society . . . signifies the whole complex system of social relationships . . . in and through which we live. . . . And its structure is for ever changing."[26]

According to Hiller: "The subject of sociology is that of human relations. These relations are social because they consist of the conduct and inclinations of persons with reference to one another. . . . Social relations are discovered through a study of rules, standards, and usages prescribing conduct between persons. All such regulations . . . are a part of the culture of a given society."[27]

Not only do those authors define society in terms of specific phenomena called social relations or human relations rather than as a system including all categories of cultural phenomena, but they recognize the need of inductive research in order to discover how a particular society is organized, instead of assuming that the organization of all societies is essentially uniform and its basic principles already known. In other words, society is becoming a heuristic concept for guidance toward future discoveries.[28]

This new conception of the task of sociology raises three important problems: (1) What are these presumably elementary phenomena, sometimes termed "human relations," sometimes "social relations," and what kind of order exists among them? (2) What is the connection between sociology and the established cultural sciences? (3) What is the connection between sociology and natural sciences?

[26]   Robert M. MacIver, *Society: Its Structure and Changes* (New York: H. Long & Smith, Inc., 1931), pp. 9, 56.

[27]   Ernest T. Hiller, *Social Relations and Structures* (New York: Harper, 1947), p. 2.

[28]   For an excellent systematic survey of this and of other new trends in sociology up to 1931, and a "suggested organization of sociological theory in terms of its major concepts," see Earle Edward Eubank, *The Concepts of Sociology* (New York: Heath, 1932). Obviously, in this book I could not refer to all the important new contributions to sociological theory made since 1931. Many of them, up to 1945, are summarized in *Twentieth Century Sociology*, eds. Gurvitch and Moore (New York: Philosophical Library, 1945).

Sociology as the Science of Order among Social Actions

Let us begin with a brief survey of the meaning of the term "human relations," which is apparently much more widely used than the term "social relations," judging from the number of publications which contain it in their titles.

We find, however, two very different conceptions of a human relation. It may be, and frequently is, conceived as a relation between *"human beings"* as biopsychological entities. It consist in any process, simple or complex, which occurs between them and affects directly or indirectly their biological functions or their psychological processes. It includes, among other things, those phenomena which human ecology, following the models of plant and animal ecology, investigates and which James A. Quinn has defined as "spatial and temporal relations between human beings as affected by the selective, distributive and accommodative forces of the environment."[29] According to this conception, human beings between whom a relation occurs need not even be conscious of each other. The lives of those human beings in New York who consume oranges produced in Florida or California or drink tea imported from Ceylon are in some measure affected by the behavior of the human beings who cultivate and gather oranges or tea leaves; yet most New Yorkers know very little about the latter in general and nothing at all about any of them in particular, and vice versa. During depressions the lives of millions of human beings are affected by changes which have occurred in the lives of millions of others who are unknown to them.

The other concept symbolized by the term "human relations" is more specific and limited. It includes essentially the same phenomena as those included in the concept "social relations" as used by sociologists. This is the meaning which Hiller gives it in the

[29]   James A. Quinn, "The Development of Human Ecology in Sociology," eds. Barnes, Becker, and Becker, in *Contemporary Social Theory* (New York: Appleton, 1940), p. 212.

paragraph previously quoted.[30] And in surveying some studies of so-called human relations, e.g., human relations in industry, we find that the meaning of this term is also almost identical with that of social relations in sociological works. As there seems to be no reason for this terminological duplication, to avoid confusion we shall drop the term "human relations" altogether and limit our analysis to *social* relations.

The simplest, elementary phenomenon which certain sociologists, e.g., Simmel, von Wiese, Hiller, denote by this term, is a single process of conscious intercourse between two individuals which affects both of them. The first essential condition of its occurrence is that both individuals be aware of each other. If neither is aware of the other, there obviously cannot be any conscious relation between them. If only one is aware of the other, as when A sees B walking on the street, but is not seen by B, this experience may affect some attitudes or tendencies of A, but it would not be called a social relation, since B is unaffected by it. Even when two individuals are aware of each other, this by itself is still not enough to produce a social relation between them. On a crowded street, many individuals see each other, but usually nothing occurs to make them mutually conscious of any influence exerted by one upon the other. The consciousness of such influence appears only when one of them, A, performs an action bearing upon the other, B, as a datum of his experience; for instance, when A tries to make B move out of his way or purposely opens a way for B to pass, asks B about the location of a street or a building, or attempts to start companionate conversation with B. Considered from B's point of view, A's action results in a situation of which A, as a datum of B's experience, is a component. B usually tends to do something in this situation; and whatever he does, both A and B are aware that A has done something practically significant to B and that it is practically significant to A how B will act under the influence of this action, or—briefly speaking—how he reacts to it.

Thus, when we investigate the simple, elementary phenomenon

[30]   Hiller's conception of human or social relations is similar to that of von Wiese.

which certain sociologists call "social relation" from the point of view of the two individuals who participate in it, rather than from that of an observer, and analyze it as a combination of their experiences and active tendencies, we find that it is not really a relation between two individuals as such, but between their *actions*. We prefer, therefore, to call it an "interaction" rather than a "relation," for the word "relation" in common language connotes a more durable interdependence. Later we shall limit the term "social relation" to rather long-lasting axionormative *systems* of numerous actions performed by two interacting agents, each of whom is a durable positive value to the other (e.g., mother and child, husband and wife). Nevertheless, even a single interaction is definitely a social phenomenon, for its chief component is a *social action* of which one individual, as given to another, is the object and which tends to influence the latter, to provoke a reaction from him. This reaction may be also a social action in this sense, as when the second individual gives verbally the directions he has been asked to give or responds positively to the initial attempt of the first to start a conversation. Or it may be a technical action, as when, without trying to influence the first individual, he moves along the way which the former opened up for him; but even in this case, his action has been socially conditioned, since he is aware that the other intended to make him perform it.

If sociology is essentially the science of human or social relations, as experienced by those who participate in them, then the primary phenomena which sociologists have to investigate are social actions, just as the primary phenomena investigated by religionists, students of material technique, economists, and theorists of art are religious, technical, economic, artistic actions. In an earlier work, we tried to analyze and classify social actions as a distinct category. We included in this category all those and only those human actions (individual or collective) which have as main values other human individuals, experienced and conceived by the agents as living and conscious beings (or collectivities composed of such individuals), and which tend to produce some changes in these main values as social objects by using as instruments some data experienced by both of them.

As most historians, ethnologists, and sociologists well know, social actions, just like other kinds of actions, are axionormatively ordered insofar as they conform with definite cultural patterns, and they can be classified according to this order. The similarities between them are primarily based on the standards by which their main objects are defined and evaluated, secondarily by the norms which they are supposed to follow. Of course, as in every realm of culture, actions which do not conform raise special problems.

We surveyed briefly in Chapter 10 one rather general cultural class of social actions—curing sick persons. Basically, all the objects of these actions are supposed to be positively valuable to the agents, though their valuation differs in degree and their definitions vary, depending upon their presumed sickness or disease. We noticed the great diversity of norms with which medical agents are expected to conform in various collectivities and saw how they change in the course of history. When investigating the problem of transgressions, we found that individuals who are judged to be transgressors are negatively evaluated by conformists according to certain standards and subjected to normatively regulated social actions, though their definitions and negative valuations differ in kind and degree, and the actions dealing with them vary accordingly.

Functionally interdependent social actions of different agents become integrated into axionormatively organized systems of various size, complexity, extension, and duration. Relatively simple are the systems of interdependent actions of two individuals who evaluate each other positively by standards which both accept, and who follow certain norms in acting upon each other. Take, for instance, companionate conversation carried on by two acquaintances in accordance with definite principles of etiquette, or the functionally interdependent sexual actions of a man and a woman each of whom tends to give maximum satisfaction to the other and to enjoy fully what the other does. Such a short-lasting system may be part of a long-lasting system—life-long companionship or enduring mutual love. Many such long-lasting systems of culturally patterned interactions between two individual agents have been investigated by sociologists and ethnologists, and the term social relations has usually been applied to them. Numerous works have been written about marriage, or conjugal relations, courtship relations, parent-child relations, kinship relations in general, relations of mutual aid and cooperation, relations between ruler and subject, employer and employee, teacher and pupil, leader and follower, etc.

Considerable research has also been done on the highly complex systems of interdependent social actions performed by the numerous individual agents who constitute together an organized social group. One class of the latter—military groups—began to be thoroughly studied in classical antiquity (Xenophon, Thucydides, Caesar, especially Polybius). Since then many other specific social groups have been investigated—legislative groups, administrative groups, political parties, craftsmen's guilds, professional groups, religious groups, clans, secret societies, lately labor unions, and various smaller, apparently less influential associations.[31]

Much less attention has been paid to social systems of the intermediary type—axionormatively ordered combinations of social relations between one individual and a number of others—e.g., a physician and his patients, a teacher and her pupils. Historians have made quite a few studies of such systems as relations between a prince and his courtiers, a military or political leader and his followers, a philosopher and his disciples, an artist and his patrons and admirers, the hostess of a salon and her guests.[32] But not until

---

[31]   Many sociologists consider that a comparative study of social groups constitutes the primary task of sociology. Cf. the statement of Charles A. Ellwood in *The Psychology of Human Society* (New York: Appleton, 1927) : "It is the concrete group, rather than the abstract society, that is the primary datum of present-day sociology" (p. vi). Cf. Eubank, *op. cit.*: "The group is the pivotal concept of sociological theory" (p. 164). Every textbook of sociology contains a section on social groups. And yet, except for a few brief and superficial essays, not a single general systematic work on social groups has been published in any language.

[32]   Other, widely different examples of such studies might be mentioned, such as Frazer's investigation of the socioreligious functions of kings and priests, in his *Golden Bough*; Sombart's *Der Bourgeois*; several studies of medicine men and shamans in nonliterate societies; Léon Gautier, *La Chevalerie*, etc. Spencer's *Professional Institutions* was the

thirty years ago did sociologists begin to investigate these systems and apply to them the general concept of social role, and they still do not agree concerning the heuristic significance of this concept.

However questionable methodically and insignificant theoretically may be certain results of recent specialized sociological researches, there is no doubt that many sociologists who investigate social actions in the sense just defined, have found and will find within the realm of their investigation the same two basic categories of order which other cultural scientists discover in their respective realms—the order of conformity of actions with cultural patterns and the order of functional interdependence which integrates conformist actions into systems. Since these orders are axionormative, due to the acceptance and practical application by agents of ideological models, and axionormative order does not exist in the world of nature, sociology as a science of social actions is manifestly a cultural, not a natural, science.

The general term *social order* has been widely used to denote axionormative order among phenomena called "social." Cooley and other sociologists have used it in an objective, scientific sense. To quite a few thinkers, however, it symbolizes an ethical, rather than a scientific, concept. For instance, Edward L. Thorndike, the famous psychologist, in his book *Human Nature and the Social Order*[33] does not define social order at all, but apparently takes for granted that it means economic and legal organization, which

---

first attempt to develop an evolutionary theory of one general class of these systems. A comparative analysis of a considerable diversity of them led me twenty-five years ago to the conclusion that all of them have certain common components: a set or circle of people with whom any particular individual interacts; an evaluative representation of him as a person by the circle and by himself; a definition of "rights" which his circle actively supports; and a definition of "duties" which he actively performs. In 1930, I borrowed from Park and Burgess the term "social role" to designate such dynamic systems of actions and have used it since in three books (two in Polish, one in English) and in several articles. Recently a general survey of the main logical classes of such systems was published by Hiller; but the author uses a static approach, and terms these classes "statuses," in the sense of "positions" in the "structure of society" (*op. cit.*, Part Six).

33   Edward L. Thorndike, *Human Nature and the Social Order* (New York: Macmillan, 1940).

should be studied not by scientific methods, but from the point of view of its goodness for man. Some French thinkers have given it a moralistic connotation, which led Gurvitch to suggest that it be altogether excluded from sociological theory.[34]

There is some reason for this confusion. If social order means *only* axionormative order, this implies that social phenomena which do not conform with established standards and norms have no order whatsoever, no regularity which would enable scientists to generalize about them; in short, that they belong under the general category of disorder as antithesis to order. This is as if biologists limited their search for natural order in their realm to anatomical structures and physiological functions of organisms and omitted the search for causal laws of relationship between organic changes and environmental influences as well as the search for regularities in the genesis of new species. Nonetheless, this term should be preserved in its objective, nonevaluative sense, for it has been helpful in distinguishing sociology from other sciences. But it should be extended so as to include those regularities of change occurring within social actions and systems which make causal generalization possible and those regularities in the genesis of new patterns and systems which may lead to evolutionary generalizations. In other words, sociologists must postulate that some kind of objective order exists among all social phenomena and discard altogether the concept of disorder and other analogous concepts.

As a matter of fact, many sociologists who specialize in investigating axionormatively ordered social actions and axionormatively organized systems of such actions have been searching for causal order in social change. Thus, quite a few attempts have been made to draw causal generalizations about the changes in social actions occurring in the course of their performance.[35] Many studies of changes in various kinds of systems of social actions, ranging in

---

34   Georges Gurvitch, "Social Control," eds. Gurvitch and Moore, in *Twentieth Century Sociology*, p. 247.

35   Most of them are included within the realm of social psychology. Cf. Florian Znaniecki, *The Laws of Social Psychology* (Chicago: University of Chicago Press, 1926) ; Lois B. Murphy and Gardner Murphy, *An Experimental Social Psychology* (New York: Harper, 1931) ; and many other works.

size and complexity from conjugal relations to governmental organizations, have been carried on and have resulted in causal hypotheses. We believe, therefore, that sociologists will soon cease
to separate studies of social change in general from studies of
social order in general.

The development of methodical genetic research has been somewhat impeded in recent times by the discredit attached to the concept of social evolution; but many historical studies have been
made about the emergence of new social systems in the course of
the last two centuries, and some sociologists are aware of the significance of these studies for sociology as a generalizing science.

The Connection between Sociology and Other
Cultural Sciences

While social actions, like all conscious human actions, are
dynamic systems of values, yet the main values included in them
differ essentially from those included in other categories of actions.
This difference is of primary importance for the function of sociology as a cultural science.

The primary value of any particular social action, as we have
seen, is a human individual, experienced and conceived by the
agent both as an object and as a conscious performer of actions.
Anthropomorphic deities are similarly conceived, but their actions
cannot be observed as human actions are. Many animals also appear similar to human beings in the experience of those who act
upon them; but this is irrelevant to our present problem since,
though the higher animals are indubitably conscious, any evidence
that they can actually participate in human culture is indirect and
inconclusive.

Now, a human individual is not only a lasting social object of
many diverse attitudes and actions, but also an agent who in the
course of time manifests many diverse attitudes and performs many
actions dealing with various kinds of objects. Most of the actions
which he performs, not only social but nonsocial—technical, religious, intellectual, aesthetic, etc.—influence directly or indirectly,
positively or negatively, some actions of others; and those who

act upon him are well aware of this. Consequently, the definition and evaluation of a human individual as a social object depend in considerable measure upon various kinds of actions which he has performed or is presumed to have performed in the past; and the predominant, if not the only, tendency of most social actions of which he is the object is to make him perform (or refrain from performing) in the future specific actions, not only social but non-social. This is, of course, not one-sided social control, but many-sided social influence, since every conscious individual in his turn, when he experiences others and acts upon them as social objects, manifests such evaluative attitudes and active tendencies. The same may be said, with some modifications, of organized social groups.

Social actions are thus cultural forces which influence the participation of human agents in every realm of culture. In our preceding chapters, we mentioned occasionally some manifestations of this influence. Let us survey them briefly.

In investigating the spread of ideological models of attitudes in a collectivity, we found that whatever the values and ways of acting to which these models refer—social, religious, technical, economic, aesthetic, etc.—their acceptance by participants in the collectivity is the result of specific social actions performed by those who tend to have these models generally accepted. These actions consist in communicating to others the standards and norms which the models include and inducing others to recognize them as valid. This is necessary, though not always sufficient, to have any model accepted. Without symbolic communication and persuasion, no consensus about the validity of standards and norms would be possible.

In surveying changes in ideological systems we noticed that, although those changes are initiated by thinkers who create new ideals, yet an ideal does not effectively modify an existing ideological system unless socially active leaders and their followers succeed in having it accepted and practically applied by influential social groups. And we saw that the stabilization of ideals into dogmas is achieved by social actions, individual and collective, of authoritative agents who tend to maintain an ideological system changeless by having it recognized as such by all present and future members of the groups which they dominate. When we discussed the expansion and recession of ideological systems, we found that both these processes are conditioned by social interaction between the adherents of different ideologies.

In our comparative analysis of culturally patterned actions performed by individuals, we included various kinds of actions, more or less complex, most of which were not social in the sense defined above. Private religious cultus, technical production of individual craftsmen, artistic performances of individual painters, sculptors, musicians, or poets, and intellectual actions of philosophers or scientists cannot be classified as social. When we passed to organized systems of specific actions performed by many individuals, we found that, though they differ from individual performances as to size, complexity, and duration, yet such differences do not justify their classification in a separate category, in contrast with individual actions, as some thinkers who identify "collective" with "social" have been doing.

Collective cultus of limited or unlimited duration is still religious, not social, activity; for the main common objects of all who participate in it are mythical beings, not living and active men. The collective construction of a building; the making, maintaining, and using of roads for motor traffic; and the continuous functioning of a factory or a mine are systems of interdependent technical actions, and must be studied by specialists in these realms. The playing of a symphony by an orchestra, just as the playing of a nocturne by an individual pianist, is obviously music, and has to be investigated by musicologists, not by sociologists. Even a collective economic system, although it requires interaction between human agents, includes as main values not men, but utilitarian products; and economists have drawn valid generalizations about such systems without investigating how producers, consumers, merchants, or bankers evaluate and act upon one another.

And yet we noticed that not only these collective systems of actions, but even the regular conformity of individual actions with cultural patterns depend upon social actions. Individuals do not automatically become participants in a collectively organized religious, technical, artistic, or even economic system; they must be actively admitted to participation, whether at their own initiative or at the initiative of others. The regular, continuous functioning of a collective system requires that deviations and transgressions which disturb this functioning be counteracted or prevented; and this, as we have seen, means *social* activity. When a collective system becomes creatively reorganized by introducing a new order, this reorganization requires continuous social cooperation between initiators of the new order as leaders and other participants as followers.

And, as every cultural scientist knows, before an individual can perform culturally patterned actions, even all alone, he must have learned how to perform them. Now, not all learning requires teaching. An individual who is already acquainted with certain cultural data and ways of acting can learn at his own initiative by observation and imitation how to perform an action unlike those he has performed before, or even a relatively new action somewhat different from any he has observed others performing. And yet he could not have originally learned to deal with any cultural data or acquired the ability to perform any culturally patterned action without being educated for a rather long period of time, for self-education is an outgrowth of education. And education consists of specifically social interaction between educators and educands. In any particular case, it consists of a sequence of culturally patterned social actions performed by an educator of which the educand is the main object, and of actions of the educand performed under the influence of the educator's actions.

Even when an individual has completed his education and performs culturally patterned nonsocial actions without anybody's guidance or cooperation, others are still interested in him and his performances; unless he lives in isolation, they are apt to manifest their interest by social actions bearing upon him. This is easily explicable when what he is doing is supposed to have some bearing on values with which the others deal. Thus, we found that private cultus is a matter of active interest to fellow believers who think that its regular performance by an individual worshiper propitiates their common deity and brings indirectly some blessing upon the whole congregation. In the realm of material technique, it is also easily understandable that, when trade developed, members of the various guilds became interested in the actions of their fellow craftsmen; and also that those who use technical products are interested in the actions of the producers, and vice versa.

But, in fact, this interest is found not only when actions of separate individuals are functionally interdependent. Ethnologists have noticed that, in many collectivities with traditional technological patterns, men who make hunting implements; women who make clothes, rugs, or domestic implements; potters, gardeners, male or female, who make any products not for sale but for their own use or the use of their families and so have nothing to gain or lose by the success or failure of others, nevertheless manifest considerable interest in each other's performances. They compare and evaluate the products by the standards and norms of the craft. They subject the performers to social sanctions—positive for those who conform and negative for those who deviate—at least in the form of personal praise or blame.

Historians of art are familiar with the interest, positive or negative, which artists working in the same realm—painters, musicians, poets—show in one another's work, and which critics manifest in the works of all of them. This interest is not limited to art itself, but extends to artists as persons and leads to numerous social actions, individual and collective, ranging from private or public approval or disapproval to the formation of schools and associations which tend to maintain the conformity of artists with established standards and norms, or to induce young artists to follow new aesthetic patterns.

The purpose of this brief survey is to justify our heuristic postulate about the function of sociology in relation to other cultural sciences. We must remember that the very existence of culture ultimately depends on conscious and active human individuals. Cultural data are the common data of successive experiences of many individuals; they grow in the course of time as agglomerated products of individual agents and are being used in the course of time by numerous individual agents. Consequently, no cultural pattern can last, no cultural systems can survive, unless the unlimited diversity of changing individual experiences of cultural data is continually uniformalized by common standards; and the many different, often conflicting, actions of individuals simultaneously and successively dealing with these data are continually regulated and integrated by common norms. This cannot be achieved by anybody but the individuals themselves who regularly cooperate in developing, preserving, and applying those standards and norms. Such regular cooperation requires conscious social interaction between them, not arbitrary and accidental, but guided by common standards of mutual experience and understanding and by common norms of conduct.

This means that, whatever axionormative order may be found among nonsocial actions dealing with nonhuman objects—material things, meaningful symbols, mythical beings, fictitious products of creative imagination, aesthetic constructs of sensory perception, abstract ideas—is conditioned by an axionormative, dynamic social order of interaction between the individuals who perform those nonsocial actions. And, however different may be the cultural patterns and systems of actions dealing with such nonhuman objects, their continued existence depends on certain essential similiarities in the social order.

These similiarities enable sociologists to generalize about the common social foundations of all categories of cultural order.[36] The development of the concept of organized social groups or associations has already resulted in the discovery that the functioning of various cultural systems—religious, industrial, economic, recently even scientific—found in collectivities with widely different cultures or civilizations, depends upon organized groups with an essentially similar social order (though, of course, with specific differences). The concept of social role, as a system of social relations between one individual and a number of others, is being applied to various kinds of culturally patterned performances of indi-

---

[36] Sociologists are gradually becoming aware that the importance of sociology for other cultural sciences *increases* in the very measure in which it *limits its task* to a comparative study of those social systems upon which the existence of every realm of culture depends. Compare the subdivisions of sociology found in *L'Année sociologique* with those in Barnes, Becker, and Becker, *op. cit.*, and later in Gurvitch and Moore, *op. cit.*

vidual agents, in nonliterate as well as in literate collectivities (intellectual, artistic, technical, economic); and its application shows that the regularity and continuity of such performances depend upon the functioning of social systems of this general class.

I have tried to use the sociological approach in a comparative study of education. However wide the differences in cultures, past and present, in which individuals have been and are now being taught to participate, there are beyond all doubt certain universal similarities of social systems on which all educational processes depend: social relations between educators and educands, which become integrated into specific social roles as education grows in length and complexity; social groups of which the educand is expected to bcome a member and which tend to regulate his preparation for membership; and schools as a specific class of social groups. Consequently, it is possible to develop a general sociological theory of those social systems which condition individual acculturation.

Of course, studies of the social order among human actions were initiated in classical antiquity by political theorists. Their emphasis on practical problems interfered with scientific objectivity, and their tendency to consider the order of a statc as all-inclusive often prevented them from noting the existence of other types of social order which are not reducible to political organization. These were the main reasons for the conflict which emerged in the nineteenth century between sociologists and political scientists, radically exemplified on the sociological side by Spencer's *Man versus the State,* and on the political side by Heinrich von Treitschke, Othmar Spann, and the totalitarian ideologists who completely rejected sociology. Such conflicts have subsided with the progress of scientific research, both among political scientists and among sociologists. Sociologists cannot deny the theoretic validity of many generalizations reached by political scientists, and political scientists no longer ignore the existence of many influential social systems, investigated by sociologists, which are not included in the structure of the state.

While sociologists no longer support the claim of Comte, Spencer, and their followers that political science is necessarily a part of sociology because the state is one of the institutions of society, yet it is highly probable that the results of theoretic research in the realm hitherto covered by political science (not the practical application of these results in political planning) will be gradually incorporated into sociology; for, evidently, the specific social systems which together compose the organization of a state can be classified together with the other social systems which sociologists are studying. Legislative groups, administrative groups, juridical groups, military groups, and political parties manifest some common, universal characteristics of all organized groups or associations. Social roles of individuals who perform specialized official functions in the government are comparable to the social roles of individuals whose functions are not official in the political sense of the term. Thus, in our opinion, sociology is definitely becoming the one and only science of social order, in the sense in which this term has been defined here.

But neither historians of culture nor cultural anthropologists are as yet willing to recognize sociology as the basic cultural science. According to them, in every civilization or culture, all categories of cultural phenomena—technical, social, economic, linguistic, magical, religious, intellectual, aesthetic, etc.—are interconnected and more or less integrated functionally; each depends on all the others, although in any particular culture one of them may be more influential than the others. Sociologists have to show not only that the continued existence of specific cultural systems depends upon axionormatively ordered social interaction, but also that the connections between specific cultural systems are not direct but indirect, mediated through social relations, and that whatever cultural integration may be found in a particular collectivity ultimately depends upon its social organization. We believe that comparative sociological analysis will prove the validity of these hypotheses.

Consider, by way of example, the connection between two important categories of cultural phenomena, religion and art. In investigating sociologically particular cases in which religious actions and artistic actions are connected, we find that in every case this connection is socially conditioned. It is due to the fact that the same individual performs two social roles: the role of a member in a religious group, and the role of an artist—sculptor, painter, musician. As an artist, recognized as such by other members of his religious group, he is expected to make special contributions to the common values of the group or to its collective cultus and is therefore granted special privileges by the group. Why certain artistic functions are positively valued by certain religious groups, but not by others, is a matter of different ideologies. If we trace such differences back to their historical origin, we shall probably find that the acceptance or rejection of specific artistic functions by a religious group was due to social factors—participation or nonparticipation of artists and patrons of art in the group during the period of its formation, cooperation or conflict between it and other groups which appreciated and supported art.

The combination of the role of artist and that of a member of a social group is also found in secular art; i.e., the painters and sculptors who contribute to the beauty of a city hall are usually members of the municipal group. Moreover, when artists are dependent upon patrons, the role of an artist functioning under the patronage of a high priest does not differ essentially from that of an artist patronized by a king, a dictator, or a millionaire, though the content of the creative work he is required to do may differ considerably.

As to the dependence of cultural integration in general upon social organization, we may mention, first, certain significant similarities and differences between so-called "preliterate" or "nonliterate" collectivities. Cultures maintained by well-organized, autonomous tribal groups seem to be better integrated than most folk cultures in the old sense of the term; i.e., those found in collectivities inhabiting areas under control of modern civilized states and lacking autonomous social organization. If, however, such a folk community has preserved some autonomy and is coherently organized, its culture remains rather well integrated, even though in the course of history many components which had no connection with its traditional patterns penetrated it. On the other hand, when intergroup conflicts frequently occur within a tribal collectivity, its culture does not seem to be functionally united. And the disintegration of tribal cultures under the impact of European colonial expansion apparently began in many cases with social disorganization.

However, more varied and more valid evidence in favor of the hypothesis that cultural integration depends on social organization can be found in the historical development of modern national cultures—Italian, French, Spanish, German, English, Swedish, Polish, Russian, American, Chinese, Japanese, etc. Each of these cultures includes a common literary language (which may be also a part of another culture, though with some differences); secular literature written in this language (epics, lyrics, drama, semi-fictitious and fictitious prose, history, biography, political and legal ideologies, general philosophy, eventually also products of cultural and natural sciences); all realms of art (architecture, painting, sculpture, music); systems of technical production; and economic systems. And each culture is viewed by its educated participants as well as by investigators as a unique, more or less integrated whole. Every national culture grows through centuries by the creative contributions of numerous individuals, although, as we have seen above, when social conflicts between nationalities are very active, creative tendencies are checked by national conservatism.

I have been investigating comparatively for many years not national cultures as such, a task beyond my competence, but the development of the social organization to which their growth and integration are due. It is impossible to summarize here the results of this investigation. The important point is that, however much these cultures differ, the development of social organization by the collectivities which create and maintain them was, and is, essentially the same. It began in various realms of culture with the emergence of social roles of creative leaders who gained followers and sponsors. And it continued with the progressive formation of social groups which promoted the organization, extension, and duration of various cultural systems. Throughout this development the common ideal of the individuals and the groups who participated in it was *social unification* of the millions of people who were supposed to share the same age-old cultural heritage (and sometimes a common semi-mythical biological ancestry), although they were divided into diverse ethnic subgroups, separate states, social classes, and sometimes even conflicting religious groups. A fully developed and integrated literary culture, superimposed through education upon more or less diversified folk cultures, regional cultures, class cultures, and religious cultures was expected to become, and actually did become, a powerful bond of social solidarity—more powerful than political, economic, or even religious bonds. But this was achieved only through the continuous cooperation of increasingly numerous, diverse social groups which gradually became functionally united into an organized highly complex society.

Bibliography of Works
by Florian Znaniecki

BOOKS IN ENGLISH

The Polish Peasant in Europe and America (with W. I. Thomas). First edition, Vols. I–II, Chicago: University of Chicago Press, 1918; Vols. III–V, Boston: Badger, 1919–1920. Second edition, 2 volumes, New York: Alfred A. Knopf, 1927.

Cultural Reality. Chicago: University of Chicago Press, 1919; pp. xv, 1–359.

The Laws of Social Psychology. Chicago: University of Chicago Press, 1925; pp. viii, 1–320.

The Method of Sociology. New York: Farrar & Rinehart, 1934; pp. xii, 1–338.

Social Actions. New York: Farrar & Rinehart, 1936; pp. xix, 1–746.

The Social Role of the Man of Knowledge. New York: Columbia University Press, 1940; pp. 1–212.

Cultural Sciences. Urbana, Ill.: University of Illinois Press, 1952; pp. i–viii, 1–438.

Modern Nationalities. Urbana, Ill.: University of Illinois Press, 1952; pp. i–xvi, 1–196. Unpublished outline translated by Vincente Herrero and published as "Las sociedades de cultura nacional y sus relaciones." Mexico: El Colegio de Mexico, No. 24 of *Jornadas*, a series of social studies, 1944; pp. 3–80.

Social Relations and Social Roles: The Unfinished Sociology. San Francisco, Calif.: Chandler Publishing Co., 1965; pp. i–xxviii, 1–372.

Compiled by Helena Znaniecki Lopata. Reprinted from Florian Znaniecki, *Social Relations and Social Roles: The Unfinished Sociology* (San Francisco: Chandler Publishing Company, 1965), pp. xx–xxviii. Reprinted by permission of the publisher.

ARTICLES AND OTHER PUBLICATIONS IN ENGLISH

"The Principle of Relativity and Philosophical Absolutism." *The Philosophical Review*, Vol. XXIV, 1915, pp. 150–164.

"Experiences of an Immigrant" (anonymous, autobiographical). *Atlantic Monthly*, 1918–1919.

"The Object-Matter of Sociology." *American Journal of Sociology*, Vol. 32, No. 4, January, 1927, pp. 529–584.

"The Poles." *Immigrant Backgrounds*, H. Fairchild, ed., in honor of W. I. Thomas. New York: Wiley, 1927; pp. 196–212.

"The Sexual Relation as a Social Relation and Some of Its Changes." Excerpt from *Verhandlungen des I. Internationalen Kongresses für Sexualforschung*, Vol. IV. Berlin-Köln, Marcus and Weber, 1928; pp. 222–230.

"Social Research in Criminology." *Sociology and Social Research*, Vol. XII, 1928, March-April, pp. 307–322.

"Education and Self-Education in Modern Societies." *American Journal of Sociology*, Vol. 36, No. 3, November, 1930, pp. 371–386.

"Group Crises Produced by Voluntary Undertakings." *Social Attitudes*, Kimball Young, ed. New York: Holt, 1931; pp. 265–290.

"The Analysis of Social Processes." *Publications of the American Sociological Society*, Vol. 26, No. 3, August, 1932, pp. 37–43.

"The Sociology of the Struggle for Pomerania." Torun: Baltic Institute (The Baltic Pocket Library), 1934; pp. 1–57.

Comment added to Herbert Blumer's *Critiques of Research in the Social Sciences, I.* New York, 1939, pp. 87–98.

"Social Groups as Products of Participating Individuals." *American Journal of Sociology*, Vol. 44, 1939, pp. 799–804.

"The Social Role of the Unemployed" (in English). *Sociologicka revue*, Brno, 1939 (volume in honor of Prof. I. A. Blaha) ; pp. 239–251.

"The Changing Culture Ideals of the Family." *Marriage and Family Living*, Vol. III, Summer, 1941, pp. 58–62, 68.

"Sociometry and Sociology." *Sociometry*, Vol. V, No. 3, 1943, pp. 225–233.

"The Impact of War on Personal Organization." *Sociology and Social Research*, Vol. 27, January-February, 1943, pp. 171–180.

"Social Organization and Institutions." *Twentieth Century Sociology, a symposium.* G. Gurvitch and W. Moore, eds. New York: Philosophical Library, 1945; pp. 172–217.

"Controversies in Doctrine and Method." *American Journal of Sociology*, Vol. 50, No. 6, 1945, pp. 514–521.

"Sociological Ignorance in Social Planning." *Sociology and Social Research*, Vol. 30, No. 2, November-December, 1945, pp. 87–100.

"William I. Thomas as a Collaborator." *Sociology and Social Research*, Vol. 32, March-April, 1948, pp. 765–767.

"Methodological Trends in Sociological Research." *Sociology and Social Research*, Vol. 33, No. 1, September-October, 1948, pp. 10–14.

Comment on John L. Thomas' article "Marriage Prediction in *The Polish Peasant*." *American Journal of Sociology*, Vol. 55, No. 6, May, 1950, article pp. 572–577, comment pp. 577–578.

"European and American Sociology after Two World Wars." *American Journal of Sociology*, Vol. 56, No. 3, November, 1950, pp. 217–221. Translated as "Europäische und amerikanische Soziologie nach zwei Weltkriegen." *Universitas*. No. 6, 1951, pp. 497–504.

"The Function of Sociology of Education." *Educational Theory*, Vol. 1, No. II, August, 1951 (publication of the John Dewey Society of the College of Education, University of Illinois). pp. 69–78.

"The Present and Future of Sociology of Knowledge." *Soziologische Forschung in Unserer Zeit* (in honor of Leopold von Wiese's seventy-fifth birthday). Köln, Westdeutscher Verlag, 1951; pp. 248–258.

"Should Sociologists Be Also Philosophers of Values?" *Sociology and Social Research*, November-December, 1952, pp. 79–84.

"Basic Problems of Contemporary Sociology." *American Sociological Review*, October, 1954, Vol. 19 (presidential address, American Sociological Society, Urbana, Ill.) pp. 519–524.

"The Dynamics of Social Relations." *Sociometry*, November, 1954 (paper read in section on theory at the 1954 meetings of the American Sociological Society).

"Social Groups in the Modern World." *Freedom and Control in Modern Society*, Morroe Berger, Theodore Abel, and Charles H. Page, eds. New York: D. Van Nostrand Company, 1954, pp. 125–140. [This item added by editor.]

"The Creative Evolution and Diffusion of Knowledge." *Three Columbia Centennial Lectures*. New York: Polish Institute of Arts and Sciences in America, 1954.

"The Social Roles of Innovators." *Midwest Sociologist*, Winter, 1955, pp. 14–19.

"Important Developments in Sociology." *Sociology and Social Research,* Vol. 40, No. 6, July-August, 1956, pp. 419–420.

BOOKS PUBLISHED IN POLISH

Cheops: Poemat Fantastyczny, Warsaw: J. Fiszer, 1903; pp. 4–84. (*Cheops: A Poem of Fantasy*)

Zagadnienie wartości w filozofji. Warsaw: Przegląd Filozoficzny, 1910; pp. 2–115. (*The Problem of Values in Philosophy,* published by *The Philosophical Review*)

Humanism i poznanie. Warsaw: Przegląd Filozoficzny, 1912; pp. 2–231. (*Humanism and Knowledge,* published by *The Philosophical Review*)

Evolucja twórcza. Warsaw: Gebethner & Wolff, 1913; pp. x–310. Translation and discussion of Henri Bergson's *Creative Evolution.*

Upadek cywilizacji zachodniej: Szkic z pograniczą filosofji kultury i socjologji. Poznań: Kimitet Obrony Narodowej, 1921; pp. xiii, 1–111. (*The Fall of Western Civilization*)

Wstęp do socjologji. Poznań: Poznańskie Tow. Przyjaciół Nauki, 1922; pp. 2–467. (*Introduction to Sociology*)

Socjologia wychowania. Warsaw: The Ministry of Education of Poland; Vol. 1, 1928, pp. 1–312; Vol. II, 1930, pp. 1–372. (*The Sociology of Education*)

Miasto w świadomości jego obywateli. Poznań: Instytut socjologiczny, 1931; pp 1–141. (*The City Viewed by Its Inhabitants,* from the study of the city of Poznań by the Polish Sociological Institute)

Ludzie teraźniejsi a ciwilizacja przyszłości. Lwów-Warsaw: Książnica-Atlas, 1935; pp. 1–379. (*People of Today and the Civilization of Tomorrow*)

ARTICLES AND OTHER PUBLICATIONS NOT IN ENGLISH

"Etyka filozoficzna a nauka o wartosciach moralnych." *Przegląd Filozoficzny,* 1909. ("Philosophical Ethics and the Science of Moral Values")

"Statystyka wychodztwa." *Wychodzca Polski,* z. 1 and 2, 1911. ("Emigrant Statistics")

"Wychodztwo a położenie ludności wiejskiej zarobkującej w Królestwie Polskim." *Wychodzca Polski,* z. 3, 1911. ("Emigration and the

Economic Status of the Agricultural Population of the Polish Kingdom")

"Studia nad filozofji wartości i elementy rzeczywistości praktycznej." *Przegląd Filozoficzny*, 1912, pp. 1–27. ("Studies in the Philosophy of Values and the Elements of Practical Realities")

"Znaczenie rozwoju swiata i człowieka." *Swiat i Człowiek*, Vol. IV, 1913, pp. 283–356. ("The Significance of the Evolution of the World and of Man")

Organizacja obywateli pracy. Poznań, 1920, pp. 1–14. ("The Organization of Workers")

Preface to Berkan, Wladyslaw, *Życiorys słasny.* Poznań: Materiały Instytutu socjologicznego w Poznaniu, I, 1923; pp. iii–xvii. (The Preface to one of the autobiographies collected and published by the Polish Sociological Institute)

"Szkice a socjoloji wychowania." Kraków: *Ruch pedagogiczny*, Nos. September-October, 1924, pp. 145–159, and November-December, 1924, pp. 209–219. ("Outline of Educational Sociology")

"Stany Zjednoczone Ameryki Połnocnej." *Nauka Polska*, Vol. IV, 1924, pp. 487–508. ("The United States of America")

"Co jest psychologia społeczna?" *Przegląd współczesny*, No. 38, pp. 370–386, and No. 39, pp. 51–87, 1925. ("What Is Social Psychology?")

"Przedmiot i zadania nauki o wiedzy." *Nauka Polska*, Vol. V, 1925, pp. 1–78. ("The Subject and Problems of the Sociology of Knowledge")

"Die soziologischen Ursachen der gegenwärtigen Krise der Demokratie." *Demokratie und Parlamentarismus, Prager Press*, 1 January, 1926.

"Zadania syntezy filosoficznej." *Przegląd Filozoficzny.* Vol. XXX, z. 2, No. 3, 1927, pp. 103–116. ("Problems of Philosophical Synthesis")

"Prąd socjologiczny w filozofji nowoczesnej." *Księga pamiątkowa ku czci w Heinricha*, Kraków, 1927. ("The Sociological Trend in Modern Philosophy")

"O wyborze zawodu." *Młodzież Sobie*, Poznań, R.I. No. 3, 1927, pp. 26–28. See shortened form in *Młodziez Sobie*, 1930, No. 3, pp. 3–4. ("On Choosing a Career")

"Sammlung u. Verwertung des soziologischen Materials." *Zeitschrift für Völkerpsychologie und Soziologie*, Vol. III, 1927, pp. 274–293.

Preface to Mirel, Franciszek, *Elementy społeczne parafi rzymskokatoliciej.* Poznań: Fiszer i Majewski, 1928; pp. ix–xix.

"Początki myśli socjologicznej." *Ruch Prawniczy, Ekonomiczny i Socjologiczny*, R. VIII, 1928, pp. 78–97. ("The Origins of Sociological Thought")

"W sprawie rozwoju socjologji polskiej." Poznań: *Programi samoobrona,* 1929, pp. 1–24. ("The Process of Development of Polish Sociology")

"Potrzeby socjologji w Polsce." *Nauka Polska,* Vol. X, 1929, pp. 486–498. ("The Needs of Sociology in Poland")

"Podstawy i granice celowego działania wychowawczego." *Zagadnienie oswiaty dorosłych: Dwie Konferencje,* Warsaw, 1930, pp. 17–32 and 200–217. ("Foundations and Limitations in the Goals of Education"—for the conference dealing with "The Question of Adult Education")

"O szczeblach rozwoju społecznego." *Ruch Prawniczy, Ekonomiczny i Socjologiczny,* R. X, 1930, pp. 285–296. ("The Rungs of Social Evolution")

"Forming the Educand." From Vol. I of *Socjologia wychowania.* Extrait du *Bulletin International de la Société Scientifique de Pédagogie,* Warsaw-Lwów, 1930, Kaiążnica-Atlas, pp. 1–16.

"Siły społeczne w walce o Pomorze." *Polskie Pomorze:* Toruń, 1931, Vols. I and II, pp. 80–108. ("Social Forces in the Struggle for Pomerania," in joint volumes)

"Studia nad antagonizmem do obcych." *Przegląd socjologiczny,* 1931, z. 2–4, pp. 1–54. ("Studies in the Antagonism to Strangers")

"Kultura amerykańska." *Ruch Prawniczy, Ekonomiczny i Socjologiczny,* R. XII, z. 1, 1932, pp. 36–39. ("American Culture")

"Polska w kryzysie swiatowym." *Dziennik Poznański,* No. 279, December 3, 1933. ("Poland in the World Crisis")

"Persönliche Erziehung und soziale Kultur." *Kölner Vierteljahrhefte für Soziologie,* 12, 1934–1935, pp. 328–356. (A translated section from *Ludzie teraźniejsi a ciwilizacja przyszłości*)

"Les Forces sociales en Poméranie." Toruń: L'Institut Baltique, 1934, pp. 1–55. (Translation of "Siły społeczne w walce o Pomorze" [1931])

"Kierownictwa a zwolennictwo we współpracy twórczej." *Kultura i Wychowanie.* Warsaw, 1934, R. I, z. 4, pp. 277–294. ("Control versus Freedom in Creative Cooperation")

"Teoria sobkostwa i towarzykosci." *Przegląd socjologiczny,* Poznań, Vol. III, 1935, pp. 83–108. ("A Theory of Selfishness and Sociability")

"Socjologia walki o Pomorze." Toruń: Instytut Baltycki, 1935, pp. 1–48. (Translated from English, "The Sociology of the Struggle for Pomerania" [1934])

"Stefan Czarnowski, 1879–1937." *Przegląd socjologiczny,* 1937, Vol. V, pp. 3–4. (obituary)

"Uczeni polscy a życie polskie." *Droga*, 1936, No. 2–3, pp. 101–116, and No. 4, pp. 255–271. ("The Educated Pole and Polish Life")

"Znaczenie socjologiczne badań Ludwiga Krzywickiego nad spoleczeństwami niższymi." *Krzywicki, Ludwik.* Warsaw: Instytut Gospodarstwo społecznego, 1938, pp. 217–248. ("The Significance of Ludwig Krzywicki's Sociological Studies of Primitive Societies")

Preface to Chałasinski, Jósef, *Młode pokolenie chłopów.* Warsaw: Państwowy Inst. Kultury Wsi, 1938, pp. ix–xvii.

"Tworczość naukowa Stefana Czarnowskiego." *Czarnowski, Stefan.* Warsaw-Poznań: Społeczeństwo-Kultura, 1939, pp. xxix–xxxvii. ("The Scientific Productivity of Stefan Czarnowski")

"Stan obecny technologii spoleczneji." *Ruch Prawniczy, Ekonomiczny i Socjologiczny*, R. 19, No. 3, 1939, pp. 317–327. ("The Present State of Social Technology")